Photoshop™
Filter Finesse

withdrawn

Bill Niffenegger

RANDOM HOUSE
ELECTRONIC PUBLISHING

New York   Toronto   London   Sydney   Auckland

Contents

CHAPTER 4

3D Effects in a 2D World   155

CHAPTER 5

Terrific Text Effects   187

CHAPTER 6

Paper, Patterns, and Textures   209

CHAPTER 7

Lighting, Halos, Fluorescent Effects   227

CHAPTER 8

Smoke, Mirrors, and More   243

CHAPTER 9

Grained and Faceted Imaging   255

CHAPTER 10

Oils, Pastels, and Other Digital Deceptions   269

CHAPTER 11

Picture Frames   285

CHAPTER 12

Gigantic Files and Seamless Composites   301

CHAPTER 13

Animation and Video Magic   311

CHAPTER 14

Power User Combinations   325

CHAPTER 15

Professional Applications   *341*

Foreword

by Kai Krause

Convert, Crop, Correct, Colorize, Clone...!

Is there a Mac owner involved with graphics in any serious fashion who does *not* have Photoshop? Not very likely. So it seemed only logical when Adobe implemented a plug-in interface allowing third parties to add new functionality. Boy, was everyone surprised when they saw the little plug-in babies grow up into full-blown stealth programs in their own right.

In the same way, it seemed only logical when Random House decided to publish this book dissecting the details of the grown-up babies. Boy, will everyone be surprised when they see that Bill Niffenegger's coverage is a magnificent web of detail and content in *its* own right.

Photoshop Filter Finesse is not a mere compendium or encyclopedia rattling down the plug-ins by specification and vendor. Nor does it simply sling manufacturers' addresses at the reader or reprint the functional descriptions as supplied in the manuals. Bill is clearly not content to enumerate the names and numbers of some software products: Rather, he sets out to redefine the purpose and creative potential of each one.

Bill Niffenegger is not a starving writer, but a "tortured *artiste*" living with his tools day in and day out. He feels the pain of limitations and the anguish of missing features and bugs, as well as the joys of the found beauty and the accidental miracles revealed during a night's aimless combinatorics. He delights in demonstrating techniques and serving up solutions, refusing to cater to the elite or pander to the lowest common denominator in the process.

Every Photoshop user should be able to benefit from *Photoshop Filter Finesse*. The pure novice may find refuge in the comprehensive overview; the casual, once-in-awhile Photoshopper will see new vistas beyond the obvious; and even seasoned designers behind jaded shades can delight in Bill's personal vision of tools applied, not to mention his incredible grab-bag of private techniques laid bare on the table.

Fleeting and ethereal, or loud and clear as "a task well done," this is (or certainly ought to be) the motivation for any of us entranced by these new tools and toys. And make no mistake: With *Photoshop Filter Finesse*, Bill gets deep into it. This is what the reader will ultimately find compelling and infectious: the sense of sheer, endless cross-connections and the myriad new processes that yield something that is hard to come by these days—a visual manifestation you may never have seen before!

I fully expect that Bill will get his share of what I consider my most delightful mail, the letters that start: "Dear Kai, I haven't seen my husband/wife in three days and it's all your fault!" This tome may cost many people their dear weekends, as they find themselves mesmerized to follow his proud footprints into uncharted worlds of imaging.

There is another important feature of Bill's book that bears mention—and I am stating this for all my software publishing colleagues: There simply is very, very little overlap between any of the effects, processes, and generators discussed and illustrated in these pages. In an almost amazing case of happy symbiosis, the serious user will emerge with the understanding that you simply *must* invest in your tools and that you simply *cannot* have enough of them. It clearly is not a case of one filter collection *instead* of the other; if anything, it is merely a question of understanding "when to use what to get the job done."

Here, Bill has made his most beneficial contribution: He has almost selflessly thrown himself into the task of unravelling the task-oriented solutions to daily problems—way beyond what you may expect a journalistic treatment of the genre to encompass.

He is nuts!

This book is nuts!

A good kind of nuts.

I wish we had many more like him to write many more books like this one.

Preface

Photoshop-compatible plug-in filters are extremely powerful enhancements to Mac and Windows graphics programs, allowing you to achieve special effects and production efficiencies that would otherwise be nearly impossible. Many of the newer-generation filters are as powerful as many free standing applications of a few years ago. This book-disk package will give you an overview of the plug-ins available on the market today, show you how to do amazing things with them (far more than their documentation describes), and provide you with your own ready-to-use library of some of the tastiest filters from today's top collections. We'll even touch on some of the more exotic filters, such as the "Sucking Fish Filter" from Tokyo.

Photoshop Filter Finesse makes some basic assumptions. It assumes that you are familiar with the basic functions of the Macintosh or PC and the system software that you are using. It also assumes that you have some knowledge of the basic imaging techniques described in the manuals of your software packages. This book is intended as an adjunct and companion piece to the *Adobe Photoshop Handbook*, itself an excellent source of assistance in adding to your imaging expertise.

The book covers the use of filters from several different angles. Chapters 1, 2, and 3 provide a complete and authoritative compendium on what's out there—what filters are, where they came from, who's selling them, and what they do. I have included short tips with many of these descriptions to suggest creative uses for the filters.

In Chapters 4 through 13, we'll go much further into the filters universe: This is the "cookbook" portion, full of techniques and recipes that will show you how to achieve incredible special effects and production magic, including powerful ways to combine filter effects. With a greater understanding of the flexibility of filters and their potential interactions with one another, you will find more opportunities to use them creatively in your projects.

The book concludes with tips and case studies (Chapters 14 and 15) of the work of some of today's top digital illustrators, including Kai Krause, Glen Mitsui, and others, showcased in a full-color gallery. Viewing the artwork of these exciting artists should provide inspiration and enjoyment.

Special offers in the back of the book will not only help you access the power of filters, but also make it easier to purchase more of them to add to your imaging arsenal. It is my hope that you will integrate the enhancing power of these new tools into your images—images that you can truly call your own.

The enclosed Toolkit Disc is packed with commercial filters, presets, paper textures, seamless tiles, work files, and other goodies that will allow you to immediately start emulating and building upon the book's techniques (see the back cover for details).

The inclusion of discount coupons for the participating third-party filter vendors, together with the unveiling of techniques for creating your own seamless textures and backgrounds, make this book a bargain in dollars saved and provide tools for new approaches to enhanced productivity.

I hope that *Photoshop Filter Finesse* will open new areas of discovery for you and that I can make you smile during the journey. Imaging is fun; with the transformative power of plug-in technology, it can take your imagination to new heights.

I am anxious to hear about any new filters and techniques for using them. . .Have some ideas? I can be reached through Random House Electronic Publishing at 201 East 50th Street, New York, New York 10022.

ATTENTION PHOTOSHOP 3.0 USERS: When you are directed in the step-by-step exercises to use the Compositive Controls mrnu option to select the opacity or the apply mode, instead use the Layers palette for these settings. To access the sliders for more control, double-click on the name of the layer in the Layers Palette. The sliders will then appear.

CAUTION: Filter enhancement of images can be addictive. It is an adventure that has absorbed literally thousands of hours of my life. What an amazing adventure awaits you!

Bill Niffenegger

Acknowledgments

Writing a first book, especially a technical one, is an all-encompassing process. Mark Siprut, coauthor of the *Adobe Photoshop Handbook 2.5 Edition* and general supporter, put it very well when he told me, "Bill, you will be having birth pangs for months on end." He was correct. I am in a euphoric state at its completion and I have some wonderful people to thank for it.

I thank my lovely wife (her face is on the cover of the book) for her unswerving support and love during my obsessive writing and imaging schedule. I thank my daughters, Natalie and Rachel, for their understanding during "Daddy's project."

A special thanks to some of the primary contributors to the book. Mike Roney, senior editor, gets my undying support for having faith in me and for his wizardry at his job. Although I'm a first-time author, he made me feel that I could write a book that I would like to buy. Anne Marie Concepción gets my golden seal of approval and thanks for her help with the Mac side of Chapters 1 through 3. She was invaluable in ferreting out the information that makes those chapters the most complete compendium ever put together about filters. I must also thank Sybil and Emil Ihrig of VersaTech Associates for researching the PC side of things, providing Windows-user tips, and doing an outstanding job of page composition. Trish Meyer was fabulous in pulling together the video chapter and doing the technical review. A special thanks to Bill Hanson for his multimedia expertise, and Jeff Foster gets my heartfelt gratitude for providing information and files for the Ultimatte filter compositing section. My long-time friend, Thomas Skomski, helped to name the book. Tom, I thank you.

The list is very, very long when it comes to filter and application support from the many commercial, shareware, and freeware software vendors. I especially thank Kai Krause and John Wilczak for many types of assistance from them and their HSC team. Aldus Corporation and Xaos Tools lent extraordinary support, as did Mike Skurski at Total Integration. Adobe Systems, Fractal Design Corporation, and Pixel Resources were a great help in lending technical assistance. I thank the many other vendors who lent their time and expertise.

The book was produced 100 percent digitally on Apple Macintoshes using SuperMac's accurately calibrated Pressiview monitor, speedy Thunder IIGX graphics card, and luscious two-page Proof Positive color printer for draft proofs. High-speed 1.3Gb optical drives from Micronet were used to archive and shuttle huge quantities of data among all the parties involved in production. The Microtek 45T slide scanner brought in brilliant transparency material. The reliable UMAX 1200SE flatbed scanner was used for numerous scans of source material. The PLI SCSI-2 cards made file transfers incredibly fast. Daystar's Photomatic software automated the file conversion process, and a 40 MHz Daystar Turbo 040 accelerator sped up layout and production functions. Optronics gave invaluable assistance, providing accurate proofs from their new Intelliproof system and producing all the fine color separations. These vendors are all high on my hit parade for providing equipment to make the book production process a modern dream. I had the best equipment, and expertise was provided to make the most of it.

And what is a computer graphics book without images? Special thanks to ColorBytes for providing the Toolkit Tiger image and to Multimedia Library for providing the Toolkit Rooster. Thanks to PhotoDisc, D'pix, Seattle Support Group, and Aris Entertainment for supplying beautiful source images to work with. My fellow fine artists who shared their work in the final chapter are especially dear to me. I hope everyone enjoys their work as much as I do.

Bill Niffenegger

The Power of Filters

Twirl pixels with the push of a button, turn a woman's face to stone and a man's hair to atomic particles, recolor, smooth, and preen an image, or reshape it into any configuration. What can do all of this? Plug-in filters. This chapter will explain what they are, how they evolved, and where you can use them.

What Filters Are and What They Do

Photoshop-compatible plug-in filters are easily installed software extensions for Adobe Photoshop and a number of other graphics programs. Both Macintosh and PC users can benefit from their power. *Special-effects* and *production* filters—those we will be covering in this book—work by manipulating the bits of data that make up a digital image. This manipulation, or "pixel processing," can create an unlimited number of permutations of the original image.

Filters can perform tasks as basic as shifting an image one pixel in a specific direction or as complex as calculating where each pixel will be placed when hundreds of thousands of them are radically distorted. The interfaces can be nonexistent or look like a control panel of a science fiction spaceship. Filters can be applied directly or show you preview windows that take you into visual realms of infinite magnification, color, and pattern. The variety and scope of filters seems endless.

Plug-in technology also allows individual manufacturers of scanners, printers, digital cameras, calibration equipment, and high-end imaging systems to create plug-ins that act as interfaces between Photoshop and their devices. However, these aren't what we define as special-effects or production filters, and so we won't be covering them in this book.

A Compressed History of Pixel Processing

Photoshop comes with a filter called "Custom," which exemplifies and accommodates the mathematical formulas of the first digital-imaging mathematicians. These early programming explorers developed equations that altered a field of pixels. These mathematical alterations were first called "convolves" and later "convolution kernels." The current Photoshop Custom filter exemplifies this do-it-yourself experimentation that fascinated the early adopters of pixel processing.

Those early math experiments bear fruit to this day by providing the mathematical *algorithms*, or formulas, which allow the sharpening and edge-finding abilities that are at the heart of digital photo-retouching and scan-enhancing.

The military's need to glean increasingly detailed information from processed satellite images furthered the explosion in mathematical digital processing. This evolution of robust image-enhancement features empowered early high-end imaging systems and graphics programs now running on today's personal computers. Painting and retouching programs began to employ the use of increasingly sophisticated algorithms and features to set themselves apart from competitors in the crowded graphics software arena.

How Filters Evolved

Initially, graphics applications on the Macintosh and PC platforms included a main feature set of functions plus special capabilities that set them apart from competitors. Some of these software packages added layer after layer of special effects to attract purchases by more digital artists. The 1990 release of Adobe Photoshop 2.0 boasted an expanded plug-in format adapted from one first developed by Silicon Beach Software for Digital Darkroom and SuperPaint. This quasistandard allowed special effects to be added to a primary standalone application. The plug-in modules could be added or removed from a folder that also contained the preferences file of the host application. This *open architecture* standard permitted third-party developers to write and market special effects filters for Photoshop.

Other painting and digital-imaging applications followed suit and also began supporting the use of Photoshop plug-in module filters. Third-party developers began to develop filters with capabilities that would have been released as full-fledged applications a year or two previously. 3D software entered the fray with the ability to apply filters to rendered objects in a still image or to a series of rendered objects in an animation sequence. That was followed by the desktop video revolution: Digital video technology makes it possible to apply some special-effects filters to individual or multiple frames of an animation or QuickTime movie.

The Photoshop filter format is now advantageous both to the manufacturers of standalone imaging applications and to the plug-in developers themselves. Thanks to in-house and third-party filter development, standalone graphics applications remain viable as they continue to evolve. And, third-party filter developers benefit by having a very developed host—the standalone application—in which to operate their "miniprograms."

How to Use and Install Filters

In Adobe Photoshop, you define the location of the plug-in filters folder by choosing File: Preferences and then selecting the Plug-Ins option. Navigate through the dialog box until you have selected your plug-ins folder. Then, restart the program.

NOTE: If you use the Windows version of Photoshop, you must place all plug-ins in the \photoshp\plugins directory, or Photoshop will not recognize them. If you need to install your plug-ins somewhere else, one workaround is to edit the PluginDirectory= line of your photoshp.ini file. This file is located in the directory where you installed Windows.

CAUTION PHOTOSHOP OWNERS: If you move your plug-ins folder or throw away the Photoshop Prefs file, which is located in the Preferences folder within the System folder, you must repeat the process of selecting the location of the plug-ins folder.

Adobe Photoshop's Filter menu accommodates both built-in filters (also called *native* filters) and any third-party filters that you add to the plug-in folder or directory. You can access plug-ins through the File: Acquire and File: Export menu options, too. The File: Acquire submenu lists filters you can use to access various formats of information, such as specially compressed files, scanners, and digital cameras. Using the File: Export submenu, you can access specialized printers or export information in formats that the normal Save or Save-As functions within Photoshop do not support.

Some filters operate without a dialog box. Others are a playground of multifaceted choices and sublime previews that guide you when applying your effects to an image.

TIP: **Macintosh Photoshop versions 2.5 and later have a Preview option in the Filters: Distort submenu. To activate this option, choose About Plug-In in the Apple menu, press and hold the Option key, and select one of the Distort filters. A checkbox in the lower left corner of the dialog box gives you the option to turn previews and sliders for these filters on or off. I highly recommend that you activate this preview feature. The color previews can save you hours of processing time by allowing you to make rapid adjustments to the filter settings before applying the filter.**

A great strategy for experimenting with filters is to apply the filter to a portion of the image. Select areas of the image that are especially significant and sensitive to obliteration. Certain distortion filters, for example, could obscure important features of your image. By testing a single filter on a small selection, you can quickly undo the application of the filter and try again. I like to use the File: Revert option in Photoshop when applying multiple filters.

TIP: **To reapply the most recently used filter, press Command-F (Macintosh users) or Ctrl-F (Windows users). To recall filters with dialog boxes and make further setting changes in the dialog box, press and hold Option- Command-F (Macintosh users) or Alt-Ctrl-F (Windows users).**

The Filter Controversy

What could possibly be controversial about filters? There are many schools of thought on the use of filters, and opinions can be quite strong. There are artists who feel that the use of filters has allowed a number of dilettantes to invade the digital art community. This point of view was especially prevalent immediately after the release of the first set of push-button paint filters, Aldus Gallery Effects: Classic Art, Series 1. The ads for the product implied that a user need not be an artist to achieve paintings that rivaled those of the masters. The filters provided great promise for the novice or Sunday painter but threatened some digital and traditional illustrators. The advent of the filters sent a shudder through parts of the industry, much in the way that the general public's ability to set type on a personal computer upset the traditional type houses.

Just as typographers screamed that there would be an avalanche of badly typeset brochures flooding the country, it came true. As the digital designers became more sophisticated, however, they produced higher-quality pieces. It simply took them a little time to develop their knowledge of typography.

The same thing is happening now in the digital graphics world. Early users of "push-button" imaging and special-effects filters overused them, applying them to everything and producing images that had a cookie-cutter familiarity.

Easy-to-achieve filter effects will continue to be used by persons searching for simple and quick solutions, and there's nothing wrong with that. For those who require a more sophisticated look, there are enough filtering tools on the market to produce fresh imaging combinations. It is the strength of the concepts behind the images that is most important. Filters are tools and, as with most artist tools, they respond to the intelligent use of the artist.

If you are a visionary artist or designer with an obsession for exploration, there is plenty of territory left to explore. The hobbyist and beginner can "power-play" months on end and possibly grow into the shoes of a great innovator in graphics. Have fun. The rest of this chapter describes software applications in which you can play with filters to your heart's content.

Filter-Friendly Applications

A number of standalone applications on both platforms take advantage of the imaging power of filters. Macintosh and PC users can extend Photoshop-compatible plug-in technology to the programs of their choice. Some of the applications described in this section integrate filters into the program, while others provide access to filters only as a postprocessing feature. Specialized information concerning program-specific implementation of filters will be discussed where applicable.

NOTE WINDOWS USERS: With Windows users growing more design-savvy every day, interest in special-effects filters for images is increasing. As a result, there is a proliferation of both the number of plug-in filter sets running under Windows and image-editing packages that accept plug-ins. Although some of these applications have been ported over from the Macintosh platform, many have been designed specifically for Windows.

TIP: Standards are a potential problem for users of Windows-based imaging products who want to work with plug-ins. Originally, Aldus and

---

GUIDE TO PC/MAC NOTATION

Mac If this icon appears before a product name, the application is Mac-only (the majority).

Pc This icon before a product name indicates that it's available only on the PC platform.

Mac **Pc** This dual icon before a product name means that it's available on both PC and Mac platforms.

Adobe initiated two differing specifications for plug-ins, with Gallery Effects representing the Aldus standard, and packages like the Andromeda filters series representing the Adobe standard. Recently, the trend has been for developers to support both standards, but you should be aware that some plug-in sets, image-editing packages, and paint applications may effectively support only one. In this book, the focus is on products that support the Adobe "Photoshop-compatible" standard. The emphasis in the profiles of "filter-friendly" Windows applications is on the *unique* features of each software package that foster especially creative uses for plug-ins.

Adobe Photoshop

This is the premier software product for image processing on either the Macintosh or the Windows platform. It is as suitable for the entry-level user who needs to modify low-resolution scans as it is for the professional prepress staffer who does color correction, photomontages, and silhouetting of 24-bit high-resolution scans or original bit-mapped art. For the creative artist, Photoshop's pioneering use of alpha channels (masks) and plug-in filters (modular special effects) presents an incredible opportunity for original and imaginative image manipulations, many of which are impossible to achieve using traditional photographic equipment.

NOTE WINDOWS USERS: Whenever you see a reference to "folder" in any discussion of Photoshop in this book, think "directory."

FILTER FACTS

Adobe Photoshop, like many other applications covered in the following pages, has two kinds of filters: built-in and plug-in. Built-in filters—also known as *native* or standard filters—are an integral part of the program and are always available in Photoshop's Filter menu. Plug-in filters—the topic

AIDS
This illustration by the author uses filter techniques demonstrated in this book.

Regalia 11
This illustration by the author incorporates textures, patterns, and finishes produced with the help of filters.

of this book—are like little special-effects programs, software add-ons that are dropped into ("plugged into") a special folder. This folder is called, strangely enough, the Plug-ins folder. Adobe includes a number of plug-in filters with Photoshop in addition to its native ones.

Although the Plug-ins folder is installed in your Adobe Photoshop folder by default, the folder can actually reside anywhere on your hard drive. The Preferences dialog box allows you to inform Photoshop where the Plug-ins folder is located. Any Photoshop-compatible filter that you add to the Plug-ins folder will appear in Photoshop's Filters menu. It's not necessary to restart the program to see newly added plug-ins appear in the Filters menu.

TIP: To see which plug-in filters are available when the Macintosh version of Photoshop is active, choose the About Plug-in option from the Apple menu. A drop-down menu will appear listing all the plug-in filters. If you're running Photoshop under Windows, you'll find the About Plug-in option in the Help menu.

Adobe Premiere 1.1

Offering an intuitive interface for capturing video and for laying out and outputting digital movies, this video- and animation-editing product is the perfect complement to Photoshop for multimedia professionals. The Windows version of Premiere is somewhat less full-featured than its version 3 Macintosh cousin. It currently lacks support for EDL, titling, motion control, and multiple tracks.

FILTER FACTS

Whatever you can do with filters in Photoshop, you can do in Premiere; all native and plug-in filters are interchangeable. Transitions and alpha channel support for superimposing images offer fruitful ground where you can put special-effects filters to good use.

CAUTION: Be aware that not all filter effects look as good in motion sequences as they do on still images. Test the filters you want to use before committing your pixels!

Aldus PhotoStyler 2.0

PhotoStyler is a comprehensive image processing package native to the Windows environment. A customizable toolbar covers selection and masking, image enhancement, and painting functions, with all current tool options accessible through an intuitive tool ribbon. In addition to the masking techniques common to most image processing programs (Magic Wand, Lasso, geometrical shapes), PhotoStyler includes a Ruby Mask mode that lets you use the Airbrush or other painting tools to select and mask discontiguous pixels and delicate areas such as hair. A Merge Control dialog box facilitates image compositing, offering complete control over color, tonal range, image channels, and transparency options when merging floating and background images. Channel and image compositing functions are also available through the Image: Compute command. Output- and production-related features include CMYK editing, the ability to create nonrectangular clipping paths for placement in layouts, on-screen channel editing, and integrated Kodak Precision Color Configure software, a color management utility that ensures consistent color results from input to printing.

FILTER FACTS

You can define a pattern from a filter effect and use the new pattern to tile a selected area, maintaining control over the positioning, color mapping, and transparency of the tiles. You can also use filter results as you would a paintbrush, painting them selectively into the image. Accessible channel-related tools make it easy to explore filter manipulation of individual image channels.

TIP: PhotoStyler's Partial Edit mode is of special interest to filter buffs who never seem to have enough memory to process large, RAM-hungry images. In Partial Edit mode, you can work efficiently with multi-megabyte images by loading just a portion of an image into RAM at a time. PhotoStyler loads the remainder of the image onto a temporary file on your hard drive, thereby speeding filter processing time and freeing up system resources.

NOTE: To integrate plug-ins into PhotoStyler's menus, use a text editor to open the ULEAD.INI file in the Windows directory and locate the [PLUG IN] heading, or create this heading if it doesn't exist. Immediately after this heading, add a line that points to the directory where the filters are located. You can add up to nine lines, each pointing to a separate directory. The syntax follows the model

```
PLUGINDIR1=c:\photoshp\plugins
PLUGINDIR2=c:\kpt
```

and so on. When you next start PhotoStyler, special-effects filters appear in the Effects menu, while input- or output-related plug-ins appear in the File: Import or File: Export submenus, respectively.

Altamira Composer 1.01

Altamira Composer is an image processing package specializing in montaging and compositing techniques. An optimized use of the alpha channel allows each element within a composition to behave as an independent, object-oriented image. This means, among other things, that images don't have to have rectangular backgrounds—everything outside the defined shape becomes transparent. With each image as a separate layer, you can change the position or stack order of any element in the composition without using traditional selection and masking techniques. You can also group, ungroup, lock, distort, and align component images as you would in a drawing or modeling program. Composer provides a large number of built-in special effects, such as shape warps, washes, and automatic drop shadows.

FILTER FACTS

Plug-ins are accessible to Altamira Composer through the Altamira Plug-In Toolkit, a sub-application that mediates between Composer and third-party software. Since each element of a composition is independent, you can select an item for filtering simply by clicking on it. You can also apply filters to multiple-selected or grouped images. Each filtered image or group maintains its shape without masking, and you have real-time control over filter transparency.

NOTE: To specify the location of plug-ins for Composer, double-click the Plug-In icon in Composer's toolbar to open the Plug-In Toolkit. Choose the Other entry in the Plug-In menu to call up a dialog box in which you can specify the directory location of the plug-ins you want to use. Your selection becomes available immediately.

Apple Photoflash

Photoflash is an application designed primarily to automate and otherwise simplify image selection, basic clean-up of scans, image compression, and image placement into page layout programs. When you start Photoflash, it scans your hard drive and presents you with a thumbnail browser view of all the images it finds. You can select images there and perform basic manipulations, such as adjusting brightness and contrast, cleaning up "dust" and "scratches," rotating, resizing, and cropping. You can also compress the entire image or just parts of it (selective compression). The built-in recorder makes batch processing faster and easier by allowing you to track and play back manipulation sequences. Photoflash supports the usual variety of image file formats.

Avid VideoShop

VideoShop is a QuickTime video-editing program that lets users combine video, audio, text, and graphics to create short-form videotapes, interactive presentations, and CD-ROM content. An intuitive "canvas" interface, a built-in titling tool, over 200 special effects, and a nondestructive editing ability make this a user-friendly yet powerful program.

Claris BrushStrokes

BrushStrokes is a budget-friendly and user-friendly 32-bit paint program with many high-end features. The interface consistently provides helpful feedback; when you select a brush, for instance, the cursor takes on the foreground color so that you know what color will be applied when you use the brush. Brushes can be used in any one of 13 modes and can be set to automatically antialias edges as you paint. A full complement of image-modification features includes masking, distortions, and some built-in special-effects filters.

FILTER FACTS

BrushStrokes can find filters that are in the System folder, the System Folder's Preferences folder, or in BrushStroke's own application folder. They appear in the program's Selection menu or the section of the Tool palette reserved for plug-ins.

Corel PhotoPaint 5.0

PhotoPaint is an image-editing application that is bundled with the ever-popular PC drawing package, CorelDRAW! Version 5.0 has been enhanced with more powerful features that Corel Corporation says will allow it to compete with Photoshop, PhotoStyler, and other major products in their class. Photoshop plug-ins can be stored in any directory specified from PhotoPaint's Preferences dialog box.

CoSA After Effects

CoSA After Effects is a special effects application for QuickTime and is designed to help Macintosh users, video producers, and broadcast professionals create high-quality video productions. The program has a unique key-frame based interface that allows you to composite layer upon layer of moving video and animation while controlling the position, rotation, scale, and opacity of each layer over time. The program comes with its own suite of filters (which can animate) and can also access third-party plug-ins.

Daystar PhotoMatic

PhotoMatic is a scriptable "batch" application for automating repetitive image processing chores. It has two parts: a plug-in filter and a standalone application. The plug-in adds a Record menu item to Adobe Photoshop, providing an easy way to record any sequence of transformations (including filter effects) applied to a given image in Photoshop. When you stop recording, the plug-in prompts you to save the script. The PhotoMatic application lets you apply those same scripts to other images, singly or in batches.

FILTER FACTS

Since the Record plug-in records any filter transformations accessible from within Photoshop, you can use any Photoshop-compatible third-party plug-in filter as part of the macro sequence. In this way, you can include filters in the script that you would use within the PhotoMatic batch-processing application.

NOTE: As of this writing, the Record plug-in filter works only with Adobe Photoshop.

DiaQuest DQ-Animaq and Quickpass

DQ-Animaq is a NuBus board that provides frame-accurate recording (video out) and digitizing (video in) for both desktop video and broadcast-quality television. You can use it in conjunction with Macintosh paint, illustration, 3D, multimedia, and image processing programs to produce video animations. You can automatically record single or multiple video-frame and real-time digital transitions onto videotape. The board can control videotape, laserdisc, and digital disk recorders. The optional Quickpass software significantly reduces the amount of time required for video recording and digitizing by applying multiple edits per pass. Videos that are digitized by Animaq contain additional SMPTE time code information readable by Adobe Premiere (see the section on Premiere earlier in this chapter).

FILTER FACTS

DQ-Animaq supports filter plug-ins as a standard feature. These plug-ins work with source video sequences on a frame-by-frame basis for rotoscoping, image processing, and special effects.

EFI Cachet

Cachet is primarily a color-correction program for attaining predictable results from a variety of output devices. Using various target and reference images (included), you can modify the settings for different output devices, such as color printers, digital proofers, web presses, and so on. Cachet saves these settings as *device profiles* that you apply to your finished image files before you output them. Since Cachet has no tools strictly for painting or retouching, it works best as an adjunct to paint programs like Adobe Photoshop.

FILTER FACTS

Cachet accepts plug-in filters for image acquisition and export (for example, CMYK and JPEG) and allows for access to many scanners and printers.

Equilibrium DeBabelizer

This program has two main functions: It intelligently translates just about any graphics file from one format to another (including cross-platform translations), and it can apply the same translations and/or transformations to a batch of graphics files (greatly improving productivity when you have a folder full of scans to despeckle, for example).

FILTER FACTS

Since DeBabelizer accepts third-party plug-ins, you can leverage its batch capabilities to apply the same special effects to a series of images. For example, you may want to use a filter from Aldus Gallery Effects with DeBabelizer to emboss a collection of images destined for an annual report. You can take a coffee break while DeBabelizer does the repetitive work.

Fauve Matisse 1.2

In the art world, the nickname "Les Fauves" ("wild beasts" in French) refers to a group of early twentieth-century artists who reveled in the use of wild, vibrant colors. Matisse was their most famous proponent, and this hybrid imaging software, which includes both painting and image processing features, bears his name. Paint features include natural media brushes, user-definable textures, and a library of lighting effects. Matisse also includes many image retouching functions found in higher-end packages, such as multiple simultaneous floating selections, histograms, tone correction, and channel-by-channel processing.

FILTER FACTS

Filter effects used in Fauve Matisse can serve as a basis for a custom texture or surface. You can choose how to apply the texture: to the image as a whole, to the currently selected object, or freehand using a paintbrush. You can also apply a filter on top of one of the preset special lighting effects, which behave like independent objects themselves until merged with the underlying image.

NOTE: Fauve Matisse recognizes plug-ins only if they are located in the plug-in subdirectory (folder) of the directory where you installed the software. If you already have plug-ins installed and set up for use with other paint or image editing packages, copy them into the \fauve\plug-ins directory or folder. The plug-ins then will appear in the Image: Plug-In Filters submenu.

Fractal Design Painter/X2

Fractal Design Painter is a paint package that simulates traditional art tools and media electronically. You can apply "brushes" that emulate oil paints, watercolors, chalk, charcoal, pencils, and many other natural tools, particularly when applied with a pressure-sensitive digitizing tablet. Several on-screen palettes control groups of tool characteristics that collectively define brush size, behavior, and expression. You can define libraries of custom brush and brush variants, stylized brush looks, and paper textures. The many preset varieties of paper textures are useful not only for providing background textures, but also for stylizing selected areas of an image. Version X2 of Painter enhances compositing capabilities by making it possible for an image to contain multiple floating object selections. Cell-painting features for animation artists are included as well.

The Windows versions of Fractal Design Painter are virtually identical to their Macintosh cousins. Only keyboard shortcuts and other minor interface-related features vary, due to differences in operating system conventions for the two platforms.

FILTER FACTS

Painter recognizes only one plug-in folder or directory at a time. To specify a different location for third-party plug-ins, press the Option key while starting Painter.

NOTE: **To specify the location of third-party plug-ins with the Windows version of Painter, press Ctrl as you double-click the Painter icon to start the program. When a dialog box titled "Choose one Plug-In from your Plug-In Directory" appears, select any single filter file from the directory that contains the plug-in set you want to use. Painter then recognizes all the plug-ins in that directory. You can access only one directory per work session.**

TIP: **To create a multicolored outline of the currently selected and feathered area in Painter, use the KPT Gradients on Path filter.**

TIP: **Use your favorite filter effects as bases for new textures in a custom Paper Library; you can then apply the new texture to image backgrounds or to selected areas. If you are using Painter X2, use Fractal's Edit: Generate Mask command after applying a filter to create an automatic mask (protected area) that follows the contour of the filter effect.**

TIP: **For a screened-back or partially transparent filter effect, apply a filter and then specify a percentage using Painter's Edit: Fade command.**

TIP: **You can save the Paper Texture snippets in sets, then resize the textures and use them to simulate the effects of paper. To create rich surfaces, apply the same paper texture set multiple times at a variety of sizes.**

TIP: **The Distort filters in Photoshop 2.5 and later are not accessible from within Painter. If you like, you can keep the Photoshop 2.01 versions of** these filters in your Plug-ins folder. The name of these filters will appear twice in the Filters menu. The second one listed is the newer filter.

Fractal Design Sketcher

Sketcher, a grayscale painting and image editing program, is designed for desktop publishers, newsletter creators, graphic artists, cartoonists, and other creative professionals working in a monochrome or grayscale environment. In some ways, you could consider Sketcher to be Painter's little brother—its reduced feature set takes up less memory (you can run it on Macs or PCs with only 2 to 4 Mb of RAM), and Sketcher also has new features designed to make working on entry-level computers easier and faster. At the same time, Sketcher shares many features with Painter, including such natural-media tools as pencils, crayons, calligraphy pens, airbrushes, friskets, paintbrushes for oils and water colors, and more.

FILTER FACTS

To make Sketcher recognize the location of your Plug-ins folder, hold down the Command key (Macintosh users) or the Ctrl key (PC users) when you launch the program. A dialog box appears in which you can specify the location of the plug-ins you want to use during the current work session.

Microfrontier Enhance

Enhance is an image-editing program that works with black-and-white or 8-bit grayscale images. Although Enhance can open 24-bit images, it converts them to 8-bit. The program includes most of the image manipulation tools and capabilities found in high-end paint programs, such as masking features, built-in filters, image resampling and resizing, and montage capabilities.

FILTER FACTS

Enhance recognizes plug-in filters only if they are located in the Scanners & Plug-ins folder within the application folder. Plug-ins appear in Enhance's Plug-in Filters menu.

Microfrontier Color It!

Color It! is an image-enhancement and painting program. Color It! provides editable tool palettes, masking features for filter processing, and multiple Undos. It also lets you work with virtual images.

FILTER FACTS

In addition to being able to access Photoshop-compatible plug-in filters from other programs (see the tip that follows), Color It! has an extensive implementation of its own native filters. These filters are not transferable to other programs and are not Photoshop-compatible. I mention Color-It!'s proprietary filter technology because of an unusual feature that can help you discover how filters work. The convolution filter dialog box, within Color It!, provides real-time preview for its Custom filter. This preview gives you direct visual feedback to numeric input in the custom convolution dialog box. Early programming mathematicians would have loved to see the fruits of their experimentation so quickly.

TIP: Color It! does not have a way to locate a plug-in folder outside of its proprietary filter folder. If you are using System 7, make an alias for each of your filters and support files, and then put them in the Color It! filter folder. This technique saves storage space on your hard drive.

Olduvai
Multi-Clip Pro 3.1

Multi-Clip lets users go far beyond the limited functionality of Apple's Clipboard. It allows you to cut and copy a huge variety of file formats to multiple clipboard "holding areas" and paste them back in any order. You can also access the contents of Multi-Clip's clipboards for cropping, scaling, and applying transformations (e.g., third-party plug-in filters). In addition to its own "Super Scrapbook," the program has some intelligent hooks to Apple's system Scrapbook.

FILTER FACTS

Multi-Clip Pro has an image-editing window that you can access by double-clicking its "clipframe," which is similar to a Scrapbook window. When you are in image-editing mode (normally just for selecting, scaling, and cropping), you can apply any third-party Photoshop plug-in filter. You can apply filters to the entire image or just to a selection. The Tool menu that appears in image-editing mode contains two commands that let you access the filters: the Plug-in Effects pop-out hierarchical menu and the Other command. Use the Other command to locate plug-ins that aren't in your default folder.

NOTE: Filters applied to Multi-Clip Pro images actually affect only the PICT preview! Obviously, Multi-Clip is not the program to use filters in if you want to write to the actual image. It does work wonderfully, however, if you simply want to paste a low-resolution

image into a word processing program or a database and you want the image to have a special, filter-applied effect.

Olduvai VideoPaint 1.5

VideoPaint is an intermediate-level color paint program that includes some 3D modeling and rendering functions as well. In addition to the usual features of paint programs, VideoPaint offers more than 50 special effects, stencil and mask tools, and built-in scanner drivers, and allows for 3D wire-frame creation and rendering.

FILTER FACTS

Video Paint can access plug-in filters anywhere on your hard drive from its Effects menu. Filters in the default Plug-ins folder appear under the Plug-ins menu option, and you can access other filters by choosing the Other option in the Effects menu.

Micrografx Picture Publisher 4.0

Picture Publisher is a native Windows image editing package. Its support for multiple object layers assists the image compositing process: You can have several floating images per file and apply constant "what-if" revisions to each. Productivity-related features include FastBitsTM, which allows you to load just a small portion of an image into memory; macro capability; one Undo per object rather than one per picture; and the option to open a low-resolution version of a file for speedier creative experimentation. For color correction functions, the Color Shield provides a quick, one-step method of selecting or protecting up to eight user-specified color ranges in an image, while the Visual Color Balance dialog box lets you preview multiple image thumbnails to which you have tentatively applied highlight-, mid-tone-, shadow-, or channel-related changes. Picture Publisher also supports editing of individual frames of .AVI (Microsoft Video for Windows) files.

FILTER FACTS

With the ability to keep multiple floating selections active and undo your changes to each independently, Picture Publisher lets you test-apply several filter variations without committing yourself. On-screen text entry and movement eases special-effects filter application to text. Frame-by-frame filtering of video files is also a useful possibility.

NOTE: Picture Publisher can recognize up to two plug-in directories at a time. To specify the directories, choose Edit: Preferences and then select the Plug-ins Preference Group. Type the path names in the Path 1 and Path 2 text boxes and then choose OK. Your plug-in directory assignments become effective immediately.

Pixel Resources PixelPaint Pro 3

PixelPaint Pro 3 is a 32-bit painting and image manipulation program that includes a large suite of specialized features. PixelLayers allows you to make multiple selections and keep them "live" for editing, compositing, and applying filters. PixelPapers are a variety of paper textures that create special effects when you apply "paint." The program also has a feature that records image transformations (including filter effects) to create scripts which you can save and later re-apply to other images.

TIP: You can apply any third-party plug-in to the mask-only portion of a document without corrupting the color portion. Here's a three-step way to obtain tie-dyed, dayglow patterns:

1. **Apply the KPT Texture Explorer to the mask and then copy it to the red channel.**
2. **Repeat with a slight variation in the Texture Explorer and copy the result to the green channel.**
3. **Finally, repeat with a variation and copy the result to the blue channel.**

You can load Gradients from Kai's Power Tools Gradient Designer into PixelPaint 3's Gradient palette by pressing and holding the Option key while clicking the Load button in the Gradient dialog box.

RayDream Designer

Designer is a still image 3D illustration, modeling, and rendering program that does ray-tracing. Like most 3D programs, Designer comes with a variety of object primitives that you can use as starting points, and it includes lighting and distance-rendering features. In version 3.0 and later, you can do "3D painting"—brushing colors and textures directly onto an object's surface.

FILTER FACTS

Designer has the ability to postprocess images with plug-in filters. Selection capabilities are supported through a special Filter selection command that allows the use of the Lasso and Marquee tools. Designer also allows users to batch-queue files for filter applications. Use Designer's Preferences command to specify the location of your plug-ins.

RayDream JAG II

Jag II is an image-enhancement software utility. It uses an edge-tracking and resolution-boosting technique to enhance black-and-white or color images by removing the jagged edges. The enhancement can be accomplished on MacPaint, PICT, PICS, Kodak Photo CD, Adobe Photoshop, TIFF, and QuickTime files. You can enhance images produced from Paint, photo-retouching, 3D modeling, animation, and multimedia applications.

FILTER FACTS

Jag II uses plug-in filters in the same way as the company's RayDream Designer application just described. Although you can plug-in filters only to 24-bit images, Jag II automatically converts lower color-depth images to 24-bit before processing. You can reduce the color depth afterwards in a separate step within the program.

Specular Collage

Collage creates screen-resolution "proxy" files of high-resolution images. After generating the proxy, you can apply intricate compositing, masking, titling, and filtering techniques to it. Since the image is at screen resolution (72 dpi on a Macintosh monitor), these procedures take far less time than if you worked directly with the original high-resolution file. When you are done, Collage renders all the proxy's image manipulations to the high-resolution file.

FILTER FACTS

One of Collage's features is a Render Preview, which will let you see a full-resolution preview of a section of the image to which you have applied a filter. Collage has its own set of production filters that are resolution-independent. These work well in conjunction with third-party special-effects filters.

StrataStudioPro

StrataStudioPro is a combination 3D modeling, rendering, and animation program. You begin by drawing objects with familiar Bezier spline curves or importing images you have created in Adobe Illustrator. The program's 3D Sculptor editing tool lets you create free-form organic objects; you can also lathe surfaces to any degree and extrude objects with bevels or sweep surfaces. Multiple rendering methods (including RayPainting) and event-based animation capabilities are fully implemented.

FILTER FACTS

Third-party filters (also called "extensions" in the program's documentation) can be applied only after you complete final 3D rendering. You specify the location of the plug-in filter folder in the program's Preferences dialog box. The menu option Options: Modify Image lets you access filters or their aliases.

StrataType 3D

This program takes 2D type or object templates and extrudes them for true 3D representation. Text can be typed directly into StrataType 3D, or the program can open PICT and/or EPS type and objects for 3D modeling, with some limitations. You can save files in native format or in DXF (a document interchange format for CAD and 3D programs). You can also apply texture and lighting effects before the final rendering.

FILTER FACTS

See StrataStudioPro (above).

StrataVision 3D

Like StrataStudioPro, StrataVision 3D is a combination modeling, rendering, and animation program. However, this program is less full-featured in that it allows only vertex (not spline-based) editing.

FILTER FACTS

See StrataStudioPro (above).

VideoFusion

VideoFusion combines the features of a QuickTime video-editing program with those normally found only in image processing applications. With VideoFusion's time-dependent parameter controls, you can set up long, complex processes and let the program do the frame-by-frame calculations. You can work in your choice of Player View, Storyboard View, or Time View modes and change the view mode on-the-fly. After a command is processed on a frame or selection, VideoFusion generates the new media and stores it in a preview window for you. For greater creative freedom and control, you can access channel information for many special effects and filters.

FILTER FACTS

You can store filters in VideoFusion's Plug-ins folder or anywhere on your hard drive. To access the ones not in the default folder, click the Directory button in the Plug-Ins dialog box. You can apply a filter to a clip from the Storyboard or to a selection from the Player or Time view mode.

Photoshop Native Filters

There are scores of filter sets on the market today, and the list for this burgeoning field grows longer by the minute. The next two chapters provide the most complete coverage of filter products available at press time. This chapter features descriptions, sample images, techniques, and specialized uses for filters that come with Photoshop, while Chapter 3 focuses on the incredible variety of filters developed by third-party manufacturers.

Photoshop comes equipped with more than 40 filters. Many of these are the standard production workhorses of the industry. The filters are arranged hierarchically in the Filter menu according to function. The native filters of Photoshop version 2.5 and later have been rewritten to take advantage of the 3210 AT&T DSP chip, which a number of acceleration boards support. Adobe also has developed a plug-in extension to access the built-in DSP chips in the Quadra 840AV.

TIP: The rewriting of Photoshop for version 2.5, and the resulting enhancements—such as previews for the distort filters and slider bars for many of the dialog boxes—are not without a price. Many of the distortion filters that were accessible to other applications are no longer compatible with those programs. If you select a Photoshop 2.5 or later distortion filter in Fractal Design Painter, an error message box pops up informing you that the filter contains resources that require Photoshop 2.5. There *is* a workaround. I have retained my distortion filters from Photoshop version 2.0 and allow both to appear in the Filters: Distort submenu. The first duplicate in the list is the old filter; the second is the new filter complete with preview. When I use Painter, I select the first filter and apply it normally. This solution will be less attractive in the future if Adobe writes new types of filters that do not adhere to a standard that other programs can access.

How We Categorize Filters

We use the following categories for both the Photoshop native filters covered in this chapter, and for the third-party sets addressed in Chapter 3.

- **Special-effects filters** have no precedent in natural-media artwork or photography and produce a unique digital result.

- **Art-effects filters** emulate natural media, such as watercolor or colored pencil, or cause an image to take on the appearance of another medium.

- **Distortion filters** displace pixels by twisting or twirling them, or by using any technique to shift their shape. When combined, distortion filters open many new possibilities.

- **Production filters** are used by prepress houses to prepare images for print, multimedia, or video output. Commonly used prepress filter examples include Unsharp Mask and Sharpen, which users apply just before an image is ready for color separation and output to film. Production filters can emulate darkroom techniques or produce new effects for print or video jobs.

- **Conversion filters** include: conversion filters proper, which transform an image from one file format to another; compression filters; format conversion filters; and special types of import transformation filters such as Photo CD. In most imaging applications, you find conversion filters in the Filters menu or in the Acquire/Export submenu under the main File menu.

- **Hardware Plug-Ins (NOT):** All filters that add modular functionality to Photoshop and other graphics applications are "plug-ins." However, not all plug-ins are "filters" as we define them. Some are no more than interfaces that allow a particular external device (such as a scanner, printer, or digital camera) to interact with Photoshop or with another graphics application. Because of the highly specialized nature of these plug-ins, we do not cover them in this book.

Photoshop Native Filter Descriptions

Here's a complete rundown of the "native" filters that ship with Photoshop, including descriptions, specialized uses, and techniques for their use.

Blur Filters

BLUR

Type	Special-effects filter
Description	The Blur filter (Figure 2–1) calculates the darker areas and edges and lightens the adjacent pixels for a softened effect.
Specialized Uses	The Blur filter can visually smooth harsh pixelated areas and noisy scans. Use the Blur filter to soften and blend the edges of a composite image.

BLUR MORE

Type	Special-effects filter
Description	Adobe states that the effect of Blur More (Figure 2–2) is three to four times the effect of the Blur filter. When a more pronounced blurring effect is required, it is more efficient to apply this filter than multiple applications of the Blur filter.
Specialized Uses	Use Blur More to soften images for further processing.

GAUSSIAN BLUR

Type	Special-effects filter
Description	The Gaussian Blur filter (Figure 2–3) affects the image according to the intensity of the user-defined settings. You can specify uniform or Gaussian application of the blurring effect. The Gaussian setting is the more sophisticated of the settings. Gaussian blurring blurs pixels using a bell-shaped curve that can soften the image while destroying some contrast.
Specialized Uses	Gaussian Blur is very useful in special-effects filtering; we will refer repeatedly to this filter in future chapters.

MOTION BLUR

Type	Special-effects filter
Description	With the Motion Blur filter (Figure 2–4), you can vary the direction and intensity of the blur effect on an image.

  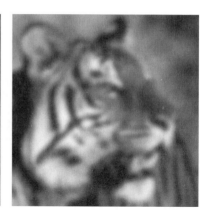

Figure 2–1
Photoshop's native Blur filter
applied to the tiger image

Figure 2–2
Blur More applied to the tiger

Figure 2–3
The Gaussian Blur filter applied at
a radius of 7

The effect is one of a photograph for which the lens
shutter speed was set too slow. You can set the pixel distance as high as 999 pixels.

Specialized Uses   Motion Blur is useful not only for showing motion streaks
on an image, but also for reducing banding in blends.

RADIAL BLUR

Type   Special-effects filter

Description   Radial Blur (Figures 2–5 and 2–6) shifts and blurs pixels
with two different methods of application. The Spin
method blurs pixels in a circular fashion, while the Zoom
method blurs pixels as if you were moving in or out of
the image. Processing for this filter is time-intensive.

Specialized Uses   Radial Blur is useful for print and multimedia special
effects, when motion needs to be indicated.

Distort Filters

DISPLACE

Type   Distortion filter

Description   The Displace filter (Figures 2–7 and 2–8) shifts each
pixel of an image horizontally or vertically. A second
image requested by the filter's dialog box, called a *displacement map* file, determines the amount of displacement.
The grayscale value of the displacement map file is the
deciding factor: Black causes the highest amount of positive displacement; white causes the greatest negative
displacement; and neutral gray (128) causes no shift.

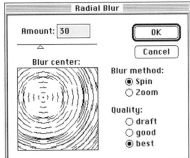

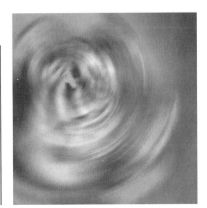

Figure 2–4
Motion Blur applied to the tiger at 45 degrees and a distance of 45 pixels

Figure 2–5
The Radial Blur dialog box

Figure 2–6
The Radial Blur filter applied to the tiger

Photoshop uses any valid Photoshop file (other than a bitmap file) to determine the displacement amount. Photoshop comes with several preset displacement maps to test the effects.

Specialized Uses   Displace can help create complex distortions that otherwise would be impossible to produce in one step.

TIP: America Online has a number of displacement maps in the Software library of the Photoshop forum. These displacement maps are provided by America Online members.

TIP: For a more in-depth discourse on displacement maps and the Displace filter, you can download Tip number seven of Kai's Power Tips in the Photoshop Forum on America Online.

TIP: To achieve textural distortions, use some of the seamless textures that we will be making in Chapter 5 (Paper, Patterns, and Textures) as displacement maps.

Figure 2–7
The Displace filter dialog box

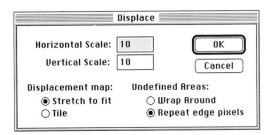

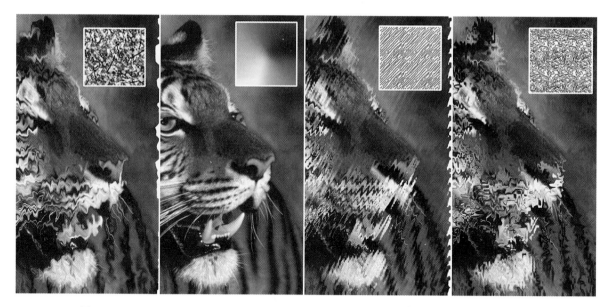

Figure 2–8 The Displace filter applied to the tiger

PINCH

Type   Distortion filter
Description   The Pinch filter (Figures 2–9 and 2–10) distorts a selection in one of two directions: toward the center (a squeezed-together look) when you define a positive percentage, or expanded outward when you define a

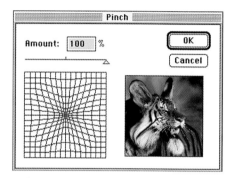

Figure 2–9
The Pinch filter dialog box

Figure 2–10
The Pinch filter applied to the tiger

negative percentage. The filter automatically blends square or rectangular selections into the background.

Specialized Uses   Use Pinch to enlarge or shrink selected areas of an image.

TIP: **If you have a circular or irregularly shaped selection, you should feather the selection to facilitate smoother blending with image areas outside the selection.**

TIP: **Heavy feathering of large selection areas yield subtle swelling and distortion effects that allow programs such as Photoshop to emulate the latest software effects for morph-like distortion.**

POLAR COORDINATES

Type   Distortion filter
Description   This filter (Figures 2–11 and 2–12) converts the rectangular coordinates of an image or selection to polar coordinates.
Specialized Uses   The Polar Coordinates filter can turn an image into a *cylinder anamorphosis*, a old-fangled art convention in which an image becomes recognizable only when you view its reflection on a mirrored tube.

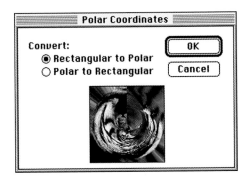

Figure 2–11
The Polar Coordinates dialog box

Figure 2–12
The Polar Coordinates filter
applied to the tiger

RIPPLE

Type	Distortion filter
Description	The Ripple filter (Figures 2–13 and 2–14) distorts the image in small, medium, or large curves that affect the image horizontally and vertically. You can set the ripple intensity by entering a number from 1 to 999.
Specialized Uses	The Ripple filter yields excellent liquid effects.

SHEAR

Type	Distortion filter
Description	The Shear filter (Figures 2–15 and 2–16), new to Photoshop 2.5, deforms a selection using a centerline to which you can add pull points. You can move the pull points to the left or right to wave-deform the selection. Options include wrapping the left and right edges of the selection around deformed areas, or allowing the background color to appear in areas that have been pulled out of the selection area.
Specialized Uses	Use the Shear filter to bend objects in a fluid manner.

TIP: **Flip the selection 90 degrees and back again when you need a vertical distortion.**

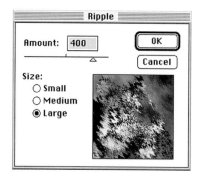

Figure 2–13
The Ripple filter dialog box

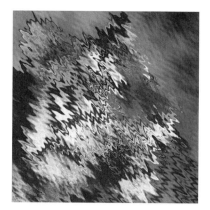

Figure 2–14
The Ripple filter applied to the tiger

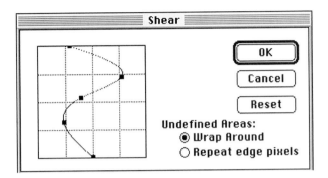

Figure 2–15
The Shear filter dialog box

Figure 2–16
The Shear filter applied to the tiger

SPHERIZE

Type   Distortion filter
Description   The Spherize filter (Figures 2–17 and 2–18) gives an
                        image the appearance of being bubbled in an outward or
                        inward direction, depending on the positive or negative
                        percentage you enter in the dialog box. You can choose
                        to affect the selection on the horizontal or vertical axis
                        only. When the selection is not square, the Spherize fil-
                        ter distorts it in a circular pattern by assigning the
                        shortest dimension as the circular distortion height.

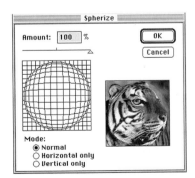

Figure 2–17
The Spherize filter dialog box

Figure 2–18
The Spherize filter applied to
the tiger

Specialized Uses   This filter produces swelling type effects and can help create distorted reflections on objects.

TIP: When using the Spherize filter, you should feather irregularly shaped selections to create smoother blending with the background.

TWIRL

Type   Distortion filter
Description   The Twirl filter (Figures 2–19 and 2–20) makes a twirling distortion on a selection, using the center of the selection as the pivot point.
Specialized Uses   The Twirl filter can create morph-like effects. It also helps blend textures.

TIP: Since the Twirl filter causes a radical displacement of pixels, you can achieve a higher-quality effect with less ripping of the image by applying the filter in increments of no more than 160 degrees at a time.

WAVE

Type   Distortion filter
Description   The Wave filter (Figures 2–21 and 2–22) distorts an image in a manner similar to that of the Ripple filter. A variety of user-defined parameters gives this filter a wide range of possible effects. You can set the number of wave

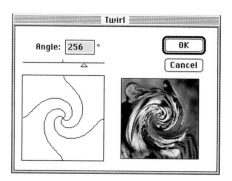

Figure 2–19
The Twirl filter dialog box

Figure 2–20
The Twirl filter applied to the tiger

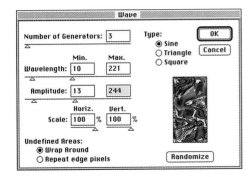

Figure 2–21
The Wave filter dialog box

Figure 2–22
The Wave filter applied to the tiger

generators (range: 1 to 999), the minimum and maximum wavelength (range: 1 to 9,999), the height or *amplitude* of the waves (range: 1 to 9,999), the horizontal and vertical scale (range: –9,999 percent to 9,999 percent), and the wave type (sine, triangle, or square).

Specialized Uses   Careful application of this filter results in liquid distortions of objects.

ZIGZAG

Type   Distortion filter
Description   The Zigzag filter (Figures 2–23 and 2–24) gives a selection the appearance of fluid into which a pebble has

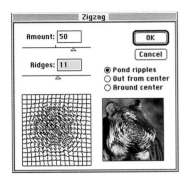

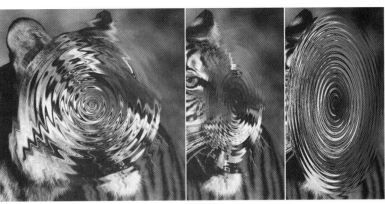

Figure 2–23
The Zigzag filter dialog box

Figure 2–24
The Zigzag filter applied to the tiger

been dropped. You can set the ripple amount (range: –999 to 999) and the number of ripples from the center to the edge of the selection (range: 1 to 999).

Specialized Uses   Zigzag produces amazing bump-maps for 3D artwork. It also helps you achieve liquid effects for selected objects.

Noise Filters

ADD NOISE

Type   Special-effects/Production filter

Description   The Add Noise filter (Figure 2–25) adds a dusting of pixels to the selection in a way that emulates film grain. The grain color is not always compatible with the image being filtered and can cause a confetti-colored look in flesh tones.

Specialized Uses   Adding noise is helpful in softening the look of stark image areas. When you are retouching photos that have existing grain texture, Add Noise helps with blending.

TIP: Noise added to a new file can serve as the beginning of a new texture when a series of additional manipulations is performed.

Figure 2–25   The Add Noise filter applied to the tiger with Amount (of noise) settings of (left to right)32, 55, and 88

DESPECKLE

Type	Production filter
Description	The Despeckle filter (Figure 2–26) detects the edge areas of a selection and retains those pixels while blurring the areas in between.
Specialized Uses	This filter can clean up noisy scans while keeping the tight details of an image intact.

TIP: Use this filter to remove moirés that result from scanning an image that had been printed previously.

TIP: Multiple applications of the Despeckle filter can simplify an image somewhat, but without altering the color the way posterization does.

MEDIAN

Type	Special-Effects/Production filter
Description	The Median filter (Figure 2–27) reads the brightness of the pixels within a selection and averages them. Median simplifies an image by reducing noise (produced when pixels of different brightness levels adjoin one another) and by averaging the differences out of the selection.
Specialized Uses	The Median filter smooths the rough areas in especially noisy scans originating from preprinted material or video frame-grabs. Median is a much neglected filter that is especially useful when you use it as the first step in creating painterly techniques.

Figure 2–26
The Despeckle filter applied to the tiger (left to right) once, four times, and ten times

Figure 2–27
Left to right: the Median
filter applied to the tiger
with a radius setting of 2,
5, 10, and 16 pixels

TIP: By defining settings between three and six, you can achieve the simplification of a broad oil brush effect. You will need to sharpen the affected image afterward, however.

Sharpen Filters

SHARPEN

Type	Production filter
Description	The Sharpen filter (Figure 2–28) intensifies the contrast of neighboring pixels. This filter acts as a general image enhancer.
Specialized Uses	Sharpen soft scans and resized images.

TIP: Since no dialog box controls accompany this filter, you should always test it on an image sample taken from a critical area of the image.

Figure 2–28
The Sharpen filter
applied to the tiger

SHARPEN MORE

Type	Production filter
Description	The Sharpen More filter (Figure 2–29) performs the same type of contrast intensification as Sharpen, but is the equivalent of approximately three passes of the Sharpen filter. Sharpen More is a timesaver if extensive sharpening is required.
Specialized Uses	Sharpen soft scans and resized images.

CAUTION: **Artifacts and extreme color shifts and contrasts can result from over-sharpening an image.**

SHARPEN EDGES

Type	Production filter
Description	The Sharpen Edges filter (Figure 2–30) affects only the high-contrast areas of a selection. The perfect candidate for this filter is an image that contains some attractive, smoothly modulated large areas with edges that are too soft.
Specialized Uses	Sharpen soft scans and resized images.

UNSHARP MASK

Type	Production filter
Description	The Unsharp Mask filter (Figures 2–31 and 2–32) is similar to the Sharpen Edges filter, except that it offers you much more control over what gets sharpened and by how

Figure 2–29
Left to right: the Sharpen More filter applied one, three, five, and seven times to the tiger

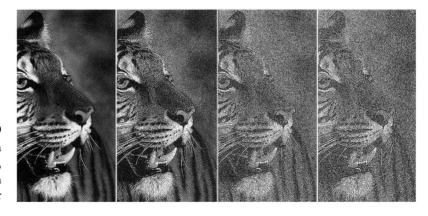

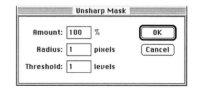

Figure 2–30
The Sharpen Edges filter applied to
the tiger

Figure 2–31
The Unsharp Mask filter dialog
box

much. You can specify the degree of sharpening (range: 1
to 500 percent) and the *pixel radius*, or number of pixels
surrounding the edges of the selection that are included
in the sharpening calculation (range: 1 to 100). In addition, you can define the brightness threshold (range: 0 to

Figure 2–32   From left to right, the Unsharp Mask filter applied to the tiger with the following
amount, pixel radius, and threshold level settings: 100%/1/1, 200%/2/2, 300%/3/3,
and 400%/4/4.

255) for the filter's color contrast calculation; lower numbers result in more extreme sharpening effects.

Specialized Uses   The Unsharp Mask filter is one of the workhorse filters for cleaning up soft, hazy scans.

Stylize Filters

COLOR HALFTONE

Type   Special-effects filter
Description   The Color Halftone filter (Figures 2–33 and 2–34) emulates the dot pattern of a four-color separation. You define the size of the dot.
Specialized Uses   Cartoon characters love to dress in this effect.

TIP: By setting very large dot pattern sizes on a photograph, you can produce an artistic effect for commercial jobs.

CRYSTALLIZE

Type   Special-effects filter
Description   The Crystallize filter (Figure 2–35) converts a selection to a random series of polygons at user-defined sizes. Each polygon's color is determined by the predominant color of the image below it.
Specialized Uses   Use Crystallize to simplify images for inclusion in brochures, ads, and multimedia.

TIP: In some cases, you can create a more appealing affect by posterizing an image (to simplify the colors) *before* applying the Crystallize filter.

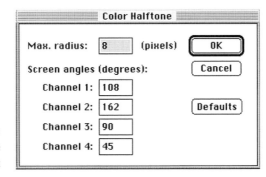

Figure 2–33
The Color Halftone
dialog box

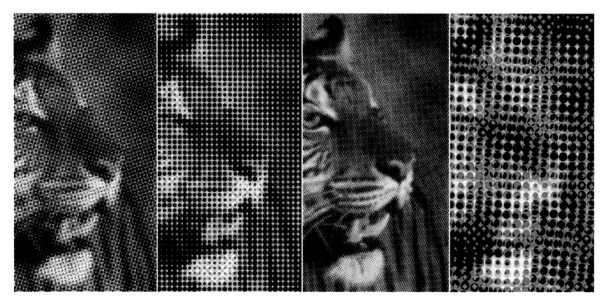

Figure 2–34   The Color Halftone filter applied to the tiger four times, each with a different set of parameters. The first tiger has a maximum halftone dot radius of 8 pixels, and the screen angles for the four CMYK plates are 108, 162, 90, and 45 degrees, respectively. The next three tigers show Color Halftone applied at the following settings (left to right): pixel radius 12, screen angles 90/180/45/0; pixel radius 4, screen angles 22/120/77/190; and pixel radius 22, screen angles 100/180/90/45.

FACET

Type	Special-effects filter
Description	The Facet filter (Figure 2–36) breaks an image into square-shaped areas of similar color. This filter processes and simplifies the color of an image, approximating a painterly look. Because the filter blocks areas of similar colors, its affect appears random.
Specialized Uses	Use Facet to break up images into artistic, flat color areas for spot color printing.

TIP: **Apply the Median filter after the Facet filter to enhance a painterly look.**

MOSAIC

Type	Special-effects filter
Description	The Mosaic filter (Figure 2–37) breaks an image down into rectangular blocks of user-defined size. Allowable

Figure 2–35
The Crystallize filter
applied to the tiger three
times, with cell size
settings of (left to right)
1, 5, and 10

block sizes range from 2 to 64 pixels. The filter determines the average color in each block and simplifies it to one color.

Specialized Uses   Mosaic simplifies images for spot-color printing and additional filtering.

TIP: **Amplify the effect of the Mosaic filter by applying the Aldus Gallery Effects: Classic Art 1 Emboss filter once.**

DIFFUSE

Type   Special-effects filter
Description   The Diffuse filter (Figure 2–38) scrambles neighboring pixels in a four-pixel cell, softening the edges in a way that makes the image appear to have been drawn on rough paper with a colored pencil. You can choose from among

Figure 2–36
The Facet filter applied
to the tiger

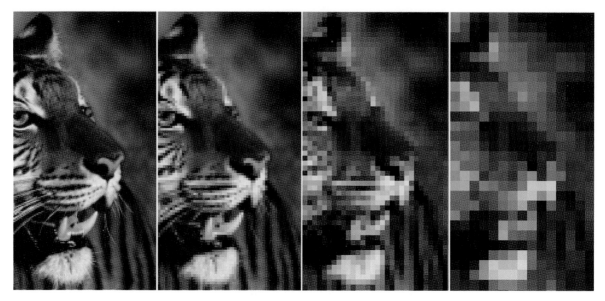

Figure 2–37   The Mosaic setting applied to the tiger with cell size settings of (left to right) 4, 8, 16, and 32, respectively.

three modes: Normal, Darken Only, or Lighten Only. Let the overall image tone determine which mode to use.

Specialized Uses   Mosaic gives images a soft-focus look.

TIP: **If you want the diffusion effect to be more pronounced on a high-resolution print job, sample the image down to 100 ppi before applying the filter and then bump the image back up to full resolution for a second pass of the filter.**

Figure 2–38
The Diffuse filter applied to the tiger using (left to right) Normal mode, Darken Only mode, and Lighten Only mode

EMBOSS

Type   Art-effects filter

Description   The Emboss filter (Figure 2–39) simulates a metal-stamped version of your image with your choice of light source direction. You can set the height of the stamped effect and the angle of the light source. If you want to reverse the stamped effect so that it appears concave, enter a negative Height number in the dialog box.

Specialized Uses   Emboss is useful for fine-art or commercial illustrations, brochures, and annual reports. It also serves well as a basis for further special filtering effects.

TIP: **For an embossed, sepia toned, hand-colored effect, first emboss an image and then colorize it with the Photoshop Hue/Saturation control set to a brownish orange. Finally, paste an original image back on it with the composite controls set to Color Only.**

EXTRUDE

Type   Special-effects filter

Description   The Extrude filter(Figures 2–40 and 2–41), new to Photoshop 2.5, cuts a selection into a series of gridded, three-dimensional chips. You can specify block-shaped sections that use the predominant color of each block as the front face, or blocks that use image areas as the front face of each block. Alternatively, you can specify a pyramid shape as the grid block. You control the size of the

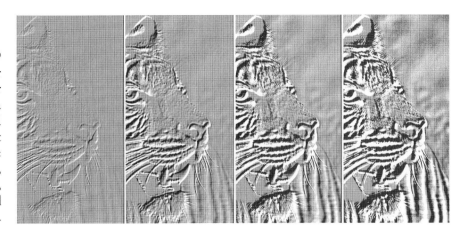

Figure 2–39
The Emboss filter applied to the tiger four times, each time with different angle, pixel height, and amount settings. Left to right: 135°/3/100%, 135°/6/200%, 135°/8/300%, and 135°/10/500%.

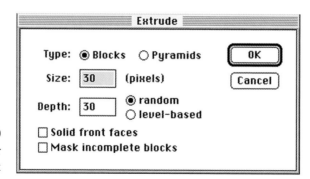

Figure 2–40
The Extrude filter
dialog box

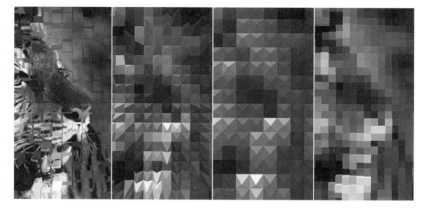

Figure 2–41
The Extrude filter
applied to the tiger with
the following Pixel Size,
Depth, and Block
settings (left to right):
30/30/random,
30/30/random/pyramids,
44/10/level-based/
pyramids, and
22/10/level-based/blocks
with solid front faces

grid block and the depth or length of the extrusion. You can also define the extrusion depth so that blocks are random in height or so that they correspond to the light and dark areas of the image. Light areas appear to extrude farther than dark areas.

Specialized Uses   The Extrude filter produces a wide variety of artistic effects and repeatable patterns.

FIND EDGES

Type   Special-effects filter
Description   The Find Edges filter in Photoshop version 2.5 and later (Figure 2–42) differs from its counterpart in previous versions. Earlier versions of the filter found the edges—points of high-contrast differences—in the image and created neon-color lines in these areas, forcing the other areas of the image to near-black. The newer version of

Figure 2–42
The Find Edges filter
applied to the tiger

this filter places the resulting colored lines on a white background instead.

Specialized Uses   Find Edges brings out details for further filter processing.

TRACE CONTOURS

Type   Special-effects filter

Description   The Trace Contours filter (Figure 2–43) is similar in effect to the Find Edges filter, except that it draws a line around the areas of contrast and renders them to each color channel.

Specialized Uses   Trace Contours brings out details for further filter processing.

TIP: For an Andy Warhol silkscreen effect, make a copy of an original image. Posterize the original and apply Trace Contours to the copy. Select the color lines that result from applying the Trace Contours filter and paste them back into the original (posterized) image. To eliminate white ghosting around the color lines, select White Matte in the Composite Controls dialog box.

TIP: After applying Trace Contours, you can achieve a beautiful, unified effect by using the Gradient tool to change the colors of the overlaid lines to a hot, contrasting blend. For a more artsy Warhol effect, you can use the Distort function in Photoshop to enlarge and stretch the lines so that they fall in slightly different locations from the corresponding shapes in the original file.

Figure 2–43
The Trace Contours filter applied to the tiger

Figure 2–44
The Fragment filter applied to the tiger

FRAGMENT

Type	Special-effects filter
Description	The Fragment filter (Figure 2–44) lays four copies of the image onto one another, offsetting each from the next.
Specialized Uses	The Fragment filter is good for the occasional "this is your mind on drugs" look.

TIP: For earth-shattering effects in QuickTime movies, use the Fragment filter to lend a movie the look of an earthquake in progress.

LENS FLARE

Type	Special-effects filter
Description	The Lens Flare filter (Figures 2–45 and 2–46) gives an image the appearance of a photograph that has been affected by a glare reflection in the camera lens. You can set the intensity of the flare within a range of 10 to 300 percent and choose the type of camera that is subject to the flare effect. Move the cross hairs in the preview display to determine the location of the flare.
Specialized Uses	Use Lens Flare to create convincing camera-lens reflections and sci-fi space effects.

TIP: You can produce halo glows and suns emerging from the edges of a distant planet by placing the originating Lens Flare center behind a masked-out planet or object.

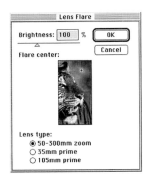

Figure 2–45
The Lens Flare filter
dialog box

Figure 2–46
The Lens Flare filter applied to the tiger image at various settings

POINTILLIZE

Type	Art-effects filter
Description	The Pointillize filter (Figure 2–47) produces a Seurat-type effect by producing, from the background color of a selected area, a series of dots based on any size you choose. In Photoshop, the background color is the color that appears between the dots of the selection.
Specialized Uses	The Pointillize filter is useful for fine-art or commercial illustrations, brochures, and annual reports.

TIP: You can produce an interesting effect by pointillizing an image using a background color that is not included in the image. Select the

Figure 2–47
The Pointillize filter
applied to the
tiger image at cell
depths of (left to right)
5, 10, 30, and
80 pixels, respectively

background color in the pointillized image and invert it. Paste the dots back into the original image.

TIP: You may find it desirable to defringe the dots in order to eliminate any hint of the old background color. Or, you may choose to leave a fringe of complementary color to heighten the pointillistic effect.

SOLARIZE

Type	Special-effects filter
Description	The Solarize filter (Figure 2–48) creates an effect similar to the darkroom effect of the same name. Solarize blends a negative and a positive, resulting in a psychedelic effect that was very popular in the sixties.
Specialized Uses	This filter provides interesting color-shift effects for fine-art and conceptual commercial illustration.

TIP: In Photoshop's Levels dialog box, use custom levels or the auto equalizing setting to bring out more vibrant color.

TILES

Type	Special-effects filter
Description	The Tiles filter (Figures 2–49 and 2–50) produces a user-defined number of tiles based on the number of vertical and horizontal tile pieces you specify. You can define

Figure 2–48
The Solarize filter applied to the tiger

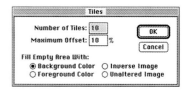

Figure 2–49
The Tiles filter dialog box

Figure 2–50
The Tiles filter applied
to the tiger image with
various settings

both the offset amount and the effect that appears
between tiles. The foreground or background color can
be selected for the intermediate spaces. You also can
select an inverted or original image.

Specialized Uses   The Tiles filter produces visual breaks in background
images for brochures and advertising.

WIND

Type   Special-effects filter
Description   The Wind filter (Figure 2–51) produces user-defined
directional lines that use the local color of an edge and
are extended at a pixel length of your choosing. To indicate this distance, the filter dialog box uses the analogy of
Wind, Blast, or Stagger rather than a specific pixel length.

Specialized Uses   Use Wind to simulate speed in a still image.

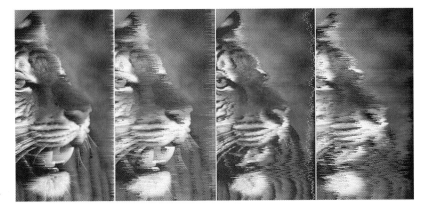

Figure 2–51
The Wind filter applied
to the tiger image with
the following settings
(left to right): Wind,
Blast, Stagger,
Blast and Stagger

Figure 2–52
The tiger image before
and after application of
the NTSC Colors filter

Video Filters

NTSC COLORS

Type	Production filter
Description	The NTSC Colors filter (Figure 2–52) alters the colors of an image to match the color gamut of NTSC television.
Specialized Uses	A standard use is the conversion of images for video presentations.

TIP: To simulate an image on a TV screen, apply the NTSC Colors filter to a normal scanned image.

DE-INTERLACE

Type	Production filter
Description	Images brought into the computer from a video source are often composed of interlaced odd and even lines. The De-Interlace filter (Figures 2–53 and 2–54) replaces one set of lines with a copy of the other, or interpolates between them.
Specialized Uses	De-Interlace can remove some motion artifacts from captured video destined for print or multimedia presentations.

TIP: Use De-Interlace to create smooth-looking QuickTime movies, even when the original interlaced images from video sources are fairly choppy.

Special-Purpose Filters

CUSTOM

Type	Special-effects/Art-effects filter
Description	Here's your chance to become a filter developer! The Custom filter (Figure 2–55) lets you modify the brightness value in a selection's pixels, using a method that

Figure 2–53
A frame-grabbed image direct
from video

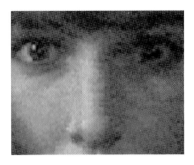

Figure 2–54
The same image after applying
the De-Interlace filter

compares adjacent pixels within a cell and sets brightness multipliers and weighted values. You choose the pixel cell scheme and enter the values in the Custom filter dialog box. Once you have entered all the desired brightness modifications, you can save the filter and use it again on another image.

Specialized Uses — The Custom filter develops your understanding of basic filter technology.

HIGH PASS

Type — Production/Special-effects filter

Description — The High Pass filter (Figure 2–56) works on the edges of color transition to eliminate areas of low intensity in an image. You can define the amount of image that you want to retain: A high number (up to 100 pixels) keeps

Figure 2–55
A variety of settings applied to the image shows how flexible the Custom filter can be.

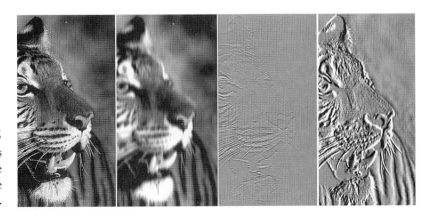

more pixels near the edge transitions, while a low number (as little as 1 pixel) retains the edges alone.

Specialized Uses   This filter is great for turning scans into line art.

MAXIMUM

Type   Production/Special-effects filter

Description   The Maximum filter (Figure 2–57) lets you identify and adjust pixel brightness by comparing adjacent pixels and applying the maximum brightness of one to the other.

Specialized Uses   This filter is useful for modifying masks and for creating a spread trap (it spreads the white areas and chokes the black areas).

MINIMUM

Type   Production/Special-effects filter

Description   The Minimum filter (Figure 2–58) compares the brightness of adjacent pixels and applies the minimum brightness of one pixel to the other.

Specialized Uses   The Minimum filter is useful for modifying masks. It creates a choke trap, since it spreads the black areas and chokes the white areas.

Figure 2–56
The High Pass filter applied to the tiger images with radius settings of (left to right) 10 pixels, 20 pixels, 40 pixels, and 80 pixels

Figure 2–57
The Maximum filter applied at a
radius of 5 pixels

Figure 2–58
The Minimum filter applied at a
radius of 5 pixels

OFFSET

Type	Special-effects filter
Description	The Offset filter (Figures 2–59 and 2–60) allows you to determine the number of pixels by which to shift a selection vertically and/or horizontally.
Specialized Uses	The Offset filter is useful for precise movement of selected areas and for producing seamless tiles.

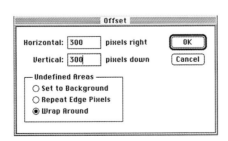

Figure 2–59
The Offset filter dialog box

Figure 2–60
The Offset filter set to one-half of
the pixel dimensions, which brings
all of the original outside edges to
the center

C H A P T E R

Third-Party Filters

An incredibly robust software industry has grown up around the development and marketing of third-party plug-in filters for Photoshop. Nevertheless, few filter sets are advertised or written about in any detail. In this chapter, we present the most comprehensive roundup of third-party filters ever assembled—including descriptions, images, specialized uses, and cool techniques for each—as well as some background information on their creators. We list these filter sets alphabetically by company name, and we use the same categories we defined for the Photoshop native filters in Chapter 2.

Keep in mind that the descriptions and techniques that follow are not substitutes for filter set user manuals. You can derive deeper operational information from the official documentation provided for each product.

Alaris

Alaris has developed a number of plug-ins that work with Photoshop and one another to streamline high-end imaging productivity.

Apertura

The Apertura suite of filters (Figures 3–1 through 3–3) assists production facilities that need access to large numbers of graphics files, particularly where Macintosh and Scitex systems must link together with efficient throughput.

TIFF

Type — Production filter

Description — AperturaTIFF is an Acquire/Export plug-in filter that lets you quickly preview (in low resolution) a large image file, select a portion of it that you want to edit, open and work on just that portion in full bit-depth mode, and save it back to the original image. With this filter, you can save enormous amounts of time when working with large, high-resolution images.

TIP: To immediately open exactly one-half or one-fourth of an image, first select an image. Then, in the preview screen for the TIFF filter, double-click the appropriate quarter- or half-image using the Marquee Quadrant Tool on the right. Double-clicking the center opens the entire image. This tip works for all the Alaris filter products.

HandshakeCT	Type	Production filter
	Description	Apertura HandshakeCT filter features the same selection-editing capabilities for ScitexCT (Continuous Tone) files as AperturaTIFF does for TIFF files.

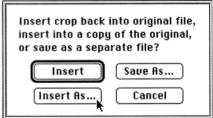

HandshakeLW	Type	Production filter
	Description	Apertura HandshakeLW filter lets you work on selected portions of ScitexLW (Linework) files without having to open the entire image, just as AperturaTIFF allows you to do with TIFF files.

Figure 3–1
The Apertura filter allows you to access any portion of a file to edit.

Figure 3–2
After editing a selection with an Apertura filter, you can either insert it back into the original file or save it as a new file.

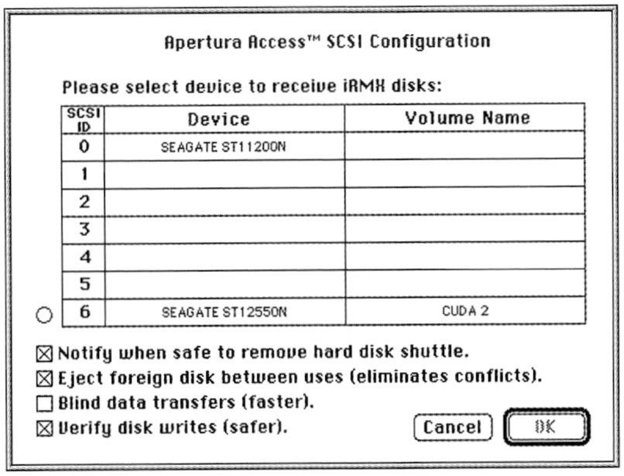

Figure 3–3
An access window allows the Apertura user to access iRMX-formatted Scitex optical disks directly.

AccessCT

Mac

Type	Production filter
Description	Apertura AccessCT lets Macintosh users edit ScitexCT images directly from foreign disks, such as iRMX®-formatted Scitex® optical disks, without any intermediate file translation or copying steps.

AccessLW

Mac

Type	Production filter
Description	Apertura AccessLW is a filter that lets you edit ScitexLW images directly from foreign disks, such as iRMX®-formatted Scitex® optical disks, again avoiding any intermediate file copying or translation steps.

TIP: If Scitex PS/2 RIPs or StarPSs are networked to your Macintoshes, you can directly open CTs and LWs across the network using AccessCT and AccessLW image modules.

Aldus

Venerable Aldus Corporation, now part of Adobe Systems, brought to market the first full-featured set of commercial third-party filters.

Gallery Effects, Classic Art, Volume 1

This package contains 16 filters that mimic classic art styles when applied to an image, such as a scanned photograph. You can either run Gallery Effects from within a standalone desk accessory or integrate it into a paint program as a set of plug-ins. Initially, Aldus positioned this filter set as an easy way for nonartists to achieve artistic effects at the push of a button. However, you can also use these plug-in tools in combination with other techniques and filters to expand artistic expression to new areas.

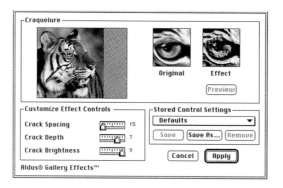

Figure 3–4
The standard Gallery
Effects dialog box gives
you the simple
parameters of the filter, a
Save Settings function,
and a preview.

All of the Gallery Effects filters have dialog boxes (see Figures 3–4 and 3–5), and all allow you to save your favorite settings by name. This allows easy batch processing of consecutive images for production.

TIP: Each of your projects can have a Gallery Effects setting named after it to assure consistency and ease of use. The default settings on the filters are more or less in a midrange. I save light and heavy settings for each filter to save time while preview-testing images.

NOTE TO WINDOWS USERS: While Gallery Effects Volumes 2 and 3 support both the Aldus and the Adobe plug-in specifications, Gallery Effects Volume 1 supports only the earlier Aldus standard. Gallery Effects Volume 1 filters might not be fully compatible with image-editing and paint applications whose Windows versions support only Photoshop-compatible plug-ins. Check with the application vendor.

  ## CHALK & CHARCOAL

Type   Art-effects filter
Description   The Chalk & Charcoal filter (Figure 3–6) replaces the
                        highlights and midtones in an image with a solid mid-

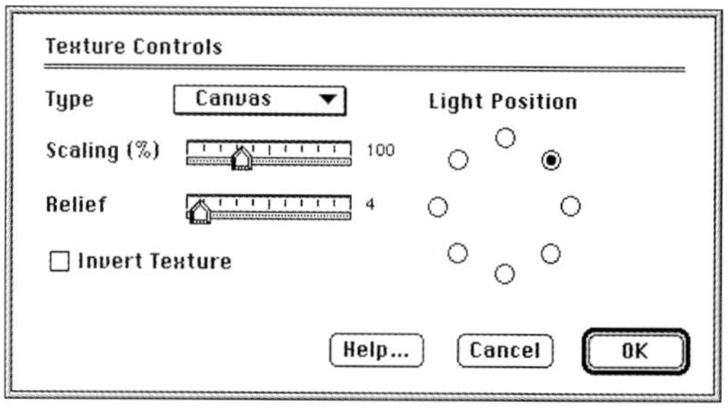

Figure 3–5
The secondary dialog
box is used in some of
the Gallery Effects filters
in Volumes 2 and 3.
Additional relief settings
and texture types are
available for your use.

Figure 3–6
The Chalk & Charcoal filter applied to the tiger image with three different sets of Charcoal Area, Chalk Area, and Stroke Pressure settings. Left to right: default settings of 6/6/1, 1/1/1, and 20/20/5.

tone gray background drawn in coarse chalk. It replaces the shadow areas with black diagonal charcoal lines. If the host application supports foreground and background colors, the Chalk & Charcoal filter uses the background color for the "chalk" and the foreground color for the "charcoal." You can set the levels at which both chalk and charcoal are applied, as well as the pressure of the strokes.

Specialized uses   Use this filter to add painterly stature to a fine-art or commercial-art project.

CHARCOAL

Type   Art-effects filter

Description   The Charcoal filter (Figure 3–7) removes the native color from a selection, creating a posterized, smudged effect along a diagonal axis. In some host applications,

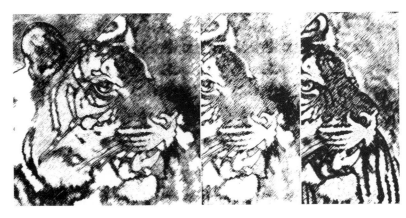

Figure 3–7
The Charcoal filter applied to the tiger with three different Charcoal Thickness, Detail, and Light/Dark Balance settings. Left to right: default settings of 1/5/50, 1/0/50, and 7/5/50.

the replacement color is black charcoal on a white paper background. In host applications, such as Adobe Photoshop and Fractal Design Painter, the charcoal strokes appear in the foreground color and the background color serves as the paper.

Specialized uses   Use this filter for fine-art or commercial illustrations, brochures, and annual reports.

  ## CHROME

Type   Art-effects filter

Description   The Chrome filter (Figure 3–8) gives an image the appearance of a 3D chrome map in which the highlights of the image represent the highest point and the shadows represent the valleys. If an image turns primarily a midtone gray after you apply this filter, use the Levels controls in Photoshop or contrast functions in other programs to give the image more punch.

Specialized uses   The Chrome filter produces metallic effects for commercial and fine-art illustration.

  ## CRAQUELURE

Type   Art-effects/Special-effects filter

Description   The Craquelure filter (Figure 3–9) creates elaborate embossing effects. The filter effect follows the values of the image and intensifies the embossing by breaking the image into a series of tighter cracks in the darker regions.

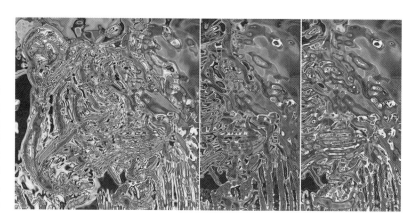

Figure 3–8
The Chrome filter applied using the following Detail and Smoothness settings (left to right): default settings of 4/7, 1/1, and 10/10.

Figure 3–9
The Craquelure filter applied to the tiger using Crack Spacing, Crack Depth, and Crack Brightness settings of (left to right) 15/6/9 (the defaults), 21/2/4, and 58/10/9.

Specialized uses   Craquelure simulates age and wear and tear for producing textures and altering photorealistic images.

TIP: The filter effect is quite striking and organic when applied to an image that contains a broad range of color or grayscale values. Flat areas take on a grid-like look. Areas with excessive flat areas may be masked out, or you can use the Dodge and Burn tool to modulate the surface of those areas.

TIP: Extremely low Crack Spacing settings for this filter result in a series of small highlighted nuggets in the tones of the selection.

DARK STROKES

Type   Art-effects filter
Description   The Dark Strokes filter (Figure 3–10) affects the light and dark areas of your image differently. It shifts dark

Figure 3–10
The Dark Strokes filter applied using Balance, Black Intensity, and White Settings of (left to right) 5/6/2 (the default settings), 1/1/2, and 10/10/10.

areas closer to black and renders them with short, diagonal paintbrush strokes. The filter shifts lighter areas of an image toward white, rendering them in longer strokes travelling in the same direction. The final result is a subtle and natural-looking posterization of an image.

Specialized uses   Use Dark Strokes for fine-art or commercial illustrations when a stronger internal contrast is required.

DRY BRUSH

Type   Art-effects filter
Description   The Dry Brush filter (Figure 3–11) finds element edges and paints them with a brush that is somewhere between oil and watercolor, adding an interesting and subtle texture to your image. This filter also reduces the range of colors in an image to areas of common color. You can set the brush size, the amount of detail shown in its strokes, and the texture intensity.
Specialized uses   Dry Brush simplifies photographs to create a more unified look for brochures and annual reports.

EMBOSS

Type   Art-effects filter
Description   The Gallery Effects Emboss filter (Figure 3–12) differs significantly from the Photoshop native Emboss filter. Colors and details are retained rather than being grayed out as with the Photoshop Emboss filter. Directional and

Figure 3–11
The Dry Brush filter applied with Brush Size, Brush Detail, and Texture settings of (left to right) 2/8/1 (the defaults), 1/1/2, and 10/1/3

Figure 3–12
The Gallery Effects
Emboss filter with Relief
and Light Position
settings of (left to right)
11/top right (the
defaults), 18/bottom,
and 25/left

embossing depth controls are available to produce tightly controlled edge enhancements.

Specialized uses	This is a workhorse filter that can accentuate any filter effect.

FILM GRAIN

Type	Art-effects filter
Description	The Film Grain filter (Figure 3–13) does not add RGB color like the Add Noise filter in Photoshop, so you don't have to worry about bizarre-looking skin tones, for example. Film Grain adds a fairly even pattern of grain to the midtones and shadow areas of your image and a heavier grain to the highlight areas, saturating them out somewhat (though you can control how intensely the highlights are treated).

Figure 3–13
The Film Grain filter
applied using Grain,
Highlight Area, and
Highlight Intensity
settings of (left to right)
4/8/10 (the defaults),
10/10/5, and20/5/0

Specialized uses	Use Film Grain to eliminate banding in blends and to visually unify elements derived from various sources.

 FRESCO

Type	Art-effects filter
Description	This is your chance to become El Greco. The Fresco filter (Figure 3–14) renders your image as though you had quickly painted it with short jabs of your paintbrush. You can set the size and detail of the brushstrokes and the intensity of the texture effect.
Specialized uses	Use Fresco when a painterly effect would add stature to a fine- or commercial-art project.

 GRAPHIC PEN

Type	Art-effects filter
Description	The Graphic Pen filter (Figure 3–15), especially effective with scanned photographs, makes an image look as though you had drawn it by hand with an ultrafine marker, using only straight lines going in approximately the same direction. (Impress your friends!) This filter uses the host application's foreground and background colors to replace any color information. Stroke length, direction, and light/dark balance are all user-definable.
Specialized uses	Use Graphic Pen for fine-art or commercial illustrations, brochures, and annual reports.

Figure 3–14
The Fresco filter applied with Brush Size, Brush Detail, and Texture settings of 2/8/1 (the default settings), 5/5/2, and10/1/3

Figure 3–15
The Graphic Pen filter applied using Stroke Length, Light/Dark Balance, and Stroke Direction of (left to right) 15/50/Right Diagonal (the defaults), 1/1/1, and 20/20/5

MOSAIC

Type	Art-effects filter
Description	The Mosaic filter (Figure 3–16) re-creates an image as though you had made it out of square tiles. You can set not only the size of the tiles, but also the width and brightness of the grout. Now, that's entertainment!
Specialized uses	Use Mosaic when a painterly effect would add stature to a fine-art or commercial-art project.

POSTER EDGES

Type	Art-effects/Special-effects filter
Description	The Poster Edges filter (Figure 3–17) transforms an image two ways. First, it *posterizes* the image (reduces the number of colors) according to the posterization level you set. Second, it finds the edges of elements in your

Figure 3–16
The Gallery Effects Mosaic filter applied using Tile Size, Grout Width, and Lighten Grout settings of (left to right) 12/3/9 (the defaults), 50/8/5, and 80/12/7

Figure 3–17
The Poster Edges filter applied using Edge Thicknes, Edge Intensity, and Posterization settings of (left to right) 2/1/2 (the defaults), 5/5/3, and 10/10/6

image and draws black lines on them. You can set the thickness and intensity of these black lines.

Specialized uses   Use Poster Edges for fine-art or commercial illustrations, brochures, and annual reports.

 RIPPLE

Type   Distort filter
Description   Despite its name, the Ripple filter (Figure 3–18) doesn't make your image look as though it got drunk on cheap wine. On second thought, maybe it does. The Ripple fil-ter adds occasional little ripples to an image, creating the impression that the image is underwater and a light breeze is blowing, refracting the light passing through the water onto your image. Ripple size and strength (how strong is that breeze?) are user-definable.

Figure 3–18
The Gallery Effects Ripple filter applied using Ripple Size and Ripple Magnitude settings of (left to right) 9/9 (the defaults), 4/4, and 15/16

Figure 3–19
The Smudge Stick filter applied using Stroke Length, Highlight Area, and Highlight Intensity settings of (left to right) 2/0/10 (the defaults), 4/10/5, and 10/15/1.

Specialized uses	This filter produces liquid effects and serves as a basis for further filtering.

SMUDGE STICK

Type	Art-effects filter
Description	The Smudge Stick filter (Figure 3–19) re-creates an image so that it appears to have been painted naturally with short, wet strokes. Darker areas of the image are smeared somewhat into the lighter ones, and the light areas lose detail and become brighter. The overall effect is soft and muted, yet vibrant.
Specialized uses	Use Smudge Stick when a painterly effect would add stature to a fine- or commercial-art project.

SPATTER

Type	Art-effects filter
Description	The Spatter filter (Figure 3–20) transforms an image into one that appears to have been created with a spatter airbrush. You can define the radius of the spray and the smoothness of the overall effect.
Specialized uses	Strong amounts of Spattering can simplify an image so that you can use it as a background for commercial- and fine-art applications.

Figure 3–20
The Spatter filter
applied using Spray
Radius and Smoothness
settings of (left to right)
10/5 (the defaults),
19/10, and 25/2

WATERCOLOR

Type	Art-effects filter
Description	The Watercolor filter (Figure 3–21) simplifies the detail of an image and detects shifts in tones. Tonal-shift edges are given a more saturated color border to simulate the pooling of watercolor paint.
Specialized uses	Use Watercolor when a painterly effect would add stature to a fine- or commercial-art project.

TIP: The Watercolor filter is the most time-consuming filter in the set. Because it simplifies shapes and detail, I find that I can obtain quite good effects on a downsampled selection. Downsampling can save an enormous amount of time, and the image can be resampled up to full resolution for the cleanup of the edges that I require for my work.

Figure 3–21
The Watercolor filter
applied using Brush
Detail, Shadow
Intensity, and Texture
settings of (left to right)
9/1/1 (the defaults),
13/5/2, and 2/9/3

Gallery Effects: Classic Art, Volume 2

The second set of 16 Gallery Effect filters retains the Classic Art name but adheres less stringently than the Volume 1 filters to the emulation of classical art techniques. You have enhanced control over the effects of some of the filters. Preview capabilities and the Save Settings option are available as in Volume 1, and a Help button has been added to each filter's dialog box, providing guidance, tips, and step-by-step instructions for specialized uses for the filter.

ACCENTED EDGES

Type	Special-effects filter
Description	The Accented Edges filter (Figure 3–22) finds the *edges*—areas of high contrast—in an image or selection and changes their look. You can define the width, brightness level, and smoothness of the edges.
Specialized uses	Use Accented Edges for fine-art or commercial illustrations, brochures, and annual reports.

TIP: To give an image more of a "hand-rendered" look, apply the Accented Edges filter first, and then one of the "painting" filters, such as Dry Brush, Watercolor, or Texturizer.

ANGLED STROKES

Type	Art-effects filter
Description	The Angled Strokes filter (Figure 3–23) re-creates the image as though it had been painted with diagonal strokes. Depending on the brightness threshold you set

Figure 3–22
The Accented Edges filter applied using Edge Width, Edge Brightness, and Smoothness settings of (left to right) 2/3/5 (the defaults), 14/22/15, and 4/48/4

Figure 3–23
The Angled Stroke filter applied using Direction Balance, Stroke Length, and Sharpness settings of (left to right) 50/15/3 (the defaults), 0/25/10, and 100/50/10

using the Direction Balance control, some areas get painted in one diagonal direction, while others get painted in the opposite direction. You can also set the stroke length and the degree of sharpening.

Specialized uses   Use Angled Strokes when a painterly effect would add stature to a fine- or commercial-art project.

NOTE: To obtain a visible stroke effect on high-resolution files, set Sharpness to a high value.

  ## BAS RELIEF

Type   Art-effects filter
Description   Using the host application's foreground and background colors, the Bas Relief filter (Figure 3–24) colorizes the image or selection and makes it appear to have been

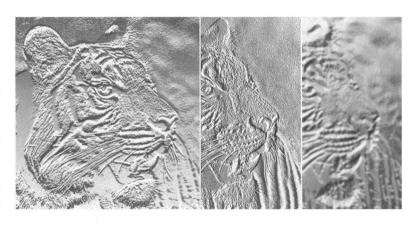

Figure 3–24
The Bas Relief filter applied using Detail, Smoothness, and Light Positions settings of (left to right) 13/3/bottom (the defaults), 15/1/right, and 8/7/top left

Specialized uses

carved in low relief. You can control the amount of detail rendered, the smoothness, and the sidelighting angle. Bas Relief is useful in developing paper textures and bump maps for 3D programs.

TIP: For an especially realistic or cool effect, apply the Bas Relief filter and then a rough or metallic texturizer filter.

COLORED PENCIL

Type   Art-effects filter
Description   The Colored Pencil filter (Figure 3–25) draws angular strokes in two directions, using the image colors for pencil color reference. The current background color in Photoshop is the paper color for this filter. You can define the lightness or darkness of the paper as the density of the pencil strokes.
Specialized uses   Use Colored Pencil for fine-art or commercial illustrations, brochures, and annual reports.

TIP: In Photoshop or Painter, change the background color just before applying the Colored Pencil filter to a selected area. This technique can create the effect of a parchment background like that seen on hand-drawn maps.

NOTE: The foreground color can vary the effect of this filter drastically.

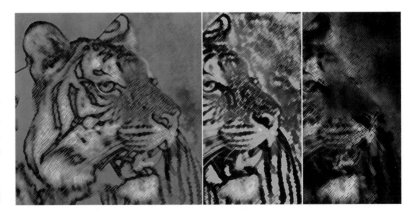

Figure 3–25
The Colored Pencil filter applied using Pencil Width, Stroke Pressure, and Paper Brightness settings of (left to right) 4/8/25 (the defaults), 9/15/37, and 3/15/0

Figure 3–26
The Diffuse Glow filter applied using Graininess, Glow Amount, and Clear Amount settings of (left to right) 6/10/15 (the defaults), 10/11/7, and 0/14/14.

DIFFUSE GLOW

Type	Special-effects filter
Description	The Diffuse Glow filter (Figure 3–26) adds translucent white noise to an image. The glow fades away from the center of the selection.
Specialized uses	Diffuse Glow is useful for fine-art or commercial illustrations, brochures, and annual reports.

GLOWING EDGES

Type	Special-effects filter
Description	The Glowing Edges filter (Figure 3–27) is similar to the Find Edges filter included with Photoshop, but with some notable exceptions. You can regulate the width and brightness of the glow effect while viewing a preview.

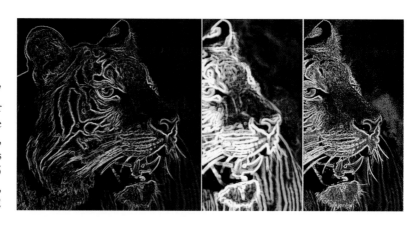

Figure 3–27
The Glowing Edges filter applied using Edge Width, Edge Brightness, and Smoothness settings of (left to right) 2/6/5 (the defaults), 7/10/8, and 1/20/2.

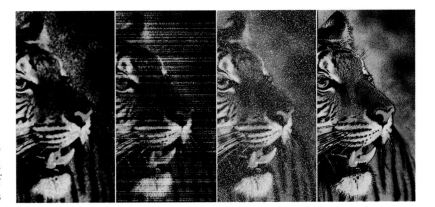

Figure 3–28
The Grain filter applied using a variety of grain types

Specialized uses   Use Glowing Edges to soften images and colorize areas for dramatic effects.

GRAIN

Type	Art-effects filter
Description	The Grain filter (Figure 3–28) adds texture to an image by simulating different types of grain, including speckles and sprinkles. You can adjust the amount of graininess and the intensity of contrast.
Specialized uses	The Grain filter offers an interesting way to add an organic feel to artificial-looking, computer-generated illustrations. It is also useful for simulating an old photograph.

NOTE PAPER

Type	Art-effects filter
Description	The Note Paper filter (Figure 3–29) combines the effects of the Emboss and Grain filters. Dark areas of the image appear as holes in the top layer of paper, revealing a background paper layer. Slider controls let you define image balance (lightness/darkness), graininess, and *relief* (depth of the embossing effect).
Specialized uses	Use Note Paper to simplify images for spot color separation and duotones.

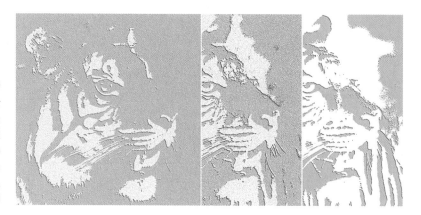

Figure 3–29
The Note Paper filter applied using Image Balance, Graininess, and Relief settings of (left to right) 25/10/11 (the defaults), 14/2/25, and 9/0/10

PALETTE KNIFE

Type	Art-effects filter
Description	The Palette Knife filter (Figure 3–30) reduces detail in an image and creates the effect of a thinly painted canvas with the fibers showing through. The filter uses a supplied or user-defined texture to simulate the exposed canvas.
Specialized uses	Use Palette Knife when a painterly effect would add stature to a fine-art or commercial-art project.

PATCHWORK

Type	Art-effects filter
Description	The Patchwork filter (Figure 3–31) makes a grid of squares filled with the predominant color of that area of the selection. You can set the size and depth of the tiles in a dialog box. The filter randomly increases and

Figure 3–30
The Palette Knife filter applied using Stroke Size, Stroke Detail, and Softness settings of (left to right) 25/3/0 (the defaults), 14/3/10, and 42/3/0

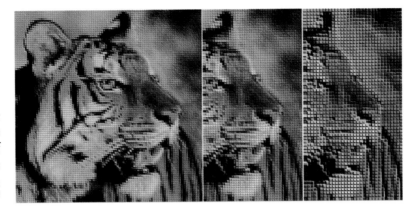

Figure 3–31
The Patchwork filter applied using Square Size and Relief settings of (left to right) 4/8 (the defaults), 6/11, and 10/19

reduces the tile sizes by emulating highlighted and shadowed edges.

Specialized uses — Use Patchwork when a painterly effect would add stature to a fine-art or commercial-art project.

PHOTOCOPY

Type   Art-effects filter
Description   The Photocopy filter (Figure 3–32) strips color from an image and leaves a visual artifact much like one from an early 1960s photocopier.
Specialized uses   This filter simplifies images for a retrocyberpunk-minimalist look.

Figure 3–32
The Photocopy filter applied using Detail and Darkness settings of (left to right) 7/8 (the defaults), 13/22, and 22/41

Figure 3–33
The Rough Pastels filter
can generate a variety of
pastelesque styles.

ROUGH PASTELS

Type	Art-effects filter
Description	The Rough Pastels filter (Figure 3–33) re-creates a selected area as though it had been drawn with pastel chalk on a textured background. Bright colors receive a thick application of chalk, and darker colors receive a thin application with more texture showing through. You can use one of the built-in textures or a user-defined one that you have saved as a PICT file.
Specialized uses	Use Rough Pastels when a painterly effect would add stature to a fine-art or commercial-art project.

SPRAYED STROKES

Type	Art-effects filter
Description	The Sprayed Strokes filter (Figure 3–34) uses the dominant colors of an image to re-create the image with

Figure 3–34
The Sprayed Strokes
filter applied using
Stroke Length, Spray
Radius, and Stroke
Direction settings of (left
to right) 12/7/Right
Diagonal (the defaults),
15/14/Left Diagonal,
and 20/25/Left Diagonal

angled, sprayed strokes of paint. You can adjust the filter's stroke length and angle.

Specialized uses   Use Sprayed Strokes when a painterly effect would add stature to a fine-art or commercial-art project.

TIP: **You can create a water reflection with the Sprayed Strokes filter by duplicating the selection, applying the Sprayed Strokes filter, vertically flipping the top half of the selection, and then darkening it.**

STAMP

Type   Art-effects filter

Description   The Stamp filter (Figure 3–35), normally used with black-and-white images, is designed to render an image as though it had been produced with a wood or rubber stamp. You can define the smoothness of the edges and the light/dark balance.

Specialized uses   The Stamp filter simplifies images for spot color work or for further manipulation.

TEXTURIZER

Type   Art-effects filter

Description   The Texturizer filter (Figure 3–36) applies a user-created or supplied texture (canvas, brick, and so on) to the image or selection. You can vary the effects of this filter by setting the light source and the relief amount

Figure 3–35
The Stamp filter applied using Light/Dark Balance and Smoothness settings of (left to right) 25/5 (the defaults), 11/19, and 6/33

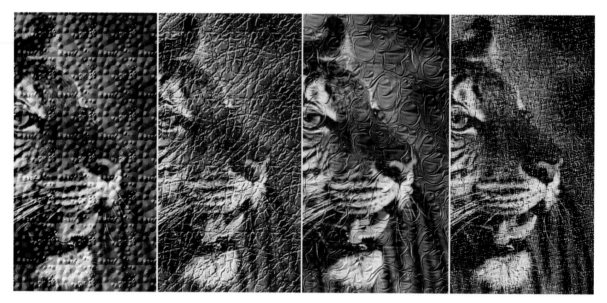

Figure 3–36   The Texturizer filter can generate a variety of textures.

Specialized uses   When used after applying other filters, the Texturizer makes an image look more organic and painterly.

  ## UNDERPAINTING

Type   Art-effects filter
Description   Similar to the Texturizer filter, the Underpainting filter (Figure 3–37) first roughly paints the image onto a supplied or user-defined texture, and then repaints the final image on top in greater detail. The final effect is a richly textured image.

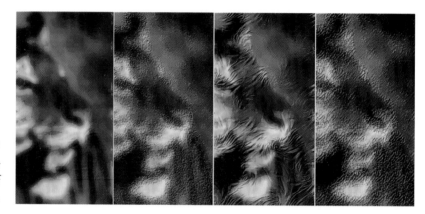

Figure 3–37
The Underpainting filter
can generate a variety of
painting effects.

Specialized uses   Use the Underpainting filter when a painterly effect would add stature to a fine-art or commercial-art project.

CONTÉ CRAYON

Gallery Effects, Classic Art, Volume 3

Type   Art-effects filter

Description   Conté crayons are darkish, crumbly crayons with a charcoal-like texture. The Conté Crayon filter (Figure 3–38) colorizes the image in this style (using the host application's foreground and background colors), resulting in a roughly textured painting with dense darks and pure whites.

Specialized uses   Use this filter for fine-art or commercial illustrations, brochures, and annual reports.

TIP: For a truer Conté effect, change the foreground color to one of the common Conté Crayon colors (black, sepia, sanguine).

TIP: Before using the Conté Crayon filter, change the background color to white with a little of the foreground color added to it for a soft, muted effect.

TIP: Conté Crayon used with a Sandstone texture resembles 19th-century Conté drawing techniques perfectly.

CROSSHATCH

Type   Art-effects filter

Description   The Crosshatch filter (Figure 3–39) creates the effect of pencil strokes crossing over one another in an image or

Figure 3–38
The Conté Crayon filter applied using Foreground Level, Background Level, and Texture settings of (left to right) 11/7/Canvas (the defaults), 4/12/Sandstone, and 12/4/Brick

Figure 3–39
The Crosshatch filter applied with Stroke Length, Sharpness, and Strength settings of (left to right) 9/6/1 (the defaults), 25/9/2, and 32/12/3

selection. The colors of the image remain true, but the rendering is rougher. You can modulate the stroke length of the hatching, the sharpness, and the intensity of the effect.

Specialized uses   Use Crosshatch when a painterly effect would add stature to a fine-art or commercial-art project.

TIP: **The Strength setting determines the number of hatching passes. The application time of the filter is longer with the Strength set to 3.**

CUT OUT

Type   Art-effects filter
Description   The Cut Out filter (Figure 3–40) affects an image as though it had been created using several layers of colored paper cutouts. High-contrast sections of the

Figure 3–40
The Cut Out filter applied using Number of Levels, Edge Simplicity, and Edge Fidelity settings of (left to right) 4/4/2 (the defaults), 2/1/1, and 7/6/3

original image appear as silhouettes. You can adjust Edge Simplicity, Edge Fidelity, and the number of levels, or layers, with higher numbers yielding a more detailed image.

Specialized uses   The Cut Out filter is excellent for spot color separation work, t-shirts, posters, and interesting collages.

TIP: After applying the Cut Out filter, an application of the Sharpen Intensity filter from Kai's Power Tools 2.0 will bring the color punch back to the image.

 GLASS

Type   Art-effects filter

Description   The Glass filter (Figure 3–41) makes an image appear as though you were viewing it through a specific type of glass. The filter includes some built-in glass effects (blocks, frosted, and so on), or you can create your own glass surface as a PICT file and apply it. You can adjust scaling, distortion, and smoothness settings.

Specialized uses   The Glass filter diffuses background images and provides liquefying effects for fine art and commercial art.

TIP: When using the surface controls with a PICT file, follow the conventions for using the Photoshop Displace filter.

Figure 3–41
The Glass filter applied using Distortion, Smoothness, and Surface settings of (left to right) 5/3/Frosted (the defaults), 10/8/Blocks, and 20/14/Tiny Lens

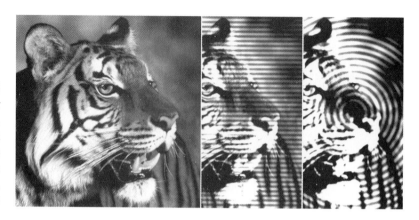

Figure 3–42
The Halftone filter applied using Dot Size, Contrast, and Screen Type settings of (left to right) 1/5/Dot (the defaults), 5/15/Line, and 7/27/Circle

HALFTONE

Type	Art-effects filter
Description	The Halftone filter (Figure 3–42) is more useful for artistic effect than for the creation of true halftones. With this filter, you can produce an image reminiscent of a traditionally created halftone but still retain the full continuous range of tones.
Specialized uses	Large halftone rosettes can convert images into contemporary illustrations.

INK OUTLINES

Type	Art-effects filter
Description	The Ink Outlines filter (Figure 3–43) uses fine, narrow pen lines to go over the details of the original image. Stroke Length and Light/Dark Intensity are user-definable.

Figure 3–43
The Ink Outlines filter applied using Stroke Length, Dark Intensity, and Light Intensity settings of (left to right) 4/20/10 (the defaults), 25/30/25, and 50/50/50

Specialized uses   Use this filter when a painterly effect would add stature to a fine- or commercial-art project.

NEON GLOW

Type   Special-effects filter

Description   The Neon Glow filter (Figure 3–44) allows you to quickly and creatively apply a neon effect to an image or to type. A button leading to the Color Picker allows you to choose the glow color, and slider controls let you set the size of the glow and determine whether to apply an outline neon effect (around the outside edges) or an inline one (a glow within the outlines).

Specialized uses   Use this filter to colorize images while softening their look.

PAINT DAUBS

Type   Art-effects filter

Description   With six different types of brushes, the Paint Daubs filter (Figure 3–45) lets you apply various paintbrush-style effects to an image or selection. You can modify the size and sharpness characteristics of each paintbrush.

Specialized uses   Use Paint Daubs when a painterly effect would add stature to a fine-art or commercial-art project.

TIP: Use the Texturizer filter to increase the natural-media look of the Paint Daubs filter.

Figure 3–44
The Neon Glow filter applied using Glow Size, Glow Brightness, and Glow Color settings of (left to right) 5/15/Blue (the defaults), 24/30/Blue, and 24/50/Blue

Figure 3–45
The Paint Daubs filter applied using Brush Size, Sharpness, and Brush Type settings of (left to right) 8/7/Simple (the defaults), 25/20/Dark Rough, and 15/30/Wide Sharp

PLASTER

Type	Art-effects filter
Description	The Plaster filter (Figure 3–46) re-creates an image as though it had been molded out of 3D plaster. Dark areas appear raised on plateaus and white areas recede into valleys (or you could invert the image first to achieve the opposite effect). The Plaster filter uses the host application's foreground and background colors to colorize the final result.
Specialized uses	The Plaster filter offers a simple way to achieve a moist 3D text effect.

TIP: Using the Plaster filter, high-contrast images such as text can be processed into liquid wonders.

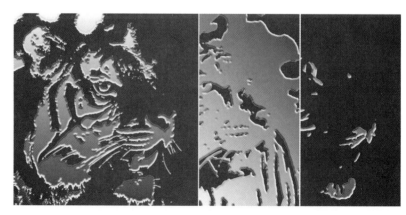

Figure 4–46
The Plaster filter applied at Image Balance, Smoothness, and Light Position settings of (left to right) 20/2/Top (the defaults), 6/8/Bottom Left, and 40/10/Top Left

PLASTIC WRAP

Type	Special-effects filter
Description	The Plastic Wrap filter (Figure 3–47) lays a surreal, reflective coating onto an image or selection. This filter highlights the surface detail of most images. You can modify the Highlight Strength, amount of Detail, and Smoothness.
Specialized uses	This filter works wonderfully for storing perishables overnight.

TIP: **The Help file of this filter describes an interesting way to achieve an "artistically altered Polaroid" look with Plastic Wrap.**

RETICULATION

Type	Art-effects filter
Description	The Reticulation filter (Figure 3–48) re-creates digitally an effect that is traditionally achieved using film emulsions. When an artist or photographer controls the shrinking and distorting of film emulsion, the resulting image appears clumped in the darker areas and lightly grained in the lighter ones. This filter allows you to control grain Density and Black/White Levels, and uses the host application's foreground and background colors to colorize the image.
Specialized uses	Use the Reticulation filter for mezzo-effects when the ordinary will not do.

Figure 3–47
The Plastic Wrap filter applied using Highlight Strength, Detail, and Smoothness settings of (left to right) 15/9/7 (the defaults), 10/3/3, and 20/8/8

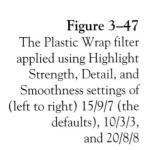

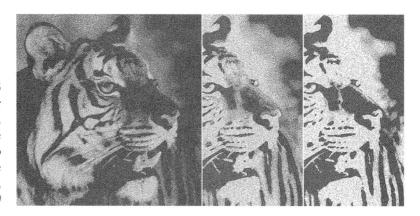

Figure 3–48
The Reticulation filter applied using Density, Black Level, and White Level settings of (left to right) 12/40/5 (the defaults), 25/25/25, and 35/40/40

TIP: Reticulation provides excellent "tooth" and grain to use as a paper texture for texturizing an image. See Chapter 5 for specific techniques.

SPONGE

Type	Art-effects filter
Description	The Sponge filter (Figure 3–49) gives your image a highly contrasted and textured "sponge-painted" look. You can set the size of the sponge "brush" and the levels of definition and smoothness.
Specialized uses	Use the Sponge filter when a painterly effect would add stature to a fine- or commercial-art project.

TIP: The Sponge filter yields especially realistic effects if you afterward pass the image through one of the rougher Texture filters.

Figure 3–49
The Sponge filter applied using Brush Size, Definition, and Smoothness settings of (left to right) 2/12/5 (the defaults), 5/17/7, and 10/25/15

STAINED GLASS

Type	Art-effects filter
Description	The Stained Glass filter (Figure 3–50) breaks up your image into single-colored adjacent cells separated by a foreground-colored border. You can change the size of the cell, the thickness of the border, and the intensity of the light shining through the glass from behind.
Specialized uses	When you need a unique effect, the Stained Glass filter is dramatic enough to require judicious use.

TIP: **You may want to posterize the image before applying the Stained Glass filter so that more adjacent cells share the same color.**

SUMI-E

Type	Art-effects filter
Description	The Sumi-E filter (Figure 3–51) is named after a traditional Japanese painting style that uses a wet brush loaded with black ink on absorbent rice paper. The Sumi-E filter re-creates your image in this style, producing rich blacks with soft, blurry edges atop the colors.
Specialized uses	Use this filter for lyrical, visual passages on fine-art and commercial jobs.

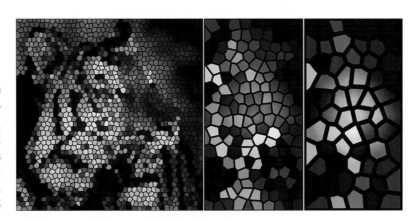

Figure 3–50
The Stained Glass filter applied using Cell Size, Border Thickness, and Light Intensity settings of (left to right) 10/4/3 (the defaults), 25/10/5, and 40/20/8

Figure 3–51
The Sumi-E filter
applied using Stroke
Width, Stroke Pressure,
and Contrast settings of
(left to right) 10/2/16
(the defaults), 10/7/20,
and 15/15/40

TORN EDGES

Type	Art-effects filter
Description	The Torn Edges filter (Figure 3–52) creates an image whose edges have the ragged, random look of torn paper. You can modify the image balance, smoothness, and contrast of the filter effect. The Torn Edges filter uses the host application's foreground and background colors to colorize the resulting image.
Specialized uses	Torn Edges reduces color for single-color and duotone printwork.

WATER PAPER

Type	Art-effects filter
Description	The Water Paper filter (Figure 3–53) causes an image to appear as though it had been painted using daubs of paint on wet, fibrous paper. The paint gets absorbed by

Figure 3–52
The Torn Edges filter
applied using Image
Balance, Smoothness,
and Contrast settings of
(left to right) 25/11/17
(the defaults), 14/5/8,
and 25/1/12

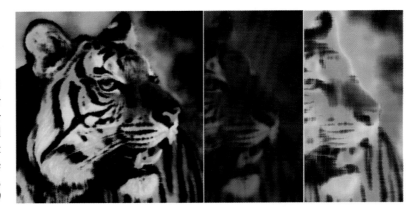

Figure 3–53
The Water Paper filter applied using Fiber Length, Brightness, and Contrast settings of (left to right) 15/60/80 (the defaults), 30/30/30, and 40/80/80

the paper's fibers and stretches out along them for a soft, blurry effect. You can set the fiber length, brightness, and image contrast.

Specialized uses   Water Paper is excellent for screened-back backgrounds in brochures and annual reports.

Andromeda Filters

Andromeda is a company that has had a long history of interaction with Adobe. Andromeda developed the original Streamline program marketed by Adobe and has long provided specialty filters for specific needs of companies. Series 1 filters are unique for motion effects and for simulating glints, sparks, geometric diffractions, reflections, and mezzo line screens. The Series 2 3D filters create three-dimensional surface wrapping effects as well as ambient, spot, and specular lighting effects, offering the user control over viewpoint and distance. The filters accept both RGB and CMYK images for processing.

Andromeda Series 1

The Andromeda Series 1 Photography Filters emulate traditional optical lens effects rather than painterly ones. Photographers familiar with the Cokin series of camera filters will find their software counterparts here. The user-definable settings of these filters, along with Andromeda's additional configurations and effects, render them much more powerful than effects that photographers can easily re-create in the darkroom.

Each of the 10 filters features a dialog box with an amply sized preview area. The filter set is unique in its ability to act upon a portion of the selection area. This ability is limited to rectangular areas; Andromeda recommends making irregular selections in the host application before applying a filter.

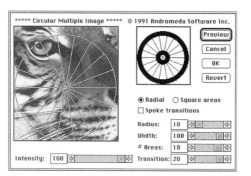

Figure 3–54
The cMulti dialog box gives you considerable control over the size, number, and shape of the multiples, as well as over the transitions between them.

 cMULTI

Type	Special-effects filter
Description	cMulti Filter stands for Circular Multiple Images Filter. cMulti (Figures 3–54 and 3–55) places a user-defined number of multiples around the original selection. The effect is much like a child's mirrored kaleidoscope. You can define rectangular or circular multiples and specify the radius, width, transparency, feathering, and number of multiples.
Specialized uses	Fool your myopic friends. Tease drunks.

 DESIGNS

Type	Special-effects filter
Description	Designs, the most intricate of the Andromeda Series 1 filters (Figures 3–56 and 3–57), lets you create a wide variety of dimensioned patterns within an image or selected area. When working with grayscale images, you

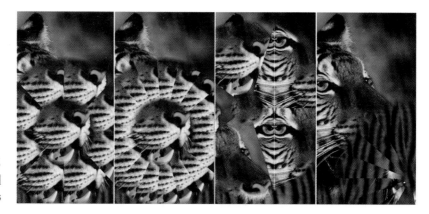

Figure 3–55
The cMulti filter applied using a variety of settings

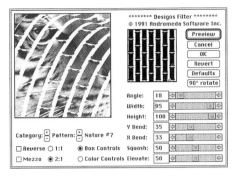

Figure 3–56
The Design Filter dialog box includes X, Y, and Squash controls for twisting the design. Many color and sizing options are also available.

can also create prehalftoned effects with the Mezzo feature. There are 13 categories of patterns from which you can choose, totaling 104 patterns altogether. When you are in Pattern mode, parameters you can define include Angle, Width, Height, Y Bend, X Bend, Squash, and Elevate. You can reverse out the pattern, antialias it, define a color and the color intensity in which it will appear, and rotate the pattern by 90 degrees. When in Mezzo mode, you can set the Intensity, Pattern, and Grain of the screen effect. A magnification preview feature lets you preview even fine-grained patterns.

Specialized uses
Use the Designs filter to composite realistic images with patterned backgrounds, create 3D and 3D texturing within an image, and prehalftone grayscale images.

Figure 3–57
You can generate many effects with the Designs filter. The Mezzo effects obtainable are not well known but can be quite useful. The second tiger from the left has a Mezzo dot applied to it.

DIFFRACT

Type	Special-effects filter
Description	The Diffract filter (Figures 3–58 and 3–59) creates a circular pattern of spoke-shaped rainbow rays radiating outward from a user-defined center point in an image. This effect resembles the one produced by a diffraction lens on a camera. You control the Radius, Length, number of Spokes, Angle, Thickness, and Intensity of the diffraction rays.
Specialized uses	Diffract is useful for drawing visual attention to bright points of light, sun reflections, or night lights within an image.

 HALO

Type	Imaging filter
Description	The Halo filter (Figures 3–60 and 3–61) spreads out the bright highlights of an image into adjoining darker areas. You control the direction, amount of Spread, Cutoff distance, Angle, and amount of Diffusion of the effect, as well as the Height, Width, and Intensity of the highlights produced.

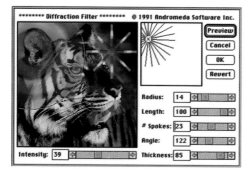

Figure 3–58
Real-time previews in the Diffract filter dialog box help in adjusting the width and intensity of the rainbow reflection. Notice the merged diffraction in the top left of the preview.

Figure 3–59
Multiple applications of the Diffract filter applied to show a variety of effects

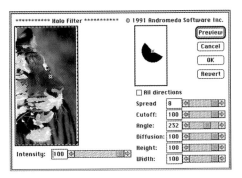

Figure 3–60
The Halo filter dialog box provides an adjustable black wedge to help visualize the spread and angle of the halo effect.

Specialized uses   Use Halo with high-contrast daylight photos, nighttime photos that feature at least some bright spots of light, and black-and-white images. Halo is less than effective with images that are dark throughout.

PRISM

Type   Special-effects filter

Description   The Prism filter (Figures 3–62 and 3–63) creates spectral color effects radiating out from the contours of an image, as though the viewer were looking through a glass prism. You define the center point from which the prismatic effect originates and the direction in which it radiates. Other options include the amount of Spread, Angle, Height, Width, and Intensity of the effect.

Specialized uses   Use Prism to enhance the effect of high-speed motion in a color photo or to add a rainbow-colored "jitter" look to an image.

Figure 3–61
The Halo filter applied to the tigers using various settings

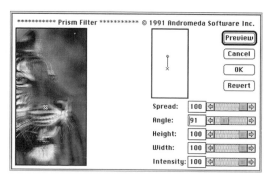

Figure 3–62
A large color preview in the Prism filter dialog box aids in the adjustments needed to jitter the colors just the way you want.

 RAINBOW

Type	Special-effects filter
Description	This filter (Figures 3–64 and 3–65) adds a rainbow arc to an image starting from the point of origin you specify. You can set the Angle, Radius, Width, and point of Origin of the arc, and can vary the color Intensity and amount of Fade. A Pot of Gold option adds a small yellow half-moon at the bottom of the arc.
Specialized uses	Add actual rainbows to images, or place this effect behind curved text or other curved objects for spectral color effects.

 REFLECTION

Type	Special-effects filter
Description	The Reflection filter (Figures 3–66 and 3–67) creates a reflection of a selected area with a user-definable amount of blending. The dialog box shows two boxes, with the

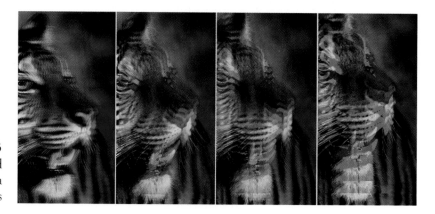

Figure 3–63
The Prism filter applied to the tigers using a variety of settings

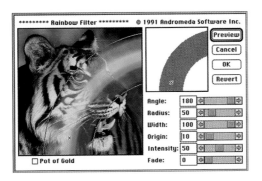

Figure 3–64
The Rainbow filter dialog box features a configurable set of rainbow parameters, including a Pot of Gold option.

Figure 3–65
A large high-intensity rainbow applied to the tiger

upper box representing the area to be reflected and the lower box representing the area that displays the end result of the reflection. You can reposition these boxes interactively and then use the sliders to control the Height and Width of the boxes, the amount of Gap between the original and the reflection, the amount of Transition (feathering), and Intensity (transparency of the reflection).

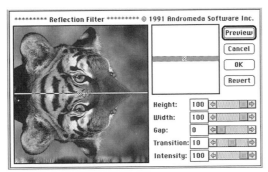

Figure 3–66
The Reflection filter dialog box allows you to see the transition between the reflection and the originating sample. You can also preview translucence.

Figure 3–67
The Reflection filter creates a perfect reflection of the upper portion of the tiger.

Specialized uses	Use the Reflection filter with images containing water to simulate realistic reflections; in images containing department-store windows or other reflective surfaces; or in commercial art to create special upside-down effects.

sMULTI

Type	Special-effects filter
Description	The sMulti filter (Figures 3–68 and 3–69) creates multiple square-shaped or parallel-line copies of an image or selected area in patterns that radiate out from a user-defined center. Users can set the center point, Angle, number of Areas, Spacing, and Intensity, and can choose from among Parallel-line effects, Square areas, or Parallel combined.
Specialized uses	This filter is useful for advertising-art effects and for fine art that emphasizes abstract or geometric shapes.

Figure 3–68
The fade function in the sMulti filter dialog box allows incremental transparency. You can move the strips by grabbing them within the preview window and dragging them to another position.

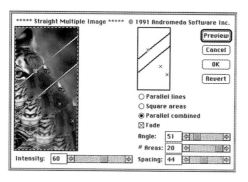

Figure 3–69
Applying the sMulti filter at various angle, tile frequency, and transparency settings results in a variety of effects.

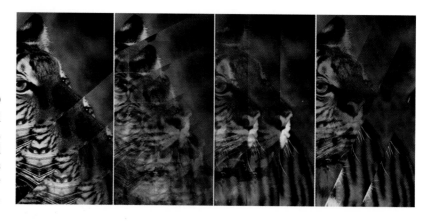

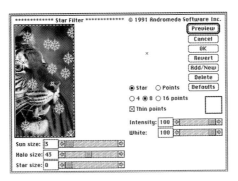

Figure 3–70
The Star filter dialog box lets you create a wide variety of star types. You can even generate multiple stars without leaving the dialog box.

STAR

Type	Special-effects filter
Description	Star (Figures 3–70 and 3–71) creates one or more stars in any color, with optional sun or halo effects. You can create multiple successive stars without having to exit the dialog box. Each star can have 4, 8, or 16 points, and you determine the Sun size, Halo size, and Star size (star arm length) using the sliders at the lower left corner of the dialog box. Other controls let you set the Thickness of the arms, the amount of Star fade, and the Intensity (transparency) of the star effect. Use the RGB color sliders to define a star color other than the default white.
Specialized uses	Use the Star filter to create special-effects suns and stars in illustrations or halo effects in front of camera or sun glare.

Figure 3–71
These variations on the Star filter show just a glimmer of your star-making options.

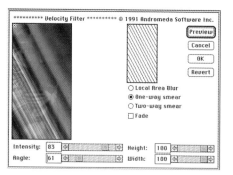

Figure 3–72
The Velocity filter
allows you to smear the
selected area locally in
one or two directions.

VELOCITY

Type   Special-effects filter
Description   This filter (Figures 3–72 and 3–73) creates sophisticated
                motion blur-type effects by smearing highlights from an
                image in the direction you specify. You can specify the
                number of Copies of the image created, the Spacing
                between copies, and the Height, Width, Intensity (fade),
                and Angle of the copies. Three additional options deter-
                mine the type of motion effect. Local Area Blur produces
                evenly spaced copies of the image with automatic fade.
                One Way Smear streaks the colors from the edge of the
                specified area along the entire area of the effect. Two
                Way Smear smears just the *highlights* from each row of the
                specified area, yielding an effect similar to a one-second
                exposure of the subject in motion.
Specialized uses Create precisely controlled motion effects in sports or
                racing photos; develop custom drop shadows in any
                direction for type or other objects.

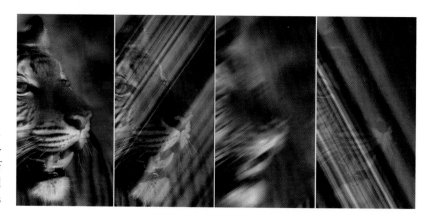

Figure 3–73
The Velocity filter
applied using a variety of
intensity, direction, and
smear settings

Andromeda Series 2

The second set of Andromeda filters is contained in one hub. Some might consider it as a single filter, but its capabilities are so vast and its interface is so deep that it deserves to be treated as a series.

3D SURFACE MAPPING

Type

Special-effects filter

Description

The filter (Figures 3–74 and 3–75) provides quick, anti-aliased, 3D renderings from within Photoshop. You have a choice of several resizable surfaces—such as Sphere, Box , Cylinder, and Plane—onto which a Photoshop image may be wrapped like paper. Several other shapes may be created by partially wrapping an image onto an invisible surface. You can crawl, rotate, or scale an image anywhere on the selected surface. "Flying" around the surface provides an infinite number of viewing angles and perspectives on each wrapped surface. A variable-intensity ambient (room) light source and a movable white light source (with its associated specular hot spot) are also provided to add visual depth. At any time during a filter session, you can display a quick, full-image preview of the rendering for a visual check. Upon completing the session, the filter renders an antialiased, full-resolution image.

Specialized uses

The 3D Surface Mapping filter is useful to artists, photographers, designers, and package engineers who need a method for generating 3D shapes within Photoshop. It can help produce dimensional graphs, image-wrapped architectural elements, and cloning sources for photographers.

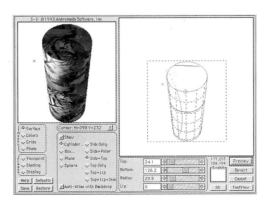

Figure 3–74
Although the 3D Surface Mapping dialog box has only one major panel, it reveals different controls for each area defined by radio buttons.

Figure 3–75   The 3D Surface Mapping filter applied using a variety of shape, lighting, and tiling options. You can drop out colors from the source image, as the cube rendering shows.

TIP: When you uncheck the Surface/Show checkbox for the 3D Surface Mapping filter, you can generate many more shapes with just the photo visible and surface invisible.

TIP: Scale down a surface using the Display/Scale/Overall slider, and then decrease Viewpoint/Distance. You will see dramatic perspectives that change surface shape.

TIP: Use the Photo/Shift to Origin control to move a corner of a flat composite (with two or three photos) to the surface origin corner for quick multisided wrapping.

Andromeda Series 3

The Mezzo filter is listed as a Series 3 filter, but it is really one filter with very extensive capabilities. Mezzo is a breakthrough product that gives you the ability to create true digital mezzotint effects.

MEZZO FILTER

Type	Special-effects filter
Description	The Mezzo Filter (Figure 3–76) converts any grayscale image into a mezzotint for printing on almost any printing device, from laser printers up through web presses. It produces true electronic mezzotint grains (a.k.a. *worms*),

Figure 3–76   The Mezzo filter makes possible a wide variety of mezzotint effects, including the ability to merge several styles together.

has controllable Unsharp Masking, and features Seamless and Random Mezzo generation. The mezzotints can be made up of grains ranging from 10 worms per inch to 300 worms per inch. The filter can also produce Mezzograms and Mezzoblends. A *Mezzogram* is a crisp, high-contrast mezzotint built using Unsharp masking. A *Mezzoblend* is a mezzotint grain (a.k.a. worms) that you can custom blend to create textured grains. The blending of mezzotints is handled either with dots or lines. Each pattern (dot or line) has several options; for instance, you could add waves to an existing elliptical line pattern and then blend it with the mezzo grain.

Specialized uses   Any designer, artist, or production facility needing high-quality mezzotint effects for brochures, letterhead, or fine-art effects will enjoy the Mezzo filter. It also provides an inexpensive imaging option for laser-printed output.

Candela

Candela currently markets filters that resolve color calibration and imaging problems using proprietary color transform technology. An encryption filter is also included in this group of filters.

ColorCrypt

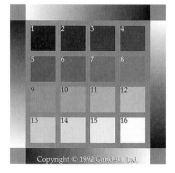

Type	Production filter
Description	The ColorCrypt filter can encrypt (scramble) any Photoshop image so as to render it unrecognizable. Run the encrypted file through the ColorCrypt filter again (don't forget your password!) and it unencrypts.
Specialized uses	CIA operatives might find ColorCrypt useful for storing and transporting their photographs of foreign despots, secret plans, and the like. Regular folk could use it for protecting the confidentiality of digitized images.

PrintCal•PI

Type	Production filter
Description	Using Candela's built-in proprietary color transform algorithms, PrintCal•PI (Figures 3–77 and 3–78) can individually calibrate up to four different color printers (such as color laser printers, dye sublimation printers, continuous-tone color film recorders, thermal wax printers, and so on) and four different monochrome printers (such as regular laser printers). The three plug-ins included in the PrintCal•PI set let you create a printed digital test pattern and enter densitometer values to correctly set the printer's gray/color balance, brightness, and contrast.
Specialized uses	Use PrintCal•PI for production facilities, service bureaus, and individual studios who need accurate calibration of multiple printing devices.

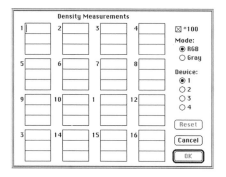

Figure 3–77
Using PrintCal•PI, you can specify
Density measurements and configure
settings for four RGB and four
grayscale printers.

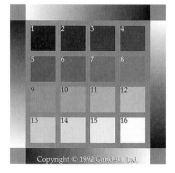

Figure 3–78
The PrintCal•PI pattern
dialog box

ScanCal	Type	Production filter
	Description	The two plug-ins and calibrated test targets that make up the ScanCal package (Figures 3–79 and 3–80) allow you to generate and store scanner calibration information for grayscale and RGB modes, and for reflective and/or transparency originals used with any scanner. ScanCal takes the Gamma C-dev's calibration into account when it calculates its own transform values for gray balance, brightness, and contrast.
	Specialized uses	Production facilities, service bureaus, and individual studios that need accurate calibration of single or multiple scanning devices will find ScanCal useful.

TIP: Use PrintCal•PI and ScanCal to calibrate your system to your service bureau's scanners and printers. You will be rewarded with more accurate output.

DPA Software

Intellihance GS/RGB/CMYK	Type	Production filters
	Description	These three filters are individual products. The GS filter is intended for grayscale images, the RGB filter for RGB images, and the CMYK filter for CMYK images. The basic metaphor for Intellihance is adjusting the control knobs on your television set—you set brightness, contrast, and so on, and all video images appear with those

Figure 3–79
A ScanCal Analyze
dialog box

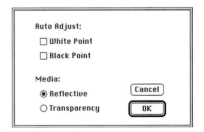

Figure 3–80
The ScanCal Execute dialog box
lets you set white and black points
to determine the overall values of
the image.

settings. Intellihance provides one main dialog box that allows you to set your preferences for contrast, brightness, saturation (RGB and CMYK only), sharpness, and despeckling (reducing inherent or scanner-produced noise). If you save those settings for use with other scanned images, Intellihance uses an artificial intelligence filter system to optimize each image, measuring it for tone curve, sharpness, etc., and adjusting it to match your preferences. For example, Intellihance will brighten images that are too dark and darken ones that are too bright. You can even apply your Intellihance settings to a folder full of images for batch processing.

Specialized uses   Use Intellihance to unify a variety of photographs of varying tones and image qualities for use in a single publication. Added feature: You can batch process an entire group of images.

IntellihancePro GS/RGB/CMYK

Type   Production filter

Description   Like DPA's entry-level Intellihance line, the IntellihancePro filters (Figures 3–81 and 3–82) are three separate products, each intended for a specific color mode. In addition to all the features of Intellihance described above, the Pro version allows you to set preferences for input (scanner) and output (press, paper, ink) calibration adjustments. It comes with a calibration strip for your scanner. Additional drop-down menus in the IntellihancePro dialog box include Descreen, Cast

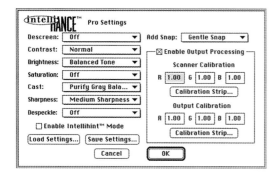

Figure 3–81
The IntellihancePro RGB dialog box features calibration readings for scanner input and general output.

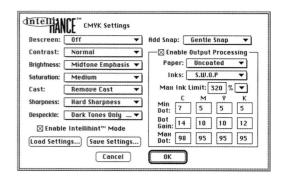

Figure 3–82
The IntellihancePro CMYK dialog box features profiles for various papers, inks, and dot gain settings.

Correction (RGB and CMYK only), Add Snap (for adding contrast at the end of the processing chain), Press Calibration/Paper (GS and CMYK only), and inks (CMYK only).

Specialized uses   Use Intellihance Pro for production-level batch processing of grayscale and four-color print jobs.

HSC Software

HSC brought to market the first plug-in suites that actually extended Photoshop's primary functions with such filters as Gradient Designer and Texture Explorer.

Kai's Power Tools 2.0

Kai's Power Tools 2.0 is a set of 33 filters that offer a wide range of capabilities. Some operate without dialog boxes, while others sport some of the most sophisticated interfaces in the digital imaging industry. When installed as plug-ins, the Macintosh versions of the filters reside in several different submenus of Photoshop's Filter menu—Blur, Distort, KPT, Noise, Sharpen, Stylize, and Video. The rationale behind this organization is that users should be able to locate a filter based on its function rather than on its manufacturer.

NOTE: It is significant that all the KPT filters will work in the CMYK Mode. This allows production houses to remain in CMYK throughout a job cycle and still have access to powerful image-processing filters.

NOTE TO PHOTOSHOP WINDOWS USERS: In Photoshop for Windows, the KPT filters appear in their own submenus, labeled KPT Extensions and KPT Filters.

NOTE TO WINDOWS USERS: Occasionally, some Windows-based imaging applications that technically support the Photoshop-compatible plug-in specification do not have all the program hooks that Kai's Power Tools needs for full compatibility. Call or write the application manufacturer for the current status of compatibility.

NOTE TO WINDOWS USERS: Version 1 of Kai's Power Tools for Windows was based on the feature set of Macintosh version 1.0d, with enhanced functionality for Windows. Version 1 for Windows presets also differed from many of the presets found in the Macintosh counterpart. The feature set and presets for Version 2 for Windows are identical to those of the Macintosh version.

BLUR SUBMENU

Smudge Darken/Smudge Lighten

Type   Special-effects filter

Description   The KPT Smudge filters (Figure 3–83), located in Photoshop's Filters: KPT Filters submenu, do not have a pop-up dialog box. They function similarly to the Photoshop Motion Blur filter, except that they affect an image in only one direction, with the added ability to darken or lighten. To achieve the dramatic effects of a more extensive application of Motion Blur, you must apply the KPT filter several times. These four filters exemplify the concept of having tools that add very specific functions to a program. Although they do not affect images as dramatically as some of the other filters in this set, they provide results that are otherwise much more difficult to achieve.

Specialized uses   By applying this filter multiple times, you can build up unique fur-like effects and textures.

DISTORT SUBMENU

Glass Lens

Type   Special-effects filter

Description   The Glass Lens filter (Figure 3–84) produces an actual ray-traced 3D sphere within a selection, complete with a highlight, an ambient light source, and a cast shadow. You can set the position of the highlight on the sphere and choose one of three light source intensities—Bright, Medium, or Soft.

Figure 3–83
Each of the four KPT Smudge filters applied 5 times on the top, 10 times in the middle, and 15 times on the bottom. Left to right: Smudge Darken Left, Smudge Darken Right, Smudge Lighten Left, and Smudge Lighten Right

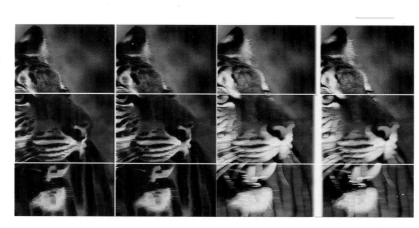

Figure 3–84
Results of applying (left to right) Glass Lens Bright, Glass Lens Normal, and Glass Lens Soft

Specialized uses   Use Glass Lens as a fine-art and editorial illustration tool when a reflective surface is needed.

NOTE TO WINDOWS USERS: You will find the three Glass Lens filters in Photoshop's Filters: KPT Filters submenu.

Page Curl
Type   Special-effects filter
Description   The Page Curl filter (Figure 3–85) curls a corner of the selection diagonally toward the center, placing a highlight down the center of the curl and a shadow on the "surface" that is revealed below it. You control how much of the page and which corner to curl.
Specialized uses   Use Page Curl as a special-effects tool for product brochures and carnival signs.

Figure 3–85
The Page Curl Filter can be applied at various sizes and in user-defined directions.

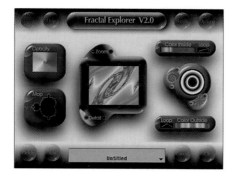

Figure 3–86
The Fractal Explorer interface permits real-time fractal space exploration without requiring numeric entry.

KPT SUBMENU

Fractal Explorer

Type	Special-effects filter
Description	Fractal Explorer (Figures 3–86 and 3–87) generates 24-bit color fractals with the help of an interface that incorporates the KPT Gradient Designer blends, including the opacity alpha channel. We then wrap the 24-bit blends around any of several types of fractal forms, with full control over looping, repeat count, and spiral angle settings. Fractal Explorer includes full previews and the ability to apply the resulting fractal in any opacity or channel operation mode. A countdown timer lets you know how long a rendering will take. You can make all adjustments to the fractal space without numeric input.
Specialized uses	Fractal Explorer is ideal for artists and designers needing colorful backgrounds and special effects, mathematics lovers who want to visualize their algorithms, game players or sci-fi fans who want to explore vast fractal space.

Figure 3–87
The KPT Fractal Explorer can produce quite unlikely results.

TIP: For a soothing meditative moment, process a beautiful complex fractal and then run the KPT Cyclone filter. A beautiful light show!

Gradient Designer

Type	Special-effects filter
Description	KPT Gradient Designer (Figures 3–88 and 3–89) greatly expands the native Photoshop capabilities for designing color ramps. The Gradient tool in Photoshop 2.5 only produces blends between the foreground and the background color, using linear or radial directions and user-definable transparency levels. The KPT Gradient Designer, on the other hand, allows you to specify up to 512 colors per gradient. It also includes:

- Looping control
- Real-time momentary pop-up 24-bit color picker
- Blended Transparency
- Presets with Hierarchical Families

Figure 3–88
The Gradient Designer dialog box provides pop-up color bars for instant color picking and up to 512 colors per custom blend.

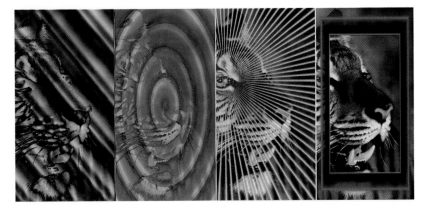

Figure 3–89
Blends from one color to another are just the jumping-off point for KPT Gradient Designer.

Specialized uses   Use KPT Gradient Designer to produce complex color blends for backgrounds, lettering effects, colorizing photos, and faux 3D effects.

NOTE TO WINDOWS USERS: You can find KPT Gradient Designer in the Filters: KPT Extensions submenu within Photoshop.

Gradients on Paths

Type   Special-effects filter
Description   Using one of the preset Gradients from KPT's Gradient Explorer filter (Figure 3–90), you can "wrap" the gradient onto any free-form path in an image. The path can be a Bezier-control type (converted to a path) or the boundaries of any selection, with or without feathering. After application, you can tweak the wrapped gradients using the controls provided with this filter.
Specialized uses   The Gradients on a Path filter is an extremely flexible tool for creating such effects as halos, neon, fog, or complex text outlines.

NOTE TO WINDOWS USERS: You will find the KPT Gradients on a Path filter in Photoshop's Filters: KPT Extensions submenu.

Texture Explorer

Type   Special-effects filter
Description   Texture Explorer (Figures 3–91 and 3–92) is a mathematical generator for textural effects, which features a number of application methods. You can automatically tile the textures over the image or stretch them over the entire selection. Rather than save storage-intensive images to tile over a selection, Texture Explorer generates user-definable tiles starting at 96 × 96-pixel square seed textures from mathematical equations all the way up to multimegabyte samplings. By providing easy-to-use buttons to change the variables of the mutation of the seed texture, Texture Explorer creates virtually unlimited possibilities for new textures. The textures interpolate the data to allow stretching over large files. Since a number of KPT filters access the alpha channel, Texture Explorer makes available a revolutionary application procedure called *procedural blend*. Procedural blend reads the grayscale intensity of the image and

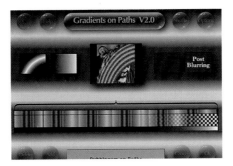

Figure 3–90
The Gradients on Paths dialog box indicates an arch here to simulate the effect on a given feathered selection.

Figure 3–91
Texture Explorer has an extensive interface that allows you to reuse your own custom gradients for texture generation. Channel operation modes are built directly into the filter and the results are visible in the real-time preview.

then applies the texture more intensively to the darker portions of the image and less intensively to the lighter portions. Reverse blend does the opposite. Since the procedural blend approach does not affect black or white areas, images can retain a full range of shadows and highlights.

The building block approach to KPT filters allows access to the gradient presets in the Gradient Designer filter. By clicking on the Rainbow Ball (Figure 3–91), you can change the color of the textures in complex ways.

Figure 3–92
Using Texture Explorer, a series of semi-translucent textures are applied to the tigers. The possibilities for textural effects with this product are extensive.

Specialized uses	Use Texture Explorer to generate backgrounds for brochures, textures for 3D bump-mapping, paper textures for Fractal Design's Painter, special text effects, and for visual exploration.

NOTE TO WINDOWS USERS: **In Photoshop, you can find the KPT Texture Explorer in the Filters: KPT Extensions submenu.**

3D Stereo Noise

Type	Special-effects filter
Description	Using a grayscale image as a starting point, the 3D Stereo Noise filter converts it into a pixellated black-and-white noise pattern that only appears to be random. (The brighter shades are remapped to white and appear more frequently, while the opposite happens to the darker shades.)
Specialized uses	The 3D Stereo Noise has one distinctive use: to create the "Stereographs" you often see in popular science and puzzle magazines. According to visual processing experiments by a researcher at Bell Labs, many people can see an incredibly sharp and deep 3D image after they stare slightly cross-eyed at a Stereograph long enough.

NOTE TO WINDOWS USERS: **The remaining KPT filters discussed in this section are available in the Photoshop's Filters: KPT Filters submenu.**

Fade Contrast

Type	Special-effects filter
Description	The Fade Contrast filter (Figure 3–93) lightens a specified area as if you used the Levels function in Photoshop to desaturate that portion of the image.
Specialized uses	Use Fade Contrast to prepare areas for text placement in brochures and collateral materials.

PixelStorm

Type	Imaging filter
Description	The PixelStorm filter (Figure 3–94) spreads each pixel in a selection 200 times over the entire selection, controlled by a "darken only" transfer mode that is built into the filter. You can set the degree of pixel diffusion to a number between 1 and 10.

Figure 3–93
The Fade Contrast filter prepares an area for text.

Specialized uses	Use PixelStorm to disintegrate images when the Diffuse filter doesn't have enough "oomph" to do the job.

PixelWind

Type	Imaging filter
Description	Like PixelStorm, PixelWind also moves pixels around within a selection, but to a much lesser degree. PixelStorm diffuses a pixel 80 times, and its built-in transfer mode enhances the image, rather than darkening it as in PixelStorm.
Specialized uses	Use PixelWind to disintegrate images when the Diffuse filter doesn't have enough "oomph" to do the job.

PixelBreeze

Type	Special-effects filter
Description	PixelBreeze applies only a 30-pixel diffusion. Since a lighten-only transfer mode is part of the filter, the end effect is a soft but somewhat noisy lightening of a selection.

Figure 3–94
From left to right: Pixel Breeze, Pixel Wind, Pixel Storm, and Universal Hue Protected Noise applied at the default settings

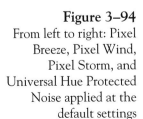

	Specialized uses
	Use PixelBreeze to disintegrate images when the Diffuse filter doesn't have enough "oomph" to do the job.

Seamless Welder

Type	Special-effects filter
Description	Using a square selection in an image as a source, Seamless Welder (Figure 3–95) calculates a smooth transition for the borders of the selection, which you can then use in a paint program's Define Pattern feature. The result is a tile edge that matches on all four sides.
Specialized uses	Seamless Welder works wonderfully when you want to make a pattern out of a complex image.

TIP: Use a pattern created with the help of Seamless Wonder as a texture map for a 3Dapplication.

Selection Info

Type	Production filter
Description	This filter (Figure 3–96) provides information on the percentage of the total image area that the selection represents and the number of pixels contained in the selection.
Specialized uses	Since Selection Info gauges the size of selections relative to the source image, it is useful as a reference in gauging the size of additional composite elements.

Figure 3–95
A small selection of the Tiger's eye was made seamless with the help of the Seamless Welder filter.

Figure 3–96
The Selection Info filter even shows the area occupied by irregularly shaped selections.

NOISE SUBMENU

Grime Layer

Type	Special-effects filter
Description	One of the oft-heard comments about computer graphics is that the images look "too clean and computer-generated." It is possible to create blends with incredibly smooth transitions and mechanically perfect edges. Grime Layer (Figure 3–97) is a filter designed to alleviate that too-clean look by generating a layer of dark pixels over the image.
Specialized uses	Grime Layer is helpful for producing starfields and removing the pristine sheen from overly slick illustrations.

Hue Protected Noise

Type	Production filter
Description	Hue Protected Noise, not Photoshop's native Noise filter, is what you should use to smooth out gradations and chunky colors. Hue Protected Noise (Figure 3–97) creates a subtle dither texture using same-color pixels, leaving the bright white and black areas virtually unscathed. The Photoshop Noise filter, on the other hand, generates red, green, and blue speckles over everything in a selection. Hue Protected Noise works in RGB, CMYK, Lab, and Grayscale modes in Photoshop. Three default settings are provided: Maximum, Medium, and Minimum; and you can modify the intensity of the filter effect within each.
Specialized uses	Hue Protected Noise is the filter of choice when you want to maintain color while preventing banding in gradations or vignettes.

Special Noises: Red, Green, and Blue

Type	Special-effects filters
Description	Each one of these three filters (Figure 3–97) uses one alpha channel (the Red Noise filter affects only the Red alpha channel, for example), is linked to a different preset Gradient from the KPT package, and has a different opacity transfer mode than the others. Applying one or more of these filters to an image or selection can result in fresh and unusual effects.
Specialized uses	The Red Noise filter is useful for depicting auto accidents. Blue Noise can simulate leaky ink pens. Green Noise can imitate that occasional grass stain.

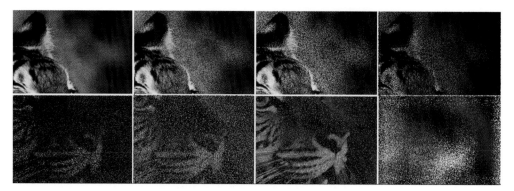

Figure 3–97   Top, left to right: KPT Hue Protected Noise Minimum, Hue Protected Noise Medium, Hue Protected Noise Maximum, Grime Layer. Bottom, left to right: Special Blue Noise, Special Green Noise, Special Red Noise, Diffuse More.

SHARPEN SUBMENU

Sharpen Intensity

Type	Production filter
Description	The Sharpen Intensity filter (Figure 3–98) will intensify the colors of an image with every application of the filter. You can set the amount of change to a number from 1 to 10.
Specialized uses	Used repeatedly, the Sharpen Intensity filter can posterize images. It is also useful for brightening up CMYK images after they have been converted from RGB, and for cleaning up scans.

Figure 3–98
The Sharpen Intensity
Filter applied at settings
of (left to right) 2, 5, 7,
and 10.

STYLIZE SUBMENU

Diffuse More

Type	Special-effects filter
Description	The Diffuse More filter randomly moves pixels around in a 100 × 100 pixel area. It's like using a broader brush than the one provided by the 25 × 25 pixel area of Photoshop's native Diffuse filter.
Specialized uses	Diffuse More adds a unique softening effect to harsh edges.

TIP: Using Diffuse More is not the same as using Photoshop's Diffuse filter four times in a row. Diffuse More uses a larger range of pixels in its diffusion calculations.

Find Edges/Invert

Type	Special-effects filter
Description	The Find Edges/Invert filter (Figure 3–99) is nearly identical to Photoshop's native Find Edges filter—it finds edges where color contrast is high and leaves a neon-like line on white. The difference is that in the KPT filter, the normally automatic Invert action is a toggle—you can turn it on or off. Thus, it is slightly more flexible than the Photoshop filter.
Specialized uses	Use KPT Find Edges/Invert when a painterly effect would add stature to a fine-art or commercial-art project.

Find Edges/Charcoal

Type	Special-effects filter
Description	The Find Edges/Charcoal filter (Figure 3–99) finds the areas of high-contrast in an image or selection and creates faint grayish lines on white on edges that pass whatever threshold you set. This filter can create widely varying results from image to image. As with KPT Find Edges/Invert, the Invert option is a toggle.
Specialized uses	Use Find Edges/Charcoal when a painterly effect would add stature to a fine-art or commercial-art project.

Find Edges/Soft

Type	Special-effects filter
Description	Using a different algorithm than any of the other Find Edges filters, KPT's Find Edges/Soft filter (Figure 3–99) finds just the smooth edge outlines for a much less harsh effect. You can toggle Invert on and off.

| Specialized uses | Use Find Edges/Soft when a painterly effect would add stature to a fine-art or commercial-art project. |

Scatter Horizontal

Type	Special-effects filter
Description	The Scatter Horizontal filter (Figure 3–99) works somewhat like the PixelStorm filter variants (see the discussions earlier in this chapter), except that it diffuses pixels horizontally only. The lighten-only transfer mode is built-in, as in PixelBreeze. You can set the strength of this filter's effect to a number from 1 to 10.
Specialized uses	Multiple applications can produce wind-like effects or placid, watery reflections.

VIDEO SUBMENU

Cyclone

| Type | Special-effects filter |
| Description | The Cyclone filter (Figure 3–100) provides an intriguing and intuitive way to devise arbitrary color maps (custom 24-bit color spaces) to apply to your images. When the KPT 2.0 package is installed, 10 different KPT-supplied "arbmaps" are copied to the KPT Support Files folder. The Cyclone filter uses these arbmaps and their interpolations to seamlessly animate a presentation of an apparently infinite number of arbmaps within the selection. When you see one you like, you can press the S key to automatically save that arbmap. If you like, you |

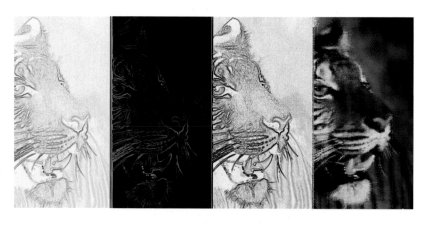

Figure 3–99
From left to right: KPT Find Edges Charcoal, KPT Find Edges Soft, KPT Find Edges—Invert, and KPT Scatter Horizontal.

Figure 3–100
The Cyclone filter can access a multitude of alternative color spaces.

can continue to watch the light show, pressing S whenever you see another arbmap you want to use. You can apply saved arbmaps to any other image within Photoshop or in any other application that supports custom 24-bit CLUTs (Color Look-Up Tables).

Specialized uses — The Cyclone filter is entertaining eye-candy for that meditative moment. It also provides powerful color restructuring for illustration and experimental art projects.

ImageXpress

ImageXpress provides a filter that automates a number of prepress preparation functions. The author of the software has an extensive background in prepress issues.

ScanPrep

M *ac*

Type	Production filter
Description	ScanPrep optimizes color separations for true color reproduction using common lithographic printing processes. This filter automatically runs up to 18 prepress image-processing operations on a scanned image in response to your settings. It makes "smart agent" decisions that it derives from an extensive, built-in lithographic database, matching your specific output and reproduction needs with the tools available in Photoshop.
Specialized uses	ScanPrep is useful for production facilities, service bureaus, and individual studios that need to automate professionally scripted color correction and color conversion for digital files.

In Software

In Software provides filters that expand color separation possibilities by extending the types of image formats available. Features include added flexibility to interface with Scitex equipment and the ability to extend the number of plate separations.

LineWorker

Mac

Type	Production filter
Description	The LineWorker filter lets you scan, import, colorize, and export Scitex Handshake Linework files from within Photoshop. You can thus bypass the intermediate steps of meticulously tracing and then colorizing scanned Scitex linework in PostScript illustration programs. When you're done colorizing linework in Photoshop, you can save the file in Scitex Linework format for import into a page layout program or for transfer to a Scitex system. Files saved in this manner are CMYK separation formats that are about 75% smaller than TIFF, Scitex CT, or EPS DCS files.
Specialized uses	LineWorker provides a much needed missing link for porting the Linework portion of Macintosh/Scitex production.

PlateMaker

Mac

Type	Production filter
Description	The PlateMaker plug-in filter lets you save files for color separation in DCS 2.0 format, which, in addition to providing the usual Cyan, Magenta, Yellow, Black, and Preview files, also makes it possible to create separation plates for spot varnishes, foil stamping, spot colors, embossing, and so on.
Specialized uses	PlateMaker is useful for service bureaus, prepress houses, individual studios, commercial printers, and anyone who needs more than the traditional CMYK separation plates.

IronMike Software

The IronMike Software company develops filters, plug-ins, utilities, and applications that help users manage the storage and retrieval of digital images—especially TIFF and JPEG images that include NAA-IPTC-formatted caption data (photographer, title, credit, keywords, etc.). The

NAA-IPTC (Newspaper Association of America-International Press Telecommunications Council) format is a standard among thousands of publications for the delivery of digitized images over Associated Press and other wire services.

commThing

IronMike's commThing filter set is a group of Acquire and Export plug-ins for transmitting and receiving digital images with NAA-IPTC captions over regular phone lines.

Specialized uses   Newspapers and multiple-location facilities of any kind who need to streamline the image file transfer over the phone will find comm-Thing useful.

commThing-TTY

Type   Production/Conversion filter

Description   The comm-Thing-TTY plug-in filter allows Mac users to send and receive JPEG files over the phone lines, either Mac-to-Mac or to an AP-Leaf Picture Desk workstation. It has a built-in TTY interface, which is a generic telecommunications interface for logging on, entering passwords, and so on.

commThing-T

Type   Production/Conversion filter

Description   The comm-Thing-T filter is an Export plug-in module that allows you to send a digital image and its NAA-IPTC caption over the phone line to another Macintosh.

commThing-DIT

Type   Production/Conversion filter

Description   The comm-Thing-DIT is nearly identical to the comm-Thing-T, except that you can transmit only to AP-Leaf Picture Desk workstations.

commThing-R

Type   Production/Conversion filter

Description   The comm-Thing-R filter is a receive-only Export plug-in. You can configure it to automatically receive

IPTC-captioned digital images using ZModem file-transfer protocol, and then open them in Photoshop.

IronMike PIK

The IronMike Plug-in Kit (PIK) is a set of Acquire, filter, and Export plug-ins that help users edit TIFF/JPEG images and their IPTC captions.

Specialized uses   IronMike PIK is useful for newspapers and multiple-location facilities of any kind who need to streamline prepress production operations.

JPEG FORMAT

Type   Conversion filter
Description   The IronMike PIK JPEG Format filter lets users open IPTC-captioned JPEG files by double-clicking their icons or by using Photoshop's Open/Save dialog box.

JPEG ACQUIRE/TIFF ACQUIRE

Type   Conversion filter
Description   The IronMike PIK JPEG Acquire filter allows Photoshop to detect and store IPTC captions within JPEG files. Users can create new captions for JPEG files as well. The TIFF Acquire filter provides the same capabilities for TIFF images.

JPEG EXPORT/TIFF EXPORT

Type   Conversion filter
Description   When users save an IPTC-captioned digital image file using the JPEG Export filter, other systems and applications (such as Leaf, AXS, Aldus Fetch, and AppleSearch) can detect the attached captions, keywords, Thumbnail, and Preview images. The TIFF Export filter provides the same capabilities for TIFF images.

ADD/EDIT CAPTION

Type   Production filter
Description   The IronMike PIK Add/Edit Caption filter (Figure 3–101) allows users to open an existing IPTC caption within Photoshop for editing, or to add an IPTC caption to an image. The Caption menu option appears in Photoshop's Filters menu.

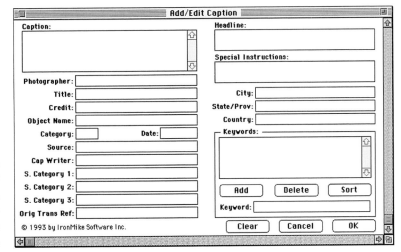

Figure 3–101
Using this screen
inIronMike PIK's
Add/Edit Caption filter,
you can link caption
information to the
associated image file.

Knoll Software

Knoll Software has an extensive knowledge of Photoshop and 3D imaging. Cybermesh helps bridge the gap between these two divergent types of programs.

CyberMesh

Type	Conversion/Special-effects filter
Description	The CyberMesh filter (Figures 3–102 through 3–104) allows you to save grayscale images as 3D models in DXF file format. CyberMesh works by interpreting gray levels of an image as heights, with black as the lowest and white as the highest level. Models can be rectangular, cylindrical, or spherical.

Traditional modeling programs provide only rudimentary tools for generating and editing these sorts of shapes. With CyberMesh, anything you can do to an image can be done to a 3D model. You can use Photoshop to paint height values, blur (smooth) areas together, punch holes in the mesh, cut and paste, resample meshes, and perform geometric distortions on the model.

CyberMesh can generate models using three different coordinate systems: Rectangular, Cylindrical, and Spherical.

Rectangular Mesh consists of points evenly spaced in the x- and y-coordinates, but uses pixel gray values to generate the z-coordinates.

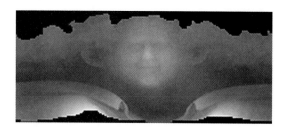

Figure 3–102
CyberMesh uses grayscale images as sources for generating 3D models.

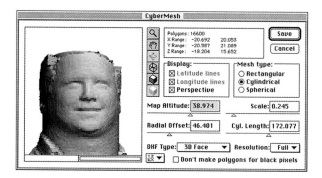

Figure 3–103
The CyberMesh filter dialog box is set to Cylindrical, which forms a dimensional head.

Cylindrical Mesh generates a cylinder whose radius is controlled by the pixel gray values. The Cylinder Length slider controls cylinder length (y-coordinate range), the Radial Offset slider controls the minimum radius, and the Map Altitude slider controls the height.

Spherical Mesh generates a sphere whose radius is controlled by the pixel gray values. The columns of the image wrap 360 degrees around the equator of the sphere, and the rows of the image wrap from the north pole to the south pole.

Specialized uses   CyberMesh is useful for artists, designers, and engineers who need organically shaped models to render in 3D programs. It is also useful for making models, such as terrain maps, that consist of many regularly spaced polygons.

Kodak

Kodak introduced the Photo CD format and provides an extensive acquire plug-in to bring Photo CD images into image editing programs.

Photo CD

Acquire

Type   Acquire module

Description   Yes, the Photo CD Acquire plug-in (Figure 3–105) makes it possible to display Photo CD images before importing them into Photoshop. This plug-in also has convenient production features that can save you time. Using Photo CD Acquire, you choose any available Photo CD resolution, crop the image, adjust its color

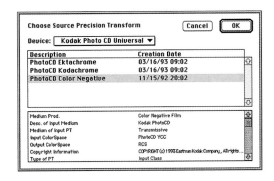

Figure 3–104
DXF files generated
using CyberMesh can
be rendered in a
3D application.

Figure 3–105
The Kodak Photo CD Acquire dialog box
gives information on the origin of the
photographic image.

	saturation and balance, and run it through any one of 21 conversion metrics for importing it into a Photoshop RGB file.
Specialized uses	Photo CD Acquire allows easy access to images stored optically.

MicroFrontier

MicroFrontier is the publisher of ColorIt, a low-priced color paint program. Their filters emulate the pattern fill functions provided within ColorIt.

Pattern Workshop

PATTERN FILL

Type	Special-effects filter
Description	Pattern Fill (Figure 3–106) allows you to select a filter set or pattern library that can hold up to 16 individual 64 × 64 pixel patterns. Pattern Fill will tile the chosen pattern within the user-defined selection.
Specialized uses	Use Pattern Fill for rapid builds of backgrounds, repeating grid backgrounds, and any operation in which repeated pattern fills play a part.

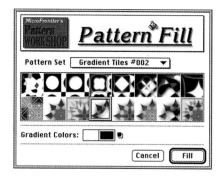

Figure 3–106
The Pattern Fill dialog
box loads 16 image
libraries of patterns.

PATTERN EDIT

Type	Special-effects filter
Description	Pattern Edit enables you to create a pattern from any user-defined selection. You can save up to 16 patterns per set. The Pattern Fill filter described above can then load and use these sets.
Specialized uses	Pattern Edit lets you create, save, and rapidly use customized pattern sets.

Performance Resources

These little-advertised commercial filters were some of the first to enter the third-party filter market.

Razza Matazz Filters

FADE

Type	Special-effects filter
Description	The Fade filter (Figure 3–107) darkens and creates a somewhat mottled effect on your image or selection by reducing the brightness of a random selection of pixels. You set the percentage of pixels to be affected; the range is from zero to 100 percent.
Specialized uses	Use the Fade filter to produce high-contrast noise for mottling over-pristine computer illustrations.

TREMOR

Type	Special-effects filter
Description	By averaging channels along a horizontal plane, the Tremor filter makes your image look as though it were shaken by an earthquake.

Specialized uses   Tremor can create more realistic depictions of real estate property in Southern California.

SEPIA

Type   Special-effects filter
Description   The Sepia filter lets you easily apply an old-fashioned look to any RGB image.
Specialized uses   Sepia permits one-step sepiatone production while still in RGB.

SPLIT 128

Type   Special-effects filter
Description   This filter scans the pixels in an image for their color values between 0 and 256. Pixels with values falling in the 0–127 range get shifted toward one end of the range, while those with values of 128–256 get shifted toward the other end. The result is a subtle posterization effect.
Specialized uses   Use Split 128 for artistic and psychedelic effects.

RGB SWAP

Type   Special-effects filter
Description   The first time you apply the RGB Swap filter to an RGB image, it shifts the Red channel color values to the Green channel, the Green channel color values to the Blue channel, and the Blue channel color values to the Red channel. The second application of the filter shifts them once more, and the third application of the filter returns the image to its original state. RGB Swap works with RGB images only.
Specialized uses   Use RGB Swap to generate rapid color shifts for special effects.

FRAMEMAKER

Type   Special-effects filter
Description   After a specified series of manual operations (including making and rotating blends), an application of the FrameMaker filter results in a "molded" picture frame.

Specialized uses	FrameMaker offers a quick-and-dirty way to create a frame around an image.

 ## MODULUS

Type	Special-effects filter
Description	The Modulus is a "mystery" filter whose results depend on the image to which you apply it. According to the documentation, final results can resemble infrared photography or neon luminescence.
Specialized uses	For that magic moment needed for a special effect, try Modulus.

 ## TRIG

Type	Special-effects filter
Description	The Trig filter provides an object lesson in trigonometry. You can apply sine, cosine, and tangent functions to an image, defining the angle (range: 1 to 5,760 degrees, positive or negative) at which to apply the function. Final results may surprise you—for example, according to the documentation, a sine value applied to a blend in multiples of 360 degrees results in columns.
Specialized uses	Trig is useful for digital imagists who want to explore the mathematical implications of color controls.

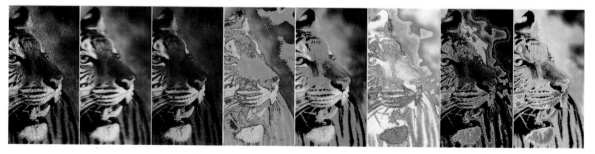

Figure 3–107   The Fade filter applied using default settings of (left to right) Fade, Tremor, Sepia, Split 128, RGB Swap, FrameMaker, Modulus, and Trig

PrePress Technologies

Two filters are provided in this set: a filter to adjust for color shifts in scanners and an interactive unsharp masking filter.

Spectre Filters

COLOR CORRECTION

Type	Production filter
Description	The Color Correction filter (Figure 3–108) compensates for the color space corruption brought about by most desktop scanners. Working in CMYK mode (and only in that mode), you use the filter's built-in densitometer to measure the color mix anywhere in an uncorrected scan. The results, as shown in Color Correction's dialog box, guide you in choosing which of the filter's six primary colors (yellow, magenta, cyan, red, green, and blue) need to be corrected. You can add six additional colors to this palette for further correction. After correcting the image, you can save the changes made to the filter's color palette as a color correction table and apply it to other scanned images.
Specialized uses	Designers, artists, service bureaus, and color houses all benefit from properly balanced, color-corrected images.

UNSHARP MASKING

Type	Production filter
Description	The Unsharp Masking filter (Figure 3–109) provides a more intuitive and interactive way to unsharp mask a scanned image than Photoshop's filter of the same name. Often, unsharp masking—which primarily sharpens edges—produces byproducts, such as unnatural color and gradation shifts, in the smooth areas of your image. Spectre's Unsharp Masking filter avoids this by identifying the smooth areas before sharpening and by applying your smoothing settings (part of the filter) as well. You can use the filter on RGB or CMYK images, and you can define sensitivity, sharpening, smoothing, and the plate(s) to be affected.
Specialized uses	Unsharp Masking is useful for anyone needing to enhance medium-quality scans or digital files with more control. It is especially helpful for interpolating when resampling small images upward.

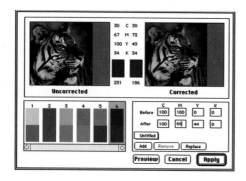

Figure 3–108
In this dialog box for the Color Correction filter, an eyedropper is used to pick colors from the base image.

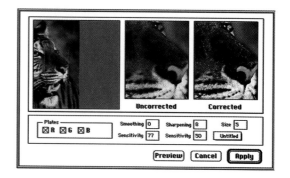

Figure 3–109
The Unsharp Mask filter dialog box sports sensitivity readings as well as previews.

Ring of Fire

Ring of Fire is a relatively new company from which we will be seeing much more in the future.

FotoMagic

This set of eight filters relies less on pixel tricks and more on powerful color-enhancement algorithms that normally are available only with specialized lab equipment and photography techniques. All filters run in either RGB or CMYK mode. The manual has a fairly well-detailed explanation of each filter in English; however, Ring of Fire's technical support line is in Japan (!).

COLOR EXPANDER

Type   Production filter
Description   The Color Expander filter (Figure 3–110) increases an image's color range by letting you define shadow values lower than zero and highlight values higher than 100. It has the secondary effect of sharpening the image. You can increase or decrease the color congruency in the entire image, in just the shadows, and/or in just the highlights. A control for adjusting the image's overall exposure is also part of this filter.
Specialized uses   Color Expander is useful for enhancing substandard color images and for creating reliable and repeatable color spaces for high-end output devices, such as Iris printers.

COLOR FILTERS

Type	Production filter
Description	The Color Filters filter (Figure 3–111) selectively modifies the color values of a group of pixels. Showing more intelligence than the color correction controls in most programs, Color Filters maintains color saturation while changing the color cast of a selected area. When you set Color Filters to add red, for example, it also proportionally subtracts green and blue from the selection. Other controls in this filter include modifiable shade, strength, and exposure, and the ability to select a foreground or background color as the color filter.
Specialized uses	Color Filters assists photographers who are comfortable with colored lens darkroom techniques to bridge the gap into digitally manipulated imaging.

COLOR NOISE

Type	Production/Special-effects filter
Description	The Color Noise filter (Figure 3–112) applies noise (modifying the color of random pixels) to an image. What makes Color Noise special is that you can set the filter to selectively add or subtract a color you choose. Other controls are provided for shade, strength, and coverage.

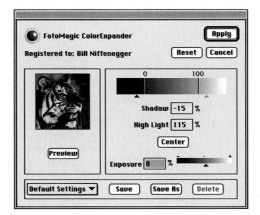

Figure 3–110
The settings in the Color Expander dialog box allow you to move beyond standard color spaces.

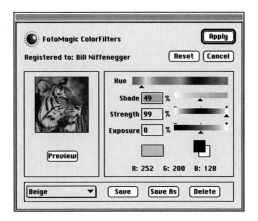

Figure 3–111
Real-time previews in the Color Filters dialog box help you select the color cast you want.

Specialized uses	Color Noise is useful for adding selective noise adjustments to individual channels or entire images. It allows control over the color space.

COLOR RANGER

Type	Production filter
Description	Color Ranger (Figure 3–113) allows you to select a blend or a gradient comprised of up to eight individual blocks of color. The selected color or blend affects the image according to the image brightness. You can set the opacity level when applying the color.
Specialized uses	Color Ranger is useful for color reduction within specified brightness ranges.

COLOR RANGER II

Type	Production filter
Description	Color Ranger II (Figure 3–114) allows you to select a blend or up to 256 individual ranges of color, which affect an image according to the image's brightness. You can set opacity levels when applying the color.
Specialized uses	Use Color Ranger II for color reduction within specified brightness ranges.

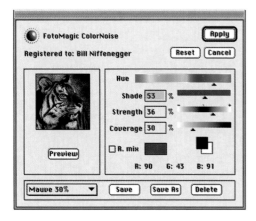

Figure 3–112
In the Color Noise dialog box, you can adjust variables that extend color control of noise and its extent.

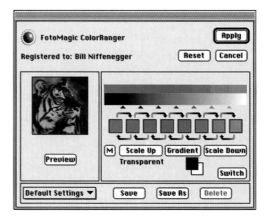

Figure 3–113
In the Color Ranger dialog box, the use of the Gradient button can yield a smooth color blend.

COLOR REVERSAL

Type	Production filter
Description	The Color Reversal filter (Figure 3–115) uses a built-in algorithm to intelligently compensate for the different color spaces involved in the process of reversing negatives to positives. You can also adjust shadows, highlights, and exposure yourself.
Specialized uses	The Color Reversal filter converts scanned color or black-and-white negatives into positive images.

 COLOR SCALER

Type	Production filter
Description	Use the Color Scaler filter (Figure 3–116) to convert color images to monochrome based on the intensity of the color values. Extensive controls help you increase contrast in shadow and highlight areas and adjust the midtone value, the hue and shade to be applied, and the exposure.
Specialized uses	Color Scaler is good for creating color casts from grayscale or color images.

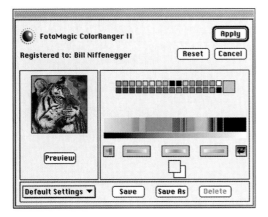

Figure 3–114
Color Ranger II permits microblends within the gradient bar. This results in a rich and varied color space.

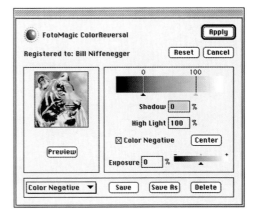

Figure 3–115
Were the Tiger a color negative, the Color Reversal filter would process it to a positive, maintaining fidelity to natural color.

COLOR SHIFTER

Type	Production/Special-effects filter
Description	The Color Shifter filter (Figure 3–117) shifts the color of your image or selection to a different color, using three slider controls for Red, Green, and Blue.
Specialized uses	Color Shifter provides alternative colorizing functions unavailable in traditional color editing programs.

COLOR SWITCHER

Type	Special-effects filter
Description	The Color Switcher (Figure 3–118) uses whatever color you select as an optical filter to dramatically change the look of an image or selection. The effect is somewhat akin to using various colored filters on an infrared camera. Interface controls let you select the filter's hue, define its shade and strength, and adjust overall image exposure.
Specialized uses	Use the Color Switcher to create pop-art or specialized scientific effects.

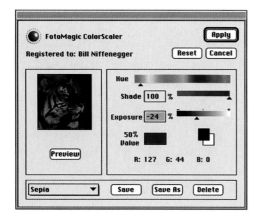

Figure 3–116
The Color Scaler filter has factory preset color casts such as Sepia.

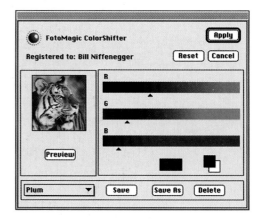

Figure 3–117
The Color Shifter filter features real-time color control bars.

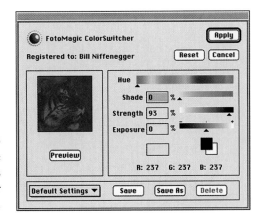

Figure 3–118
You can achieve colored-gel-like effects with the Color Switcher filter.

Savitar

Savitar provides a device-independent scanner calibration system.

ScanMatch

Type	Production filter
Description	The main purpose of ScanMatch is to match an original image to its appearance on your monitor after scanning. You scan a printed color chart (included) and use the ScanMatch software to match color values. The end result is a ScanMatch Transform plug-in filter optimized for your particular scanner and monitor, which you can then apply to other scanned images.
Specialized uses	Since ScanMatch has no capabilities for matching monitor colors to final output, this filter is useful mainly for people who have already calibrated that part of the equation, and/or for people who produce screen presentations.

Second Glance Software

These plug-ins are of special interest to silkscreen artists, fabric designers, small print shops, and in-house color producers. Each one optimizes the use of color for output on low-end devices.

PhotoSpot

This set includes several filters and export functions designed to create high-quality spot color output at low cost, using color reduction technology.

ACETONE

Type   Production filter

Description   Acetone (Figure 3–119) permits rapid color reduction by remapping the tones in an image to a set of user-specified colors.

Specialized uses   Using Acetone, silkscreen artists can reduce output costs. In-house color producers can use this filter to simulate a line art look.

  CHROMASSAGE

Type   Production/Special-effects filter

Description   This filter (Figure 3–120) allows sophisticated color table manipulation, color cycling, and "injection" of color using 24-bit color space.

Specialized uses   The colorizations and psychedelic artwork made possible by this filter are ideal for multimedia artwork, serigraphy, and t-shirt production.

  CHROMAPOINT

Type   Production filter

Description   ChromaPoint (Figure 3–121) uses a proprietary diffusion process to create optimized low-resolution color output on PostScript color printers. ChromaPoint-processed

Figure 3–119
The Acetone filter reduces colors to a manageable number.

Figure 3–120
With the Chromassage filter, you can select groups of new colors and drag them into the existing set of colors for an image.

images take less time to print and create smaller file sizes than conventional ones.

Specialized uses ChromaPoint's "hinting" for photographs is ideal for in-house color publishers whose final products are composite color documents.

  LASERSEPS

Type Production filter

Description LaserSeps (Figure 3–122) uses a proprietary diffusion process to output CMY or CMYK color separations that retain a smooth, continuous-tone look even at low line screen frequencies.

Specialized uses This plug-in is a boon to small quick print shops, textile printers, and in-house color users who need to create color separations on 300dpi color printers.

  PAINT THINNER

Type Production filter

Description Paint Thinner (Figure 3–123) lets you remap a selected range of image colors to a single spot color.

Figure 3–121
This image, custom dithered using ChromaPoint, is ready for output on an ink jet or thermal color printer.

Figure 3–122
LaserSeps produces custom-dithered separations. (Note: Because this product produces separations, the screen shot cannot properly indicate the high-quality separations possible with this product.)

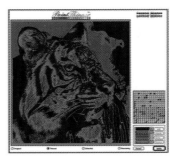

Figure 3–123
With Paint Thinner, you can specify custom color replacements for entire areas of color.

Figure 3–124
Four spot separations
generated with
PhotoSpot, with the
final image on the right

Specialized uses   With this filter, small print shop operators gain increased control over the quality of color mapping when preparing full-color jobs for color-reduced output.

 ## PHOTOSPOT

Type	Production Filter
Description	PhotoSpot (Figure 3–124) is an export filter that produces spot color separations automatically. PhotoSpot uses a naming scheme that supplies color names for each separation file. You can then import the Photoshop or TIFF separation files into a page layout program and align them to produce spot separations.
Specialized uses:	Use PhotoSpot to produce color separations for silkscreen displays, banners, t-shirts, brochures, and pinball machine backscreens.

TIP: When you export a PhotoSpot-separated image to QuarkXPress, PageMaker, Freehand, or Illustrator, all spot colors you assigned to the image automatically become part of the host application's color palette.

Southwest Software

**Color Encore
for Scanners**

Type	Production filter
Description	Color Encore (Figure 3–125) is a calibration plug-in for any scanner. It uses a supplied target image that you scan yourself. Color Encore calculates adjustments to all future scans using the differences between your scan and the test image.
Specialized uses	Color Encore is useful for artists, service bureaus, and designers who need accurately calibrated scanners for print ouput.

Storm Technology

Storm Technology is well known for its compression expertise. Many of its products are directly tied to NuBus boards. PicturePress is a filter that gives you access to advanced compression technology without dependence on add-in boards.

PicturePress

Type	Compression filter
Description	PicturePress is actually a powerful and flexible image compression program, of which its PicturePress plug-in is only a part. The plug-in allows you to JPEG compress or decompress images at one of four preset lossy levels. (*Lossy* refers to how many pixels you'll allow the program to drop from the image when compressing it. The more lossiness, the smaller the compressed file.) You can compress RGB, CMYK, and grayscale images, and you can do selective compression when working with RGB or CMYK images. Unlike traditional JPEGschemes, PicturePress lets you decompress and recompress files without image degradation.
Specialized uses	PicturePress is an aid to service bureaus, prepress houses, and individual studios that must archive, send, and receive large files without the problematic image degradation that results from traditional JPEG compression.

Total Integration

As the company name implies, Total Integration's filters are designed to greatly increase speed and productivity when editing high-resolution files in a variety of formats and across platforms.

Specialized uses	Filters from Total Integration aid production professionals and print illustrators who need timesaving enhancements when altering sections of large files.

FASTedit/CT and FASTedit/CT PRO

Type	Production filter
Description	FASTedit/CT (Figure 3–126) lets you open only those portions of Scitex CT image files that you need to edit. Once editing is complete, the plug-in appends the edited areas back into the original file. FASTedit/CT supports both CMYK and grayscale Scitex CT files. FASTedit/CT PRO (Mac only), a different product, adds the ability to do similar work with Scitex mask files.

Figure 3–125
A Color Encore dialog
box assists in setting
up a new calibration(s)
set for your individual
scanner(s).

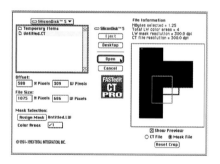

Figure 3–126
The FASTedit filters, no matter
which format, provide you with a
visual guide for grabbing a selected
portion of an image into Photoshop.

FASTedit/DCS

Type

Description

Production filter

FASTedit/DCS (Figure 3–126) supports 5-file DCS files from Adobe Photoshop and a variety of other sources. With this plug-in module, you can preview, select, and open portions of entire DCS files. Once editing is complete, the plug-in transparently appends the edited area back into the original DCS file.

FASTedit/TIFF

Type

Description

Production filter

FASTedit/TIFF (Figure 3–126) lets you to preview, select, and open portions of entire TIFF files. Once editing is complete, the plug-in seamlessly appends the edited area back into the original TIFF file. FASTedit/TIFF supports RGB, CMYK, grayscale, and bitmap TIFF file formats.

Handshake/LW

Type

Description

Production filter

The Handshake/LW filter lets Macintosh users open and edit proprietary linework files from the Scitex system, Freedom of Press PRO, RIPLink, Visionary Interpreter for PostScript, Scitex ColorFill, and the Scitex gateway. By using this filter, you can avoid having to waste costly production time on a proprietary workstation. Handshake/LW gives you an economical method to edit, change color areas, trap, and implement all features available for manipulating images in Photoshop. In addition, all file formats supported by Photoshop can be opened from and saved to Handshake linework format.

IRIS/CT

Type Production/Conversion filter

Description The IRIS/CT filter acquires and exports IRIS CMYK FEP (Front End Processor) image files. By adding a PC Ethernet card or removable media drive to the FEP, any Photoshop user can prepare and download files to an IRIS FEP for output as an ink jet proof. Previously downloaded files can be acquired back into Photoshop for further manipulation, reducing the amount of reprocessing and transfer time from the prepress, PC, and Macintosh environments. All file formats supported by Adobe Photoshop can be opened from and saved to IRIS FEP image format.

FASTedit/VUE

Type Production filter

Description This plug-in module gives the user the ability to preview, select, and open portions of entire VUE files, the file format used by Live Picture. Once editing is complete, the plug-in transparently appends the edited area back into the original VUE image file.

FASTedit/ Filmstrip

Type Production filter

Description FASTedit/Filmstrip lets you preview, select, and open specific frames of entire Filmstrip files created by Adobe Premiere. Once editing is complete, the plug-in transparently appends the edited area back into the original Filmstrip file.

FASTedit/2.5

Type Production filter

Description This plug-in module lets you preview, select, and open portions of entire Photoshop 2.5 files. It includes support for Photoshop 2.5 files saved with alpha channels. Once editing is complete, the plug-in transparently appends the edited area back into the original Photoshop 2.5 file.

Figure 3–127
With Epilogue PS, you can open EPS files and files from Adobe Illustrator, QuarkXPress, or Aldus Trapwise in Photoshop as RGB or CMYK images.

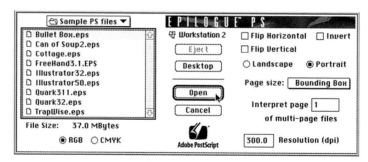

Epilogue PS

Type	Production filter
Description	Epilogue (Figure 3–127) is a collection of applications and modules based on the Configurable PostScript Interpreter from Adobe. The heart of the entire system is the Epilogue Server. This server is the network-accessible, PostScript Interpreter that communicates with the application modules including Epilogue PS, the Adobe Photoshop plug-in module. Epilogue PS lets you RIP any PostScript or Encapsulated PostScript file for further image manipulation or processing, thus allowing complete PostScript flexibility and productivity.
Specialized uses	Epilogue PS is useful to artists, designers, color houses, and service bureaus that need to rasterize Postscript files into Photoshop for further manipulation.

Ultimatte

Ultimatte boasts an impressive reputation in the movie industry for its blue-matte motion picture systems. PhotoFusion is Ultimatte's first foray into the still-image filter market.

PhotoFusion

Type	Production/Special-effects filter
Description	Based on the method by which video images are composited, PhotoFusion can automatically isolate foreground images and capture all their detail. PhotoFusion's exacting linear mask generations allow full control of flaring and tint corruption in surrounding areas. As a result, you can produce flawless composites that would be extremely difficult to duplicate using traditional masking methods.
Specialized uses	PhotoFusion is useful for professional photographers and photoillustrators with access to bluescreen photography

who require extremely accurate composites of translucent elements, such as hair, smoke, bubbles, and reflective liquids. PhotoFusion is especially effective when you complete the process by compositing the extracted portion of an image onto a new file within the filter.

NOTE: Although this chapter does not include them, PhotoFusion includes a number of dialog boxes to assist you. To see and undertand these more fully, please refer to the Seamless Compositing section in Chapter 11.

Xaos Tools

Known for its high-end Silicon Graphics animation programs, Xaos Tools has made a strong commitment to developing more powerful filters in the near future.

Paint Alchemy

Xaos Tools promotes the Paint Alchemy filter (Figures 3–128 and 3–129) as a "brushing engine." This filter applies brush strokes to user-defined selections. Rather than transforming images in a uniform manner, Paint Alchemy does so selectively, based on their hue, saturation, and brightness characteristics. Using an index-card-like interface, you can customize random transparency, color, angle, and stroke size. The filter comes with 36 preset paint brushes, and another 50 brushes are available through an auxiliary product called Floppy Full of Brushes. The intricate series of settings and the numerous brushes and style presets make this powerful tool a thousand filters in one.

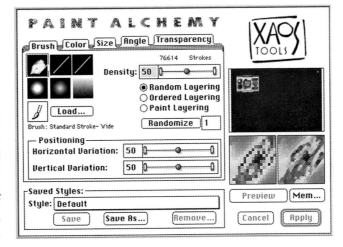

Figure 3–128
The interface of the Paint Alchemy dialog box resembles layered index cards in a recipe box. There is plenty of variability buried in those layers.

Figure 3–129
A variety of standard
Paint Alchemy styles
and some of my custom
ones have been applied
to the tiger image.

Specialized uses   Paint Alchemy is valuable for the artist, designer, and digital experimenter who wants a configurable brushing engine for fine-art and commercial-art projects.

TIP: Reviewing and altering the Paint Alchemy style presets is a good way to begin creating your own custom styles.

TIP: The Paint Alchemy manual recommends that you select a small portion of the image to speed up the preview process. I heartily second that advice to allow you the maximum time to experiment with settings. Choose an especially important portion of the image to get the best view.

MAC MEGATIP: When you open Paint Alchemy or call up another style or brush, the module searches the plug-in folder to find all of the styles and brushes. I have more than 500 items in my plug-in folder and you can imagine how this searching slows me down. Here is an elegant, timesaving solution provided by Trush Meyer, of CyberMedia in Calabasas, California:

1. Put your Paint Alchemy plug-in icon in a folder with all your brushes and styles.

2. Place this folder in the main Photoshop folder—not in the Plug-ins folder as directed by the documentation.

3. **Make an alias of the Paint Alchemy plug-in icon residing in the folder and place that in the Photoshop Plug-ins folder. This eliminates the need for Paint Alchemy to scan the entire plug-in set in order to run and results in substantial timesaving.**

Terrazzo

Type	Special-effects filter
Description	The Terrazzo filter (Figure 3–130) produces a number of user-definable tiling effects in a given selection. Going beyond seamless tiling, this filter merges the selection in seamed or seamless patterns that it triangulates, flips, merges, and antialiases in one step. You can alter the size and position of the selection area by pulling on a sizing tab or by dragging the selection around in the preview window. You can save tiling patterns and use them at a later date.
Specialized uses	Terrazo is of interest to designers and artists needing backgrounds for fine and commercial art. Anyone who uses repeating patterns in their work—fabric designers, industrial designers, and wallpaper or wrapping paper designers, for example—would find this filter helpful.

Figure 3–130 A variety of tile styles produced by using the Terrazzo filter on selected portions of the Tiger image

> **TIP:** Tile your tile. That's right. Pick an area of interest and tile it to pick up the color and feel you like. Then, use Terrazzo on this tiled image, but open up the size of the selection area in the preview. If you liked the first layer of tiling, you may really like the second layer. Scaling the selection is the key to more options.

Shareware and Freeware Filters

Adobe's marketing of its Third-Party Plug-in Developer's Kit has reached independent developers as well as commercial ones. The following filters, organized by their creator's names, are available on America Online, CompuServe, and other national and local bulletin boards.

You will notice more personal notes by me in this section, because I admire these folks, who are true experimenter types—tinkerers with code. These examples of rabid interest and innovation will most likely grow into full-fledged tools for the computer imager of the future.

Adobe/Spectural

AV/DSP

Type	Special-effects filter
Description	People using Photoshop on the AV Macs (the 660 and the 840) should get this free filter immediately. It enables the AV's built-in DSP chip to accelerate most filter operations from 10 to 300 percent. Adobe currently distributes it on bulletin boards and at trade shows.
Specialized uses	AV/DSP is intended for any AV Mac user who wants more speed when working with specific "Adobe Charged" filters that allow access to the power of the built-in DSP chips.

Paul Badger

Paul is an artist who has written some very potent filters. He has kindly agreed to include his set of filters in the Toolkit disc. Figure 3–131 shows samples of images to which some of his filters have been applied.

LUMPY NOISE

Type	Special-effects filter
Description	Paul wanted to be able to set the size of the grain generated by a Noise filter, so he wrote this filter to complement it. Lumpy Noise gives you access to some

interactive settings, including lump size, color variability, and lightness or darkness.

Specialized uses   Lumpy Noise is useful for artists, designers, and illustrators who want more control over the grain applied in a Noise filter.

TIP: While it can slow application time, try setting the noise size for the Lumpy Noise filter very high. You can form unusual flowerettes using this technique. Apply the Gallery Effects: Volume 1 Emboss filter on top and you have an innovative painting.

VECTOR GRAPH

Type   Art/ Special-effects filter

Description   Vector Graph is a specialized embossing filter that produces an effect resembling chiseled metal.

Specialized uses   Use Vector Graph to generate backgrounds for publications, special fine-art effects, and lettering.

TIP: Vector Graph works best on grayscale images.

TIP: This filter leaves some aliased artifacts. For additional refinements, slightly blur the Vector Graph image and then apply the Emboss filter.

Figure 3–131   Paul Badger filters applied to the tiger image. The first four tigers show variations of the Lumpy Noise filter; the two tigers on the right show examples of using the Vector Graph and Radar filters.

RADAR

Type	Special-effects filter
Description	Paul developed Radar (Figure 3–131) especially for animators who want to add a radial sweep to a single animation cell or to a series of cells.
Specialized uses	Radar is of interest to animators who want to produce a sweeping color effect over the same image or over evolving images.

Jim Bumgardner

The Expression filter (Figure 3–132) has been around the BBS boards since 1992 and has evolved with each change in Apple technology. The interface has evolved to the point where it has lost much of the early math-phobia imtimidation factor.

 EXPRESSION 3.0

Type	Special-effects filter
Description	Expression 3.0 has an avid following among those who understand fractal mathematics. The filter is constantly evolving and being updated and is available on America Online.
Specialized uses	Expression 3.0 is of interest to the mathematically-minded multimedia enthusiast who wants to animate fractals over time. It is also useful for generating patterns and textures.

Jeff Burton

Jeff Burton has one simple special-effects filter, yet he is a prolific writer of a type of plug-in not covered in this book—those for accessing a variety of hardware devices and file formats. Jeff is a valuable rescource for those who need interfaces to hardware and formats not easily accessed.

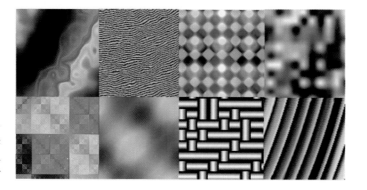

Figure 3–132
A variety of texture patches produced with the Expression filter

BACKSWAP

Type	Special-effects filter
Description	Simple and to the point, Backswap inspects your image, and everywhere it finds a pixel in the current background color, it paints it with the foreground color.
Specialized uses	Backswap is useful for anyone who wants to do that.

Chris Cox

Chris was a college student when he wrote this set of filters (Figure 3–133). I use the Fractal Noise filter in several major examples in this book. Chris has been kind enough to include his filter set in the Toolkit disc for you to enjoy.

 AVERAGE

Type	Art-effects filter
Description	The Average filter averages the colors within a selection and paints the selection with that color.
Specialized uses	Chris says he uses this filter on multiple selections within an image to create an overall stained-glass effect.

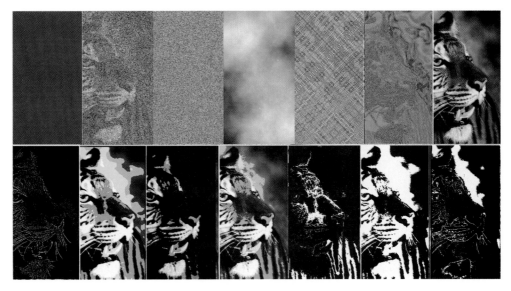

Figure 3–133 The effects of Chris Cox's filter set are shown on these variations on the tiger image. Top row, left to right: Average, BisShift, Total Noise, Fractal Noise, Plaid, Psycho, UnAlias. Bottom row, left to right: Edge 3x3, Erosion, Dilation, Skeleton, ColorKey, ChromaKey, FastKey.

TIP: After creating the "panes" of your stained glass using the Average filter, choose a Find Edges filter to create the borders between the panes.

BITSHIFT

Type	Special-effects filter
Description	The BitShift filter rotates the bytes in a selection by a specified number of bits in the range of one to seven.
Specialized uses	This filter produces unusual colorizing effects, depending on the image and its edges.

TOTAL NOISE

Type	Special-effects filter
Description	The Total Noise filter applies a completely random generation of noisy pixels to a selection. Unlike most other Noise filters, Total Noise ignores the pixels that are present in a selection when performing its calculations.
Specialized uses	Total Noise is useful for producing band-free noise for further processing, such as making custom textures.

FRACTAL NOISE

Type	Special-effects filter
Description	The Fractal Noise filter fills an image or selection with a wispy noise pattern. This filter paints only one channel at a time, so it fills a color selection with gray noise—you'll need to colorize it afterwards.
Specialized uses	Fractal noise is useful for artists and designers who need a quick and inexpensive way to produce cloud-like effects.

PLAID

Type	Special-effects filter
Description	This filter creates symmetrical patterns in each color channel of an image or selection.
Specialized uses	Plaid is useful for the artist or designer who wants a linear pattern for backgrounds and golfer's pants.

PSYCHO

Type	Special-effects filter
Description	The Psycho filter creates random, sine-wave-based color maps and applies them to RGB and CMYK images or selections.
Specialized uses	Psycho is good for artists and designers who want to experiment with radical color shifts in their artwork and who are in a random kind of mood.

UNALIAS

Type	Special-effects filter
Description	UnAlias looks for edges and corners in an image and blurs them, reducing stair-stepping of bitmaps.
Specialized uses	UnAlias is useful for removing jagged edges from scanned-in faxes and low-resolution linework.

EDGE 3X3

Type	Special-effects filter
Description	Edge 3x3 is a simple and fast alternative to Photoshop's Find Edges filter. It locates and selects borders between high-contrast areas in an image.
Specialized uses	Edge 3x3 is useful for digital artists who need to have linework surrounding black-and-white drawings.

EROSION

Type	Special-effects filter
Description	Working within the limitations of the threshold value you set, the Erode filter calculates the sum of the pixels in your selection and sets pixel(s) to white if they exceed the threshold value. The overall effect is a reduction of the dark regions in your image.
Specialized uses	Erosion is useful for artists and designers who want an alternative to customary posterizing techniques.

DILATION

Type	Special-effects filter
Description	The Dilate filter performs pixel calculations similarly to the Erode filter just described, but with the exception that it enlarges the dark regions of your image.
Specialized uses	Dilation is of interest to artists and designers who want to simplify images dramatically for posters, invitations, and fine art.

SKELETON

Type	Special-effects filter
Description	Skeleton reduces the dark areas of an image or selection down to their approximate *centerline* or skeleton.
Specialized uses	This filter can be useful in cleaning up scanned text prior to OCR operations. It is also helpful for selectively posterizing images, depending on the threshold you set.

COLORKEY

Type	Special-effects filter
Description	The ColorKey filter turns an image or selection into a mask, based on how closely the individual pixels approach the value of the foreground color. You can set the tolerance to a value in the range from zero to 999.
Specialized uses	ColorKey is useful for artists, photo retouchers, and designers who want to make quick selective masks and are familiar with channel operations.

CHROMAKEY

Type	Special-effects filter
Description	ChromaKey works similarly to ColorKey (see the foregoing description), in that it produces a mask based on the current foreground color. ChromaKey, however, is slower but more controllable, because it lets you set tolerances based on Hue, Saturation, and Value.
Specialized uses	ChromaKey is useful for artists, photo retouchers, and designers who want to generate quick selective masks and who are familiar with channel operations. In this version, you can produce grayscale masks with much more delicacy than a bitmap mask.

FASTKEY

Type	Special-effects filter
Description	Like ColorKey and ChromaKey above, FastKey generates masks based on the foreground color. FastKey, however, bases its calculations on a single RGB value, that of the foreground color. There is no facility for setting tolerance levels.
Specialized uses	FastKey is of interest to artists, photo retouchers, and designers who want to generate a quick mask from pre-posterized images.

John Knoll

The Knoll brothers, John and Thomas, developed Photoshop. Obviously, they have developed much more filter technology than is represented in these offerings. Please read Chapter 2, "Photoshop Native Filters," to realize the full magnitude of their accomplishments.

CROSS-STITCH

Type	Special-effects filter
Description	The Cross-stitch filter transforms your image into a cross-stitch pattern, suitable for printing to a 300 dpi laser printer (the filter uses symbols instead of color names to show color stitch areas. You choose the "thread" colors when you convert an image to Indexed Color from RGB prior to applying the filter.
Specialized uses	Sorry, John, we're still trying to figure it out. We do know that if you want to do a cross-stitch pillow, you could delineate the areas for different-colored threads with this filter and (Do people still make time for this?) do some cross-stitching.
Caution:	Radically reduce the number of levels of tone in the image when you use Cross-stitch, or you will get a printout with a huge list of symbols and a "hash from hell" look.

Thomas Knoll

ANGLES

Type	Production filter
Description	The Angles filter doesn't actually affect your image at all. It's a way to measure the angle between any two points in your image for whatever reason. To obtain a measurement, just drag the rectangular selection marquee from one point to another and choose Angles from the program's Export menu.

Specialized uses   This is a useful measuring tool to aid in creating accurate composites.

Sucking Fish Series

The Sucking Fish, or Koban Zame, Series filters are a pair of plug-ins that are distributed throughout the electronic bulletin boards of Asia. These filters are "mailware"; if you like them, you send e-mail to the author, Naoto Arakawa. You can access the e-mail information through the "About Plug-ins" option in the Apple menu.

DEKO-BOKO

Type   Special-effects filter

Description   The DeKo-Boko filter (Figure 3–134) produces chiseled-edged rectangles around the perimeter of a selection. You can set the width of the chiseled area and determine whether the illusion of dimension is toward you or away from you. The filter lightens and darkens the underlying image in beveled strips to create its illusion.

Specialized uses   DeKo-Boko lets you create multimedia buttons easily. It can also be used to create block-like areas for text placement in presentations and brochures.

MR. SA'KAN

Type   Special-effects filter

Description   The Mr. Sa'Kan filter (Figure 3–135) produces brick-like rectangles within a selection. You can set the width, color, and graininess of the mortar between the bricks. You can also specify the pattern of the bricks so as to produce stacked, irregular, or random arrangements. The filter creates its illusion by lightening and darkening the underlying image in rectangular shapes.

Specialized uses   Mr. Sa'Kan features a rapid method for producing a block of bricks for any occasion.

Figure 3–134
The DeKo-Boko filter forms a block effect by lightening and darkening strips of the underlying image.

Figure 3–135
The Mr. Sa'Kan filter produces bricks with mortar of any color.

Kas Thomas

Kas was unsatisfied with most of the "ice water" contrast routines found in other filters, so he wrote this one.

WARM CONTRAST

Type	Production filter
Description	Warm Contrast offers a one-step procedure for adding a warm contrast to your images.
Specialized uses	Use Warm Contrast to give a warm and rosy glow to any image.

4

3D Effects in a 2D World

Need an image of Herculean pillars to represent the stability of that new corporate client? How about some cool 3D buttons for your next interactive multimedia presentation? Techniques in this chapter will help you meet those pressing deadlines without missing your lunch hour.

Anyone who has worked with 3D programs knows how long it can take to render an object. The play *Waiting for Godot* comes to mind. Photoshop plug-ins can alleviate the time-numbing rendering that robs you of productivity and experimental fun. Creating pseudo-3D artwork with filters is not only enjoyable, it can also help you achieve exciting new effects and images that might elude you as you climb the steep learning curve of 3D software. Even the more expensive spline-based modelers that produce fluid organic shapes can be emulated using filters.

Andromeda's new Series 2 3D filter is a powerful 3D rendering tool that you can use within your paint programs. There are also other filter combinations for 3D effects that might not be immediately evident to even the seasoned digital illustrator. Quickly-rendered 3D objects that have been imaged in relatively inexpensive programs (Adobe Dimensions or RayDream AddDepth, for example) can be enhanced with filters. Filters can improve the slick surfaces of these objects to such a degree that they appear to have been rendered in high-end programs, such as the ones used to make movies like *Jurassic Park*.

Spheres, Raindrops, and Lozenges

In the 3D rendering world, the sphere belongs to a category of shapes called *primitives*—simple objects on which more complex forms are based. Spherical shapes constitute a powerful jumping-off place for many styles of imaging. Adobe Photoshop's Spherize filter will bump out any pattern or photo. For our purposes, though, we will use some third-party filters to start the imaging circus and go from there.

In traditional 3D programs, *ray tracing*, which is characterized by extremely clean highlights and shadows, is one of the more advanced rendering techniques. The KPT Glass Lens filters do an excellent job of providing a "ray-traced" quality within Photoshop and other filter-friendly applications. KPT Spheroid Designer is also an excellent source for these effects. It has realistic bump-mapped textures and can set multicolored multiple light sources. The Andromeda 3D filter can wrap textures and images around spheres while allowing masterful control over light sources and image angles. Once the sphere is in place, you can manipulate the shape in many different ways using our arsenal of additional filters.

The image that serves as the basis for all the special effects described in this chapter is a gridded sphere on a neutral gray background, which I produced with the help of the Andromeda Series 2 3D filter. This single monochrome sphere with gridlines should help you visualize the various techniques. When experimenting with this chapter's techniques, and on your own, always use a neutral background with enough space around the spheres and lozenges to permit distortions.

Remember that these techniques are only a starting point. You can combine and build on these simple variations to produce totally new images.

Spheres

Filters We Will Use
- Adobe Photoshop: Polar Coordinates, Twirl, Shear, Zigzag, Ripple, Pinch, Wave
- Andromeda Series 2: 3D Filter

To practice a variety of sphere-distortion techniques, do the following:

1. Make a 600 × 600 pixel square grayscale file and fill it with 50 percent gray.
2. Make a sphere using the KPT Glass Lens filters, the Andromeda 3D filter, or KPT Spheroid Designer.
3. Experiment with some of the selection and distortion techniques shown in Figures 4–1 through 4–4.

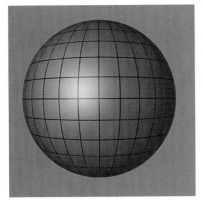

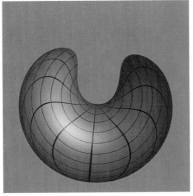

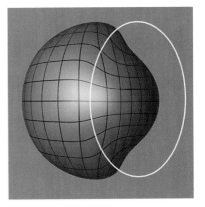

Figure 4–1
The Andromeda Series 2 3D filter was used to create this master sphere. The gridlines are intended to help you visualize the distortion effects in the following examples more clearly. This shape is the base image for all the images that follow.

Figure 4–2
The Photoshop Polar Coordinate filter was applied to the entire image with the Rectangular to Polar option active.

Figure 4–3
The Photoshop Pinch filter was applied, at a setting of 100, to a selection that had been feathered at 66 pixels.

Lozenges

Using the sphere shape as a basis, you can easily create stylized lozenges using a variety of techniques. Here is how to make a basic lozenge.

1. Make a square grayscale file and fill it with 50 percent gray.
2. Make a sphere using the KPT Glass Lens filters, the Andromeda 3D filter, or KPT Spheroid Designer in the center of the file.
3. Select the entire file and compress the entire image toward the right side of the file, using the Photoshop Image: Effects: Scale option. Move the compressed sphere into the center of the file, making sure the entire background of the file remains filled with 50 percent gray.
4. Experiment with some of the selection and distortion techniques shown in Figures 4–5 through 4–9.

This compression of the spherical shape is a simple act, but it opens up many more shaping options for you.

Level 2 Spheres (Distorted Spheres and Lozenges)

Once you have created the distorted spheres and lozenges just discussed, you can further distort them for new effects. The amount of change that distortion filters (Pinch, Spherize, and Ripple, for example) can exact in a single pass is limited. However, a second application of distortion filters has a dramatic effect on the previously altered spheres. Figures 4–10 through 4–13 illustrate effective Level 2 distortion techniques.

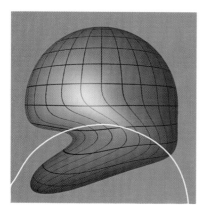

Figure 4–4
The Photoshop Wave filter was applied to a selection that had been feathered at 66 pixels.

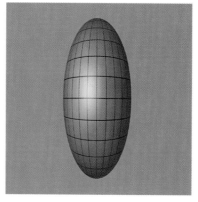

Figure 4–5
This lozenge was made by compressing the master sphere with the help of the Photoshop Image: Effects: Scale command.

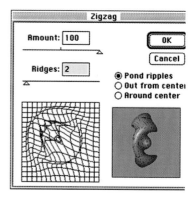

Figure 4–6
The Photoshop Zigzag dialog box settings used to produce Figure 4–7

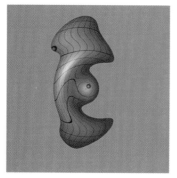

Figure 4–7
The Photoshop Zigzag filter was applied to the entire image with the Pond Ripples option active.

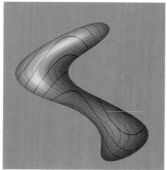

Figure 4–8
The Photoshop Wave filter was applied to the entire image with the Repeat edge pixels option active.

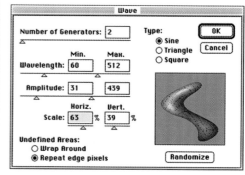

Figure 4–9
The Photoshop Wave dialog box settings used to produce Figure 4–8

Tear Drops Faster than You Can Grab a Hanky

You can pull spheres around like taffy if you understand the selection processes and distortion filters. Let's try some wet tear tricks.

Filters We Will Use

- Kai's Power Tools 2.0: Glass Lens Bright, Glass Lens Normal, Glass Lens Soft
- Andromeda Series 2: 3D Filter
- Adobe Photoshop: Pinch

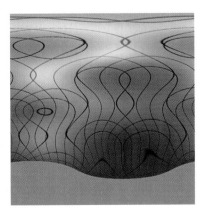

Figure 4–10
Applications of the ZigZag and
Polar Coordinates filters produced
a smooth undulating form.

Figure 4–11
Applications of the Wave and
Polar Coordinates filters produced
an extremely elongated shape.

Figure 4–12
Applications of the ZigZag filter
followed by the Twirl filter
produced a smoothly curved object.

Figure 4–13
Applications of the Shear filter
followed by the ZigZag filter
produced a dancing figure-like form.

Producing teardrop shapes is very simple. The trick lies in not focusing your distortion directly on the glassy spheres that are to become your teardrops.

1. Make a 600 × 600 pixel grayscale file and fill it with 50 percent gray.
2. Produce a number of spheres on the left half of the image, using the KPT Glass Lens filters, the Andromeda Series 2 3D filter, or KPT Spheroid Designer.

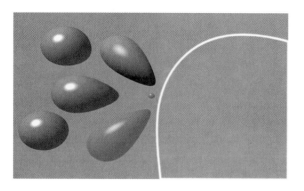

Figure 4–14
Applying the Pinch filter on a feathered selection distorts objects near the selection area.

Figure 4–15
Applying the Pinch filter inside a feathered selection sucks the objects toward the center.

3. Make a circular selection on the right half of the image and feather by 66 pixels.
4. Apply the Photoshop Pinch filter repeatedly at a setting of 100 until you achieve the desired amount of teardrop shaping (Figure 4–14).

Alternative Teardrops

An alternative method for distorting spheroids is to pinch them totally inside a selection, as illustrated in Figure 4–15.

Pillars, Chiseled Blocks, and Studded Collars

The need for three-dimensional objects arises often in both print and multimedia graphics. You can use 3D effects for multimedia buttons, text boxes, brochures, fine art, and just plain fun. Prismed and raised surfaces can be powerful design elements for backgrounds and artistic imaging. The next few sections show how to create a variety of pillars, blocks, and collarlike effects.

Pillars

Pillars and their variations can be useful in rendering interior scenes and as design elements. You can place text on them with good effects, and the possible adornments to their surfaces are endless.

You can easily add dimensional effects to rectangles by applying gradient blends that simulate light striking a rounded surface. After placing the blends, you can vary the shapes by applying distortions to the rectangle.

You can also produce true ray-traced pillars using Andromeda's Series 2 3D filter. From the standpoint of emulating the pillar's angle of view, this filter allows much more flexibility than the use of selections and gradients alone.

PILLARS FROM GRADIENTS

The first basic pillar technique is quite simple and effective. To simulate light on the surface, we will start with smoothly blended gradients and then alter the gradients for special effects.

Filters We Will Use
- Kai's Power Tools 2.0: Gradient Designer
- Toolkit Disc: Basic Pillar preset for KPT 2.0 Gradient Designer

1. Make a 200 × 900 pixel grayscale file with a 50 percent gray background.
2. Make a rectangular selection inside the file. You will apply the filters to this selection.
3. Apply the Basic Pillar gradient in the Toolkit submenu of KPT Gradient Designer (Figure 4–16).
4. Experiment with various preset gradients in KPT Gradient Designer (Table 4–1 lists the presets that are useful for creating pillar effects). Next, experiment with making your own gradients, using color effects that work for your projects.

Basic Gradients (submenu)	Earthtones
	Soft Gray Folds
Metallic (submenu)	Brushed Aluminum, Solid
	Cool Metal Jacket
	Cool Tube
	Coppertone Cymbalism (make linear and turn to proper angle)
	Gentle Gold
	Golden Center
	Green Tube
	Large Metallic Cylinder
	Sax and Violets
	Southwestern Metallic Tube
	Warm Tube
Toolkit (submenu)	Basic Pillar
	Basic Pillar Slightly Backlight

Table 4–1
KPT Gradient Designer Presets That Can Form Pillar Effects

NOTE: Some of the KPT gradient presets need to be aligned with the angle of your pillar.

TIP: To change the location of the highlight on your gradient pillar, press and hold the Option key and drag the gradient strip to the left or right while watching the results in the preview window.

FLUTED COLUMNS IN TWO STEPS

In this exercise, you will apply a specially prepared gradient (supplied on the Toolkit disc) to achieve the look of a Neoclassical fluted column.

1. Apply the Fluted Column A gradient (located in the Toolkit submenu of KPT Gradient Designer) to a rectangular selection (Figure 4–17).
2. Apply the Fluted Column B gradient (also in the Toolkit submenu) over the top of your fluted rectangle (Figure 4–18).

ADD A TWIST TO YOUR PILLARS

Once you create the fluted column just described, it's easy to create a spiral effect on its surface. Just retain the rectangular selection, go to KPT Gradient Designer and select the Fluted Columns Spirals C gradient from the Toolkit menu, and then apply the gradient (Figure 4–19). Notice that the application of the diagonal gradient in Procedural-Apply mode responds in a wrapping fashion, creating the illusion of spirals.

MOOD-LIT PILLARS

Filters We Will Use
- Andromeda, Series 2: 3D

The Andromeda filter produces a basic pillar as a default. Because this method actually renders a true 3D image, the angles of the view and light hitting the pillars are user-definable, making many more variations possible. Since the Series 2 filter uses the rectangular selection to wrap the pillar, you can use any image to form the pillar's surface. Figures 4–20 through 4–22 show examples of the Andromeda 3D filter at work.

Chiseled Blocks

The cube is another important primitive that is used time and time again in imaging. Simple rectangular selections with soft drop shadows can simulate raised panels or multimedia buttons. Let's examine some of the variations.

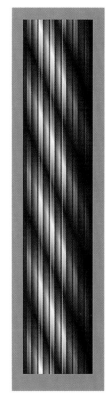

Figure 4–16
A basic pillar produced by applying a single filter

Figure 4–17
A specially prepared gradient from the Toolkit disc is applied to a rectangle.

Figure 4–18
A translucent gradient is applied over the first gradient to create the illusion of a fluted pillar.

Figure 4–19
Applying another specially prepared gradient creates a spiral effect on the column's surface.

Filters We Will Use

- Aldus Gallery Effects, Classic Art, Series 1: Emboss
- Kai's Power Tools: Gradient Designer, Texture Explorer

QUICK BLOCK

Here is a quick technique for obtaining a nice block for buttons or text uses.

1. Create a 400 × 400 pixel image area filled with 50 percent gray.

2. Use KPT Gradient Designer to create a gradient. First, select the color None on both ends of the Gradient Bar by clicking one of the ends of the bar and pressing the mouse button until the Eyedropper

Figure 4–20
The Andromeda
3D Cylinder
shape applied
with default
lighting and
positioning

Figure 4–21
The Cylinder
shape is
enhanced by
adjusting the
light source
controls within
the filter.

Figure 4–22
The viewpoint
and light source
controls were
used to provide
a different
vantage point.

appears. Select the color None from the drop-down Color Spectrum Bar and release. Repeat the color selection on the other end of the gradient bar. You should be seeing a checkerboard pattern across the entire gradient bar.

3. Drag the Moveable Bracket (located above the gradient bar) toward the left until approximately 1/5 of the gradient bar is selected.

4. Click the end of the Gradient Bar at the left edge within the bracket and, while pressing the mouse button, select a shadow color from the drop-down Color Spectrum Bar. This short blend of color will form the chiseled portion of the block you are making (Figure 4–23).

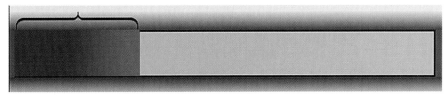

Figure 4–23
The gradient bar shown
with proper settings

5. Select the Rectangular Burst mode and Sawtooth B to A using the Normal apply mode. (Refer to the KPT manual for locations of these setting areas.)

6. Apply the gradient you just made (Figure 4–24).

RENDERED BLOCKS

The Andromeda Series 2 3D filter can produce blocks easily. Playing with the lighting on these blocks can produce additional drama.

1. Make a 400 × 400 pixel image area filled with 50 percent gray.

2. Apply the Andromeda Series 2 3D filter using the default box shape setting (Figure 4–25).

NOTE: Select the Photo dialog box within the filter dialog box and turn off the Show function so that the grayscale block contains no image patch (Figure 4–26).

TEXTURED BLOCKS

Building on the block you just created in the previous section, you can add texture to further enhance visual realism.

Figure 4–24
A quickly rendered
chiseled block is
the result.

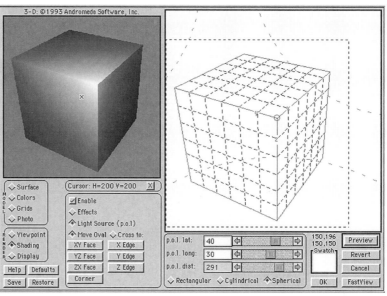

Figure 4–25
A basic default block produced
with the Andromeda 3D filter

Figure 4–26
The dialog box allows you to forego placing an image on the block.

1. Select the block without the background.
2. Apply KPT Texture Explorer using the preset Effects Textures: Sandy Speckles. Set the pixel size to 96 × 96 pixels. Set the apply mode to Procedural Blend (Figure 4–27).

NOTE: I chose Sandy Speckles because of its subtlety. The light textural nature of this preset allows it to be procedurally blended quite effectively on the block. Heavy or grid-style textures in Texture Explorer would lessen the illusion of 3D. Try some other combinations as shown by the examples in Figure 4–28.

3. To add even more punch, apply Gallery Effects Emboss using the settings Relief 6 and Light Position Top.

Studded Collars

Now that the title has grabbed your attention, let's examine some variations on the Adobe Photoshop Extrude filter. You can produce studded collars with this filter, which is also useful for backgrounds, for simulating metallic spaceships, or as a distortion tool for taking images in new directions.

Figure 4–27
A texture applied to
the block with KPT
Texture Explorer
Procedural blend

Figure 4–28   Textural variations applied to the block

Filters We Will Use
- Adobe Photoshop: Extrude, Polar Coordinates
- Kai's Power Tools 2.0: Gradient Designer

First, let's examine the grayscale potential of the filter.

STUDLY GRADIENTS

Here they are. . . studded collars at your command.

1. Make a file 900 pixels wide × 300 pixels high with a white background.
2. Use a gradient tool (KPT Gradient Designer or your program's gradient tool) to create a gradient that blends from black at both ends to white in the center. Apply it in Normal mode (Figure 4–29).
3. Apply the Photoshop Extrude filter using the settings Pyramids, Size 30, Depth 30 (level-based). See Figures 4–30 and 4–31.

FROM A STUDDED COLLAR TO A CURVED METAL SHELL

Start with the studded collar you created in the previous section and build on it to create the next effect.

1. Using a background color of white, expand the canvas area to 900 × 900 pixels. Rotate the file by 90 degrees (Figure 4–32).
2. Add 50 pixels to the top and bottom of the file so that the studded collar is surrounded by white area.
3. Apply the Photoshop Polar Coordinates Filter using the Rectangular to Polar setting (Figure 4–33).

Figure 4–29
Gradient Designer blend ready for studs

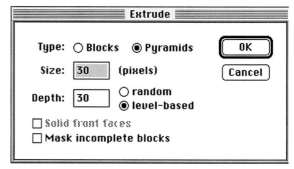

Figure 4–30
Extrude Filter settings for the studded collar

Figure 4–31   Your finished collar should look like this.

STUDDED WALL OF ANCIENT STEEL

The Photoshop Extrude filter has a random height setting that can produce the illusion of a studded metal wall.

1. Make a 500 × 500 pixel RGB image area filled with 50 percent gray.

2. Apply the Photoshop Extrude filter using the settings Pyramids, Size 30 pixels, and Depth 15, Random (Figure 4–34).

3. To obtain a more realistic metallic effect, apply the KPT Texture Explorer preset Minerals: Luminous Tourmaline in the Difference mode at 96 × 96 pixels (Figure 4–35).

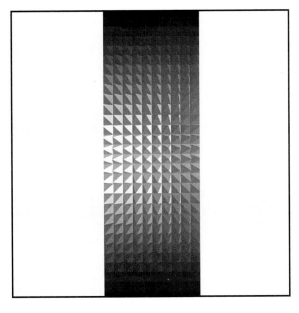

Figure 4–32
The studded collar
should be in the center
of a square.

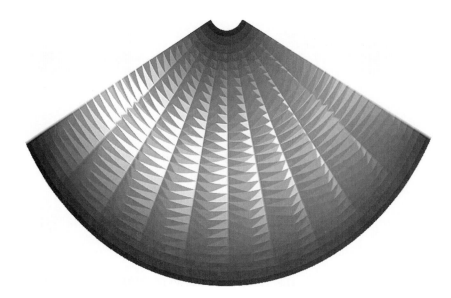

Figure 4–33
The Extrude filter coupled with the Polar Coordinates filter yields this quilted metal look.

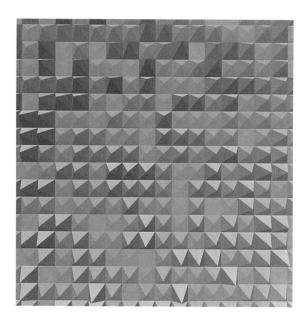

Figure 4–34
The wall features a randomly studded surface.

Figure 4–35
The studded wall has a richer appearance when texturized.

Cones and Wet Rope

Cones and wet rope in the same section may seem incongruous, but the techniques you use to create both effects can be multiplied exponentially to generate near-infinite imaging power.

Cones

Another basic building block for faux 3D is the cone. Let's examine several approaches to constructing and embellishing cones while strengthening their three-dimensional look.

CONES DIRECTLY FROM GRADIENTS

You can make cones using KPT Gradient Designer if you select None as a color. By making radial gradients with only a pie-slice of the gradient visible, you can create cones using any color or combination of colors.

Filters We Will Use

- Kai's Power Tools 2.0: Gradient Designer

1. Make a grayscale file using dimensions of 500 × 500 pixels.
2. Apply the KPT Gradient Designer preset Toolkit: Cone on Black.
3. With the background color set to black, use the oval marquee to surround the cone and form a curved selection on its bottom. Inverse the selection and delete. This step effectively strips away the bottom of the file, leaving a rounded cone bottom as shown in Figure 4–36.

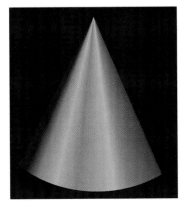

Figure 4–36
KPT Gradient Designer can make cones in one pass of the filter.

CONES FROM DISTORTION

The techniques you learned in the sections on making pillars will come in handy in this section. Simple tube-like gradient blends can be distorted to make cones.

Filters We Will Use

- Kai's Power Tools 2.0: Gradient Designer

1. Open a new a 500 × 400 pixel grayscale file with a white background.

2. Apply the KPT Gradient Designer preset Metallic: Gentle Gold after aligning the gradient vertically (Figure 4–37).

3. In Photoshop, use the distort handles to pull the top corners together toward the center of the image. I also recommend pulling both handles down a bit to create extra room at the top of the image (Figure 4–38).

4. Use the Elliptical Marquee to surround the cone and form a curved selection on its bottom. Invert the selection and delete as in Figure 4–39. This effectively strips away the bottom of the file and leaves a rounded cone bottom (Figure 4–40).

CONEY ISLAND WRAPPERS

Because of the shape of a cone, wrapping textures on them can really enhance the illusion of 3D. Since there is no true 3D cone filter, all the texture wraps are totally faux. The implication is that if you can wrap textures on cones, you can wrap them on virtually anything. Two examples of cone texture wraps follow.

Filters We Will Use

- Kai's Power Tools 2.0: Gradient Designer
- Andromeda, Series 1: Designs

Example 1

1. Create a cone using the techniques in the "Cones Directly From Gradients" section.

2. Open KPT Gradient Designer and select the preset Translucent: Moiré Shadows.

3. Change the preset to Circular Sunburst and the apply mode, in Options, to Procedural Blend mode.

4. Move the center of origin of the gradient stripes up to a point where curved stripes appear to be wrapped around the cone as in Figure 4–41.

5. Apply the gradient for a result like the one in Figure 4–42.

Figure 4–37
KPT Gradient Designer
metallic blend

Figure 4–38
A cone is formed by distorting
the gradient.

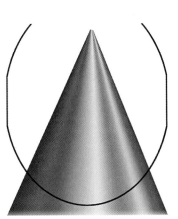

Figure 4–39
The black line shows the extent
of the oval marquee.

Figure 4–40
The completed cone

Example 2

1. Make a cone using the techniques described in the "Cones Directly From Gradients" section.

2. Open the Andromeda Series 1 Designs filter and select the Patterns Basic #6 design. Use the Bend and Squash controls to create the illusion that the diamond shapes are wrapping around the cone (Figure 4–43).

3. Apply the Designs filter (Figure 4–44).

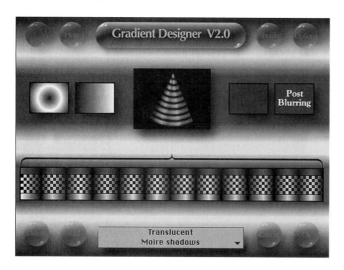

Figure 4–41
Adjusted rings made by moving the Circular Sunburst center of origin

Figure 4–42
Procedural Blend mode in Gradient Designer makes these rings appear to be wrapped around the cone.

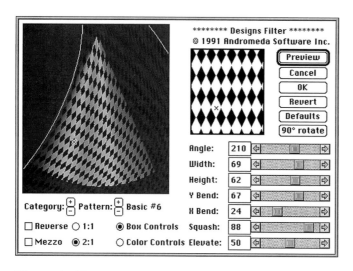

Figure 4–43
Note the adjustments to the X, Y, and Squash settings in the Andromeda Designs Filter.

Figure 4–44
Diamonds are just one of many patterns that can be applied to surfaces.

Wet Rope

Filter technology offers two basic techniques for making sinuous rope that can wind all around and through your images.

GRADIENTS WITHIN STROKED PATHS

Filters We Will Use

- Kai's Power Tools 2.0: Gradient Designer

1. Open a new 400 × 400 pixel RGB file with a white background.
2. Use a brush with hard edges to make a wide black line, or stroke a pen path using a 35 pixel solid black brush (Figure 4–45).

   NOTE: If you are using a program other than Photoshop, use any method available to make a thick solid curving line that you can then select.

3. Select the black line.
4. With KPT Gradient Designer, create a gradient for the rope. The color you want on the outside of the rope should appear on the right edge of the Gradient Bar, and the color for the inside of the rope should appear in the remaining area to the left.
5. Set the blend style (the top left adjustment box) to Circular Shapeburst.
6. Apply the filter for the result shown in Figure 4–46.

Figure 4–45
A wide black line is needed to properly see the results of the gradient.

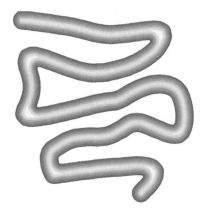

Figure 4–46
The Circular Shapeburst follows the round ends of the rope.

NOTE: Make sure that the bordering color is only a narrow area on the right of the Gradient Bar (Figure 4–47), or it will fill too much of the rope width.

THE ULTIMATE ROPEMAKER

Gradients applied using KPT Gradient Designer can be quite dramatic and it is an area that is well worth exploring. To achieve even more drama, use KPT Gradients on a Path, the ultimate ropemaker.

Filters We Will Use
- Kai's Power Tools 2.0: Gradients on Paths

1. Open a new 400 × 400 pixel RGB file with a white background.
2. Draw a winding rope-like loop with the Lasso tool or with any tool that gives you a sinuous flowing selection. For this experiment, avoid drawing the undulations of your rope too close together.
3. Feather the selection by the number of pixels that you want as a rope width. I suggest a 10-pixel feathering effect.
4. Apply the KPT Gradients on Paths filter using the preset Hot Plasma Tube (Figure 4–48).

THE ROPE OVERFLOWS

When the feather of a selection causes it to overlap any adjacent feathered areas, the results can become much more interesting.

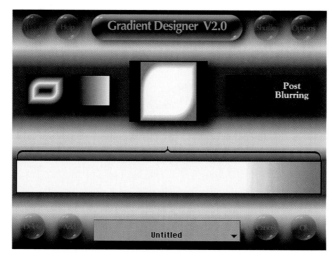

Figure 4–47
Note the compressed color on the right side of the gradient bar.

1. Make a 400 × 400 pixel RGB file with a white background.
2. Draw a winding rope-like loop using the Lasso tool or any tool that yields a sinuous flowing selection. Draw the winds of the rope lines so that they pull closer together in places.
3. Feather the selection by the number of pixels you want as a rope width. For this test, feather 35 pixels.
4. Apply the KPT Gradients on Paths filter using the preset Copper Pipe (Figure 4–49).

Golden Jewelry

The techniques described earlier for distorting spheres into organic shapes can be taken a step further to produce full-color illustrations that display an organically flowing realism.

Filters We Will Use:
- Kai's Power Tools 2.0 : Gradient Designer, Glass Lens Bright
- Adobe Photoshop: Polar Coordinates, Wave, Twirl

1. Open a new RGB file with square pixel dimensions.
2. Select a rectangular area that spans the middle of the image and is centered vertically.

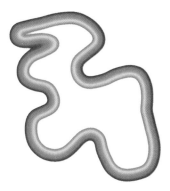

Figure 4–48
A simple feathered selection can become a blended rope.

Figure 4–49
A very different organic effect happens when the paths merge together.

3. Open KPT Gradient Designer and select the preset Metallic: Metal Sweep Cymbal. Turn the Radial preview into a horizontal rod by selecting Linear Directional Gradient, Sawtooth A to B, and then pulling the directional rod straight up and down.

4. Apply the Gradient to the rectangular selection (Figure 4–50), and then deselect.

5. Apply the Photoshop Polar Coordinates filter to the entire file using the Rectangular to Polar setting. The result is a ring of gold as shown in Figure 4–51.

6. Add a rectangle over the gold ring and fill it with KPT Gradient Designer, using the same golden rod setting but applied in Darken Only apply mode (Figure 4–52).

7. Apply the Photoshop Wave filter, distorting the image without ripping the image from the sides of the file (Figure 4–53).

8. Apply the Polar Coordinates filter, using the Rectangular to Polar option (Figure 4–54).

NOTE: If the metal tubes are not perfectly horizontal, the chain will not meet at the top. I have purposely placed them slightly off true horizontal for demonstration purposes.

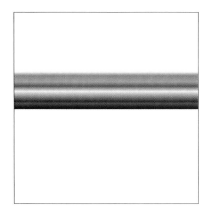

Figure 4–50
A bar of gold is formed by applying a KPT Gradient Designer metallic gradient in Linear Apply mode.

Figure 4–51
Photoshop's Polar Coordinates filter pulls the ends of the bar into a ring.

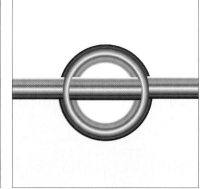

Figure 4–52
A second bar is composited through the ring of gold.

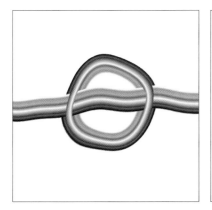 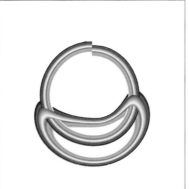 

Figure 4–53
A slight jitter is added with the Photoshop Wave filter to add visual interest.

Figure 4–54
The Photoshop Polar Coordinates filter is applied again, generating more organic forms.

Figure 4–55
A twirled sphere is added to form a decorative element where the two ends of the tubes did not meet.

9. Use the Elliptical Marquee tool to select a circle around the mismatched top seam, and then apply the Photoshop Twirl filter using a setting of –490.

10. Keeping the selection active, apply the KPT Glass Lens Bright filter (Figure 4–55).

11. You can achieve many variations on this technique by using the other Photoshop Distort filters to distort the image (Figure 4–56). A practical demonstration of these techniques is shown in Figure 4–57.

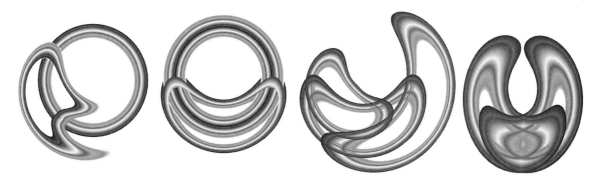

Figure 4–56   Many variations of organic forms are possible with this technique.

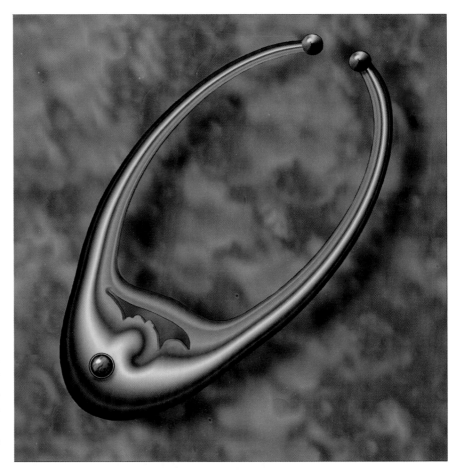

Figure 4–57
Using the 3D technique described in the "Golden Jewelry" section, this necklace was made without using modeling software. The background is a texture produced using Kai's Power Tools 2.0 Texture Explorer and further synthesized using the Clone, Burn, and Smudge tools in Photoshop.

Ancient Pillars

The techniques described earlier in this chapter provided basic instructions for producing pillars. Now, let's bring more visual interest into play. Pillars aren't just slick and shiny. They can be crusty and gnarly. They can be tiled and exotic. They can be twisted and ultratwisted. Where history goes, filter imaging techniques can follow. With Photoshop filters, any historical pillar type can be produced and new styles developed.

In this section, we will examine advanced applications for creating transparent blends and textures. These 3D texture techniques will help you produce professional finished art with amazing realism.

Filters We Will Use
- Kai's Power Tools 2.0: Gradient Designer, Texture Explorer

1. Open a new 200 × 900 pixel RGB file.
2. Apply the Basic Pillar gradient in the Toolkit submenu of KPT Gradient Designer (Figure 4–58).

NOTE: Each of the following experiments starts with the making of a basic pillar. Save one as a master file to copy for later experiments.

3. Apply KPT Texture Explorer using the preset Metals: Green Steel Lattice. Set the pixel size to 128 × 128 pixels and the apply mode to Multiply (Figure 4–59).
4. Select the entire file and copy. Paste the selection on top of itself.
5. Flip the selection horizontally, keeping the selection active (Figure 4–60).
6. Select the Edit: Composite Controls option in Photoshop and apply the Lighten Only mode.
7. Deselect the floating selection and use the Image: Adjust: Levels or Brightness/Contrast options to lighten the image a bit (Figure 4–61).

Notice how the Multiply mode in KPT Texture Explorer allows the blend from the Basic Pillar to remain visible. These combinations can inspire hours of searches for the amazing pillar effect.

Plastic Variations on Ancient Pillars

This second variation is powerful.

Follow all the instructions in the Ancient Pillar section. When you reach step 7, do not deselect the floating selection.

When you next use the Levels controls or the Brighten Contrast controls, you can watch in real time as the interaction of the areas changes shape. You are molding the pillar just as if you were sculpting it (Figure 4–62).

NOTE: The Preview option must be checked in the Levels and/or the Brighten Contrast dialog box if you want to see the changes as you make them.

Ancient Pillar Super Variations

To illustrate the rich vein of exploration available through these techniques, I have prepared six more variations (Figures 4–63 through 4–68). All of these examples are performed on a basic pillar.

NOTE: Pay close attention to the different apply modes used in these examples. Notice that some of the copied layers are flipped vertically rather than horizontally. Lighten the images at the end for better results.

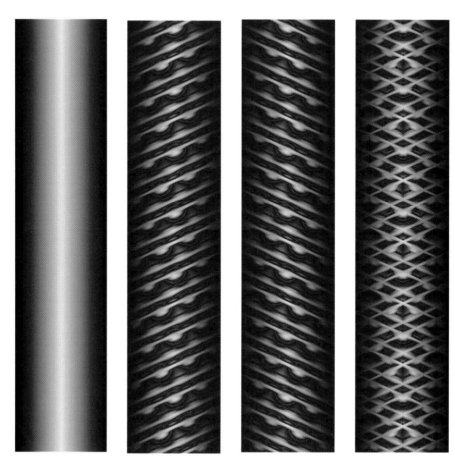

Figure 4–58
All these experiments start with a Basic Pillar.

Figure 4–59
A KPT Texture Explorer texture is applied in Multiply mode.

Figure 4–60
The texturized pillar is copied, pasted, and flipped on itself.

Figure 4–61
Use the Photoshop composite controls to allow only lighter sections of the layer beneath to become visible.

ANCIENT PILLAR TWO-STEP VARIATIONS

The two examples shown in Figures 4–67 and 4–68 involve one extra step each. In the first variation, you add a graininess to the pillars with a preliminary application of KPT Texture Explorer; in the second, you use KPT Fractal Explorer for that purpose.

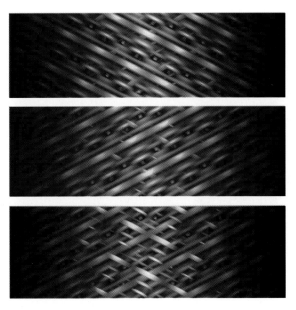

Figure 4–62
As you adjust the lightness and contrast of the top
composite layer, various bands of metal seem to be
emerging and receding.

Figure 4–63
The KPT Texture Explorer preset Eerie:
Liquid Metal Vortex was applied in Multiply
mode. The horizontally flipped layer was
composited in Darken Only mode.

Figure 4–64
The KPT Texture Explorer preset Nature,
None of your Beeswax, was applied in Multiply
mode. The horizontally flipped layer was
composited in Lighten Only mode.

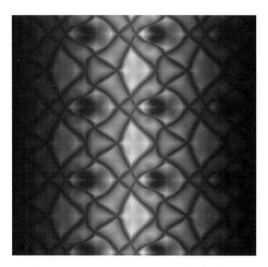

Figure 4–65
The KPT Texture Explorer preset Metals:
Sensuous was applied in Multiply mode. The
Vertically flipped layer was composited in
Darken Only mode.

Figure 4–66
The KPT Texture Explorer preset Wood:
Another Wood Pattern was applied in
Multiply mode. The horizontally flipped layer
was composited in Darken Only mode.

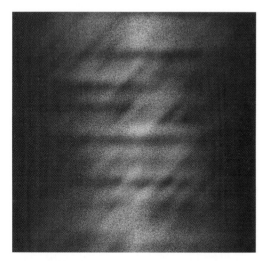

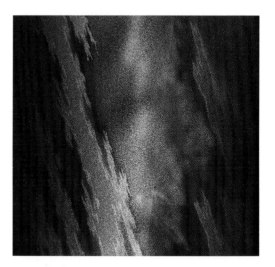

Figure 4–67
The KPT Texture Explorer preset Noise:
Lucid Polarized Noise was applied in Reverse
Blend mode. The KPT Texture Explorer
preset Minerals: Mars Observed was applied
in Procedural Blend mode. The horizontally
flipped layer was composited in Darken
Only mode.

Figure 4–68
The KPT Texture Explorer preset Noise: Lucid
Polarized Noise was applied in Reverse Blend
mode. The KPT Fractal Explorer preset
Shredded Gold, with the inside color set to
transparent, was applied in Lighten Only
mode. The horizontally flipped layer was
composited in Color mode.

Figure 4–69
The first application of a translucent gradient creates a spiral effect.

Figure 4–70
The second application of the gradient, using smaller segments, produces a complex, intertwining pillar.

SIAMESE-TWIN TWISTED PILLAR

Filters We Will Use

- Kai's Power Tools 2.0: Gradient Designer

You can produce a different and more complex type of column using our Basic Pillar and a preset of KPT Gradient Designer. It is the double application of the filter that produces this intense, rich, and complex pillar.

1. Make a Basic Pillar as described at the beginning of the "Ancient Pillars" section.
2. Apply the KPT Texture Explorer preset Noise: Lucid Polarized Noise applied in Procedural Blend mode.
3. Apply the KPT Gradient Designer using the preset Translucent: Shadow Tubes Diagonal with the Repeat option set at 2 (Figure 4–69).
4. Apply the KPT Gradient Designer using the preset Translucent: Shadow Tubes Diagonal with the Repeat option set at 6. Pull the direction bar down to the 10 o'clock position as in Figure 4–70. Lighten the final image.

NOTE: The Direction Bar is the first box to the right of the preview window in the KPT Gradient Designer dialog box. To adjust the angle of the gradient, press and hold the mouse button over the radiating bar while dragging downward.

5

Terrific Text Effects

The ability to produce quality type on a desktop was the pivotal factor in making desktop computers thrive in the design world. Until recently, only one holdout to manual dexterity has remained—the calligraphic effects and hyper-airbrushed paintings of the lettering experts. The sheen of metal or the glow of a neon halo around text required great feats of manual skill.

Now, however, you can produce these effects using the wonderful expanded toolkit of plug-in technology. No textural effect is out of reach with filters. New filters even allow multiple-colored fills that follow every nuance of letter forms.

These techniques can produce sublime effects. They can also produce hideously overdesigned, illegible typography. Since I am totally unrestrained by cautious art directors, I will humor you with a lettering extravaganza that may not show up on the next Fortune 500 annual report project. These same techniques, though, can be applied with more muted tones worthy of the boardroom in any corporation.

If you wish to follow along with the techniques described in this chapter, create the following Master Text File.

Master Text File

To create the Master Text File that serves as the basis for all the exercises in this chapter, follow these steps:

1. Create a 900 × 300 pixel RGB file with a white background.

2. Pick a font that you like and that can be antialiased. Type in the word or words of your choice in black. Be sure to leave some space around the letters and around the edges of the file. Refer to the example shown in Figure 5–1.

3. With the text still selected, clear the RGB chanels to white and save the selection in Photoshop. Save the file as Master Text File.

MACINTOSH USERS TIP: To make life easier, make the file a Stationery Pad file by selecting the icon of the unopened Master Text File while you are in the Finder. Select Get Information from the File menu in the Macintosh Finder. Click on the Stationery Pad option box in the Get Information dialog box. Now you can open up a new untitled image with type each time you open the Master Text File, without fear of overwriting the original.

Multicolored Text

Filters We Will Use

• *Kai's Power Tools*: Gradient Designer

The addition of color can alter the mood and tone of text radically. Plug-in filters can help you produce simple color blends, more complex color bursts, and more.

In this section, you will discover techniques for applying color in a variety of ways and examine some multistep applications of color blends that can add new zing to your projects. We will start with simple color blends and progress to more and more complex color enhancements.

MYSTICAL

Figure 5–1　The Master Text File can be used in all the exercises and example in this chapter.

Color Shaping

By using color blends that swell and burst across a series of letters, you can create the illusion of added dimension.

It is easier to illustrate the concepts behind your colorizing options if we use KPT Gradient Designer presets. Please make your own gradients and settings and try variations of these concepts.

Rising Sun Text

Want a smooth, airbrushed glow on your text that seems to emanate from the bottom, blushing out to the top and corners? Of course you do! And here is how.

You can use any set of colors with the following technique. With a different selection of hues, you could even call this section "Setting Sun Text."

1. Open a copy of the Master Text File and load the selection.
2. Open the KPT Gradient Designer using the preset Julia Set Gradients: Global Glow Ball.
3. In KPT Gradient Designer, move the center of origin by pressing and holding the mouse button inside the preview window of the dialog box. Drag the center of origin downward toward the bottom of the text to produce the effect of the sun rising (Figure 5–2).

Bulging Color Text

There are times when placing 3D text in a project headline would be sheer overdesign. When a hint of bulge is appropriate, though, why not do it with color?

Any color scheme will do. The goal is to obtain lighter values in the center and darker ones on the outside edges of the blend. Take your choice: Bulge from top to bottom or from side to side.

1. Open a copy of the Master Text File and load the selection.
2. Apply the KPT Gradient Designer using the preset Metallic: Sax and Violets (Figure 5–3).

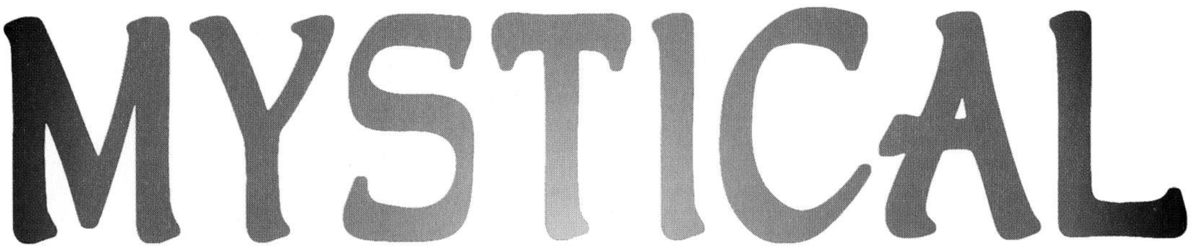

Figure 5–2   You can position glows of color within text before applying the filter.

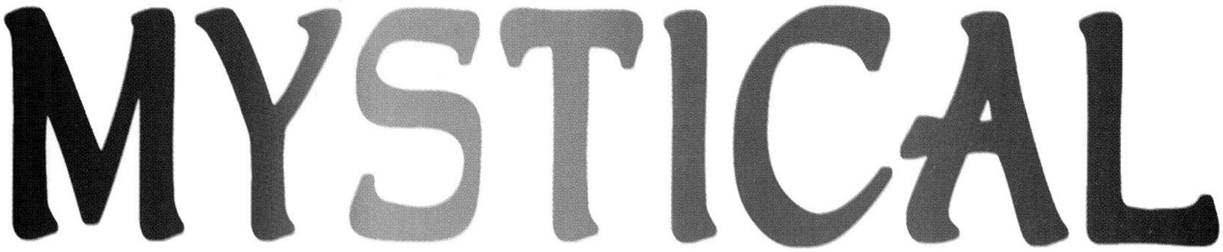

MYSTICAL

Figure 5–3   Blends with color highlights can simulate bulging type.

BULGING OPTION

1. Open a copy of the Master Text File and load the selection.
2. Open KPT Gradient Designer with the preset Metallic: Sax and Violets.
3. Pull the Gradient Direction Bar straight down; this step changes the orientation of the gradient from vertical to horizontal. Apply the gradient (Figure 5–4).

NOTE: The Direction Bar is the first box to the right of the preview window in the KPT Gradient Designer dialog box. To adjust the angle of the gradient, press and hold the radiating bar while pulling downward.

Radiating Text

Remember the days of upbeat packaging? Sunrises with their sparkling rays glowing across a loaf of bread? Revisit optimism in a 90s way with a filter technique that can put a blush on a milk-and-honey complexion.

The technique described here shares common elements with the one described in the "Rising Sun Text" section of this chapter—specifically, the ability to move the center of origin on a radial blend. Do you want your rays shining up or down?

MYSTICAL

Figure 5–4   Changes in color highlight positions alter the direction of the bulge.

1. Open a copy of the Master Text File and load the selection.
2. Open the KPT Gradient Designer using the preset Metallic: Golden Leonardo.
3. Move the center of origin in KPT Gradient Designer by pressing and holding the mouse button inside the preview window of the dialog box. Drag the center of origin downward toward the bottom of the text.
4. Pull the Gradient Direction Bar around until you like the intensity of color in the gradient preview box. (Refer to the "Bulging Options" section of this chapter for instructions on rotating a Gradient Bar. Apply the gradient (Figure 5–5).

Megacolored Text

Who said that one application of color is enough? Color on your color. When in doubt, throw on some more color. Granted, my samples may be ready for the circus, but these techniques work with the subtler ranges of color as well.

If you keep hearing about chops and channel operations and it scares you, try these easy multiple applications of color using the apply modes. Watch your fears fade into nothingness.

1. Open a copy of the Master Text File and load the selection.
2. Apply the KPT Gradient Designer using the preset Another Category: Another Radial Preset. That certainly should be enough color for anyone, but a second application of color makes the illustration even more interesting.
3. Open the KPT Gradient Designer using the preset Misc.: Bright Pastels 2.
4. Go to Options in the KPT Gradient Designer dialog box and select Difference mode. Apply the gradient (Figure 5–6).

Figure 5–5 Text can feature radiating colors with a user-definable center of origin.

MYSTICAL

Figure 5–6   Multiple applications of color add interest to text.

To experiment further, perform step 4 once again and watch the preview box as you select each apply mode in the options area of the KPT Gradient Designer dialog box.

It has never been easier to examine and understand the workings of the channel apply modes. This used to be pretty arcane information. Now you can see the changes immediately without waiting.

Swirling Color

Just when you thought you had enough color to go around, I show you how to make it go around and around within your text. You carry out this technique outside the text selection then paste it into the letter forms.

Filters We Will Use

- *Kai's Power Tools 2.0:* Gradient Designer
- *Aldus Gallery Effects, Classic Art, Series 1:* Ripple

1. Make a 900 × 300 pixel RGB file with a white background. You will use this file to create a swirling colored area that you can select and paste into text.

   NOTE: The extra file for the texture is necessary. Some of the distortion filters can pick up traces of color outside the selection area. This results in white area invading the otherwise pristine text selection and spoiling the job. The use of a separate file also lets you move the color swatch inside the text, thereby providing more options for a pleasing composition of swirls.

2. Apply the KPT Gradient Designer using the preset Basic Gradients: Soft Fairy Tale Colors.

3. Apply the Gallery Effects Ripple filter to the entire file, using a Ripple Size of 15 and a Ripple Magnitude of 20.

4. Select the rippled color file you just made and copy it to the Clipboard.

5. Open the Master Text File and load the selection.

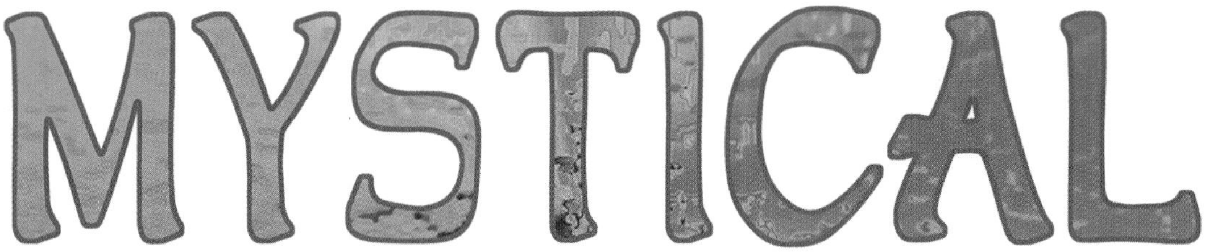

MYSTICAL

Figure 5–7   Rippled sheets of color can be repositioned within the text.

6. Select Paste Into and paste the ripple color image into the text file selection.

7. Click inside the lettering and drag the rippled color around until you are happy with the composition (Figure 5–7). Figures 5–8 and 5–9 show some additional variations.

Color within the Lines

The next technique would have made even your strictest teacher happy. You can color within the lines of your text and add colored lines on colored lines—always perfectly adjusted. Perfectionists, take note.

Using KPT Gradient Designer's Shapeburst functions, you can specify very complex blends that follow the natural forms of your letters. The Master Text File has rounded text shapes, so select the Circular Shapeburst

Figure 5–8
Variations of rippled color can suggest hammered metal.

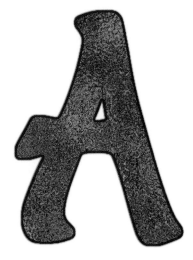

Figure 5–9
When the ripples become very tight, new textural effects are formed.

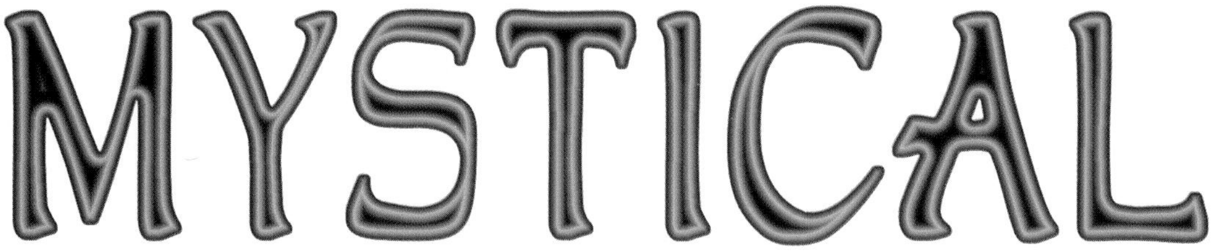

MYSTICAL

Figure 5–10   The KPT Gradient Designer filter, applied in Circular Shapeburst mode, follows the contours of these letterforms faithfully.

apply mode hidden in the top left rectangle in the KPT Gradient Designer dialog box. Use of the Circular Shapeburst mode assures you that no hard corners will mar your rounded text.

1. Open a copy of the Master Text File and load the selection.
2. Apply KPT Gradient Designer with the preset Metallic: Metallic Torus. Be sure to select the Circular Shapeburst apply mode (Figure 5–10).

Figures 5–11 and 5–12 show some additional variations on the theme of coloring within the lines.

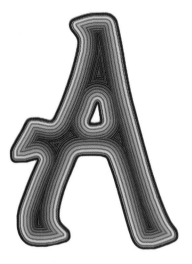

Figure 5–11
A variation of the color-within-the-lines technique

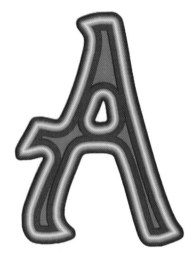

Figure 5–12
The color-within-the-lines technique taken to its extreme

Rounded-Corner and Embossed Effects

Knowing how to add dimension and 3D textures to the text of your design projects is very handy. This section will get you started. Once you understand the basis of these techniques, you can combine them with the texturizing techniques featured in the next section to obtain some truly unique effects.

The 3D text technique and the color-within-the-lines technique discussed in the previous section have many similarities. When you craft the blends carefully, text can appear molded and embossed. The following exercise illustrates the technique using a KPT Gradient Designer preset; you can also experiment on your own. Try different fonts and letterforms, too—the results will vary according to the shapes that are being filled.

These rounded-corner and embossed techniques yield results that are very different from some of the lettering effects—channel operation formation of text effects, known as *chopping*—that are currently popular. For many people, these techniques may be easier to master than chopping and will create effects that suffice for most projects.

1. Open a copy of the Master Text File and load the selection.
2. Apply the KPT Gradient Designer using the preset Metallic: Metallic Torus. Be sure to select the Circular Shapeburst apply mode. Change the mode to Grayscale and back to RGB. Save the file as 3D Master Text File (Figure 5–13).

I prepared a single letter (see Figure 5–14) for easier viewing of future text exercises.

Option To create chiseled type with control over the direction of light and shadow, apply the Photoshop Emboss filter to the selected text (Figure 5–15).

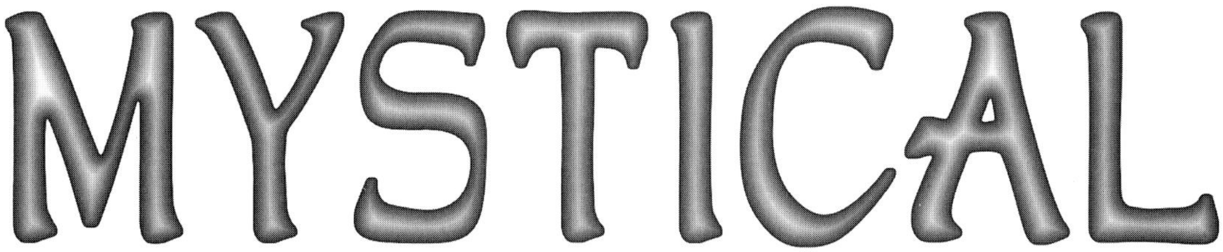

Figure 5–13 When the width of the blend is properly sized, a perfect three-dimensional text effect is produced.

NOTE: We will refer frequently in this chapter to Figures 5–13, 5–14, and 5–15. If you would like to try these exercises, save a master copy of each and have some fun. You can save time by selecting the text and saving the selection.

Texturizing Text

Once you master the grayscale shapes, you can easily apply other filter effects to the text. Stone effects of all sorts are simple to achieve, as are reflective surface effects. We will add a few twists in this section, using the Gallery Effects, Classic Art, Series 2 Texturizer filter.

Keep in mind that we do not want to obliterate the 3D text effects we have created already. We want to emboss, erode, and mutate them, but still save some semblance of the forms. This means that the channel apply modes and transparent glazes of texture and color become a priority.

Rocky Text

Let's reproduce the rich texture of stone and invent some new variations of our own. For the sake of clear examples, you will apply the techniques to a single large letter. (These techniques work just fine on the 3D Master Text File as well.)

Filters We Will Need
- *Kai's Power Tools 2.0*: Gradient Designer, Texture Explorer
- *Aldus Gallery Effects, Classic Art, Series 1*: Emboss
- *Aldus Gallery Effects, Classic Art, Series 2*: Texturizer

GRANITE EVOLVING TO MARBLE

You can build multiple transparent textures on top of the 3D text for some gritty effects.

1. Open a copy of the 3D Master Text File and load the selection.
2. Apply the KPT Texture Explorer using the preset Effects Textures: Impressionist Flowers. Select the Procedural Blend apply mode option and a pixel size of 96 × 96 pixels (Figure 5–16).
3. Apply the KPT Texture Explorer again using the preset Effects Textures: Impressionist Flowers. Select the Procedural Blend apply mode option and this time use a pixel size of 256 × 256 pixels (Figure 5–17).
4. To give more interesting definition to the stone, apply KPT Texture Explorer a second time, this time using the preset Effects Marble: White Valpollicella Marble. Select the Multiply apply mode option and a pixel size of 128 × 128 pixels (Figure 5–18).

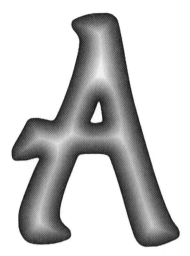
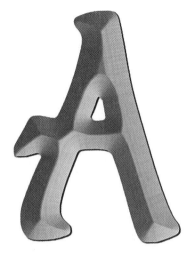
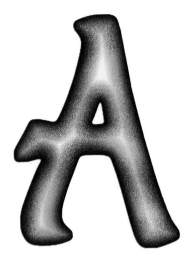

Figure 5–14
The same techniques produced both the 3D Master Text File and this text. This letter features a wider gray-to-black blend created in the KPT Gradient Designer Gradient Bar.

Figure 5–15
To sharpen the edges and cast a shadow on the text, the Photoshop Emboss filter was applied with an angle of 141 degrees, a height of 10 pixels at 100 percent.

Figure 5–16
A single application of the KPT Texture Explorer set to the Procedural Blend apply mode yields a passable granite effect.

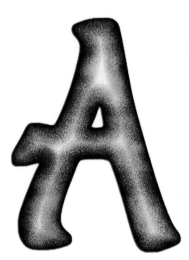

Figure 5–17
A second application of KPT Texture Explorer, using a larger-scale pattern, enhances realism.

Figure 5–18
A third application of KPT Texture Explorer, using a marble pattern, adds a new look.

Notice how the custom apply modes allow complex multiple filter applications without obscuring the 3D shaping of the text.

This is a rich vein to mine, pun intended. To take advantage of the possibilities, use the text shapes you already created and try some of your own textures on them. The apply modes and scale are your allies in the quest.

FRUITFUL DISCOVERIES IN ROCKY TERRITORY

Figures 5–19 through 5–24 present, for your inspiration and amusement, the results of several different filter combinations that yield rock-like texture effects. Keep in mind that some of these examples may be a bit too wild for certain clients.

 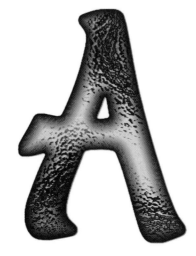 

Figure 5–19
The KPT Grime Layer filter and Gallery Effects Emboss provided the grit. The color is a homemade gradient applied using KPT Gradient Designer in the Procedural Blend apply mode.

Figure 5–20
The color background, created in the "Swirling Color" section of this chapter (see Figure 5–8), was pasted into the 3D text. The Photoshop composite controls were set to Darken Only apply mode.

Figure 5–21
The radiating color background was applied using KPT Gradient Designer in Procedural Blend apply mode. The Gallery Effects Emboss filter was applied with a Relief setting of 12 and a Top Right light position. A homemade texture in KPT Texture Explorer was applied using the Multiply apply mode.

Figure 5–22
A homemade texture in KPT Texture Explorer was applied using the Procedural Blend apply mode. The Gallery Effects Emboss filter was applied with a Relief setting of 12 and a Top Right light position.

Figure 5–23
A homemade texture in KPT Texture Explorer was applied using the Procedural Blend apply mode at a setting of 1024 × 1024 pixels. A second homemade texture in KPT Texture Explorer was applied using the Difference apply mode at a setting of 128 × 128 pixels. The Gallery Effects Emboss filter was applied using a Relief setting of 7 and a Top Left light position.

Figure 5–24
A homemade soft green-to-brown radial gradient was applied using KPT Gradient Designer in Procedural Blend apply mode. A homemade texture in KPT Texture Explorer was applied using the Difference apply mode. The Gallery Effects Emboss filter was applied with a Relief setting of 6 and a Top Left light position.

Advanced Techniques

A professional can never have enough text effects in his or her bag of tricks. Here are a few goodies to add to your effects lineup.

Filters We Will Need

- *Kai's Power Tools 2.0*: Gradient Designer, Gradients on Paths
- *Aldus Gallery Effects, Classic Art, Series 1*: Ripple
- *Adobe Photoshop*: Motion Blur

Fire Fire   Although filter techniques that produce flaming text without manual manipulation do exist, I have found them to be a bit too predictable. Here are several techniques for producing flame text effects that leave room for your own personal flair. Keep in mind that the computer-generated end results may be of limited usefulness without the personal touch of the hand-done stroke.

The application of a single filter is the most difficult part of this technique. Then it's easy—just push and pull the correct combination of red and yellow around to create cozy, fireside-flaming words. I have added a second option for those who need especially active flames. Don't get burned!

HANDS-ON FLAMES

Have fun with the hand-pulled flames on this one.

1. Open a copy of the Master Text File.
2. Select All and fill the background with black. Load the selection and fill the text with red.
3. Feather the selection by 3 pixels.
4. Apply the KPT Gradients on Paths using the preset Hot Plasma Tube.
5. Deselect the text. Use the Smudge tool to pull the yellow and red up to form flames. Use a quick zigzag motion as you pull up. Be sure that the Smudge tool has a soft feathered brush setting and that the opacity range is from 50 to 75 percent (Figure 5–25).

COALS WITH GLOWING EMBERS

Here is another hot one with no handwork.

1. Open a copy of the Master Text File.

Figure 5–25   Red text is embellished with a thin, hot orange line. The Smudge tool pulls both colors up to form flames.

2. Select All and fill the background with black. Load the selection and fill the text with a top-to-bottom red-to-black blend as shown in Figure 5–26.

3. Feather the selection by 3 pixels.

4. Apply KPT Gradients on Paths using the preset Hot Plasma Tube (Figure 5–27).

5. Apply the Gallery Effects Ripple filter to the selected text. Set both Ripple Size and Ripple Magnitude to 4.

6. Deselect the text. Use the Rectangular Marquee to select the top of the text and all of the black background directly above the text.

7. Feather the selection by 6 pixels and apply the Photoshop Motion Blur filter with a setting of –90 degrees and a Range of 44 pixels.

Figure 5–26   A blend from black to red prepares the text for a glowing ember effect.

Figure 5–27   KPT Gradients on Paths provide a glowing edge to text.

Figure 5–28   The Gallery Effects Ripple and KPT Hue Protected Noise Maximum filters heat up the visual effect.

8. Apply the Gallery Effects Ripple filter with a Ripple Size of 7 and a Ripple Magnitude of 10, and then apply KPT Hue Protected Noise Maximum (Figure 5–28).

Wet Text

After fire comes water. (I may be accused of practicing alchemy for making that statement.) Fluidity is a virtue, and creating fluid text can be fun. Next time you are "flogging 'gators" to get that water company ad done, you will thank me.

Translucency is the prime goal in this faux technique. Once you define the edges with a filter pass, a little Dodge-and-Burn tool work finishes the task. This specific technique works best when the background color is consistent.

1. Open a copy of the Master Text File.
2. Fill the background using the KPT Gradient Designer preset Strong Hues: Light Yellow Haze.
3. Load the text selection and feather until the outline starts to soften the forms, creating a slightly melted shaping.
4. Make a custom KPT Gradients on Paths gradient.

NOTE: The new KPT Gradients on Paths preset is created in KPT Gradient Designer, not Gradients on Paths.

a. Open KPT Gradient Designer.
b. Click on each end of the Gradient Bar while selecting None as the color. The Gradient Bar should now be a black-and-white checkerboard.

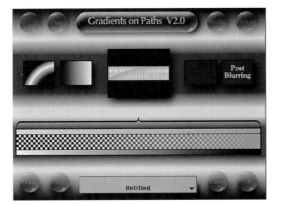

Figure 5–29
The transparent gradient was made in KPT Gradient Designer and transferred into KPT Gradients on Paths.

    c. Click on the right side of the Gradient Bar and select a color from the image background that is dark enough to serve as the outer edge of the fluid.

    d. Verify that you are using the Normal apply mode and that the Sawtooth A to B setting is selected.

    e. In the top left rectangle of the KPT Gradient Designer dialog box, select Gradients on Paths (Figure 5–29).

5. Apply the new KPT Gradients on Paths setting (Figure 5–30).

6. With the text still selected, use the Dodge-and-Burn tools to highlight and shadow the appropriate areas of the lettering (Figure 5–31).

Figure 5–30   KPT Gradients on Paths provides a translucent edge, which is the foundation of a wet effect.

Figure 5–31   Selective use of the Photoshop Dodge-and-Burn tools make the type look much more liquid.

QUICK DRENCHED TEXT

Here is a technique for those who want to learn about channel operations for special text effects. If you have promised to take the time to learn about channels but are too busy to do it, this technique is for you. Get ready for a wet ride on an easy slide toward liquid text without touching a channel.

Filters We Will Use

- *Gallery Effects, Classic Art, Volume 3*: Plaster

1. Open a new grayscale file with a black background.
2. Place white type on the image and select All.
3. Apply the Gallery Effects Plaster filter using the default setting (Figure 5–32).

You can colorize or add texture to this text easily, using the other techniques described in this chapter.

Metallic Writing

Metallic text effects are popular things to "hammer out" for multimedia, print, and presentation projects. This section demonstrates some simple-to-accomplish effects as well as slightly more involved ones that are well worth the few extra steps required.

Filters really help to get the job done when it comes to metallic effects. With a little planning, you can obtain some clean, shiny, or gritty metal ready for the printing press or the video screen.

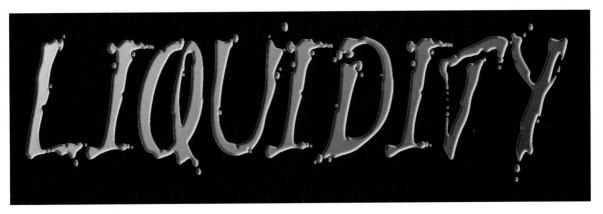

Figure 5–32   The Gallery Effects Plaster filter can create liquid text effects instantly.

GOLD CARD-QUALITY TYPE

Careful modulations of color creates realism in the painting of shiny metal. Sharp highlights create the illusion of shininess, and soft blends of color generate a satiny bronzed finish. Changes in color create the illusion of shifting reflections that occur on real metal surfaces. It used to be difficult to reproduce these effects electronically—until Kai's Power Tools Gradient Designer came along.

This section demonstrates two different approaches to gold effects. The first approach uses a direct application of opaque color blends that simulate gold. The second approach simulates the color changes that are visible when light shines across gold. By applying the transparent colors of a gold gradient, you can maintain the underlying shapes.

Filters We Will Use
- *Kai's Power Tools 2.0*: Gradient Designer, Texture Explorer

Color-Me-Gold Type   Colorizing rounded forms can be quite effective, as the following "enriching" technique shows.

1. Open a copy of the 3D Master Text File that you created in the "Rounded-Corner and Embossing Effects" section of this chapter. Select the text.
2. Apply KPT Gradient Designer using the preset Metallic: Golden Leonardo 3 in the Procedural Blend mode (Figure 5–33).

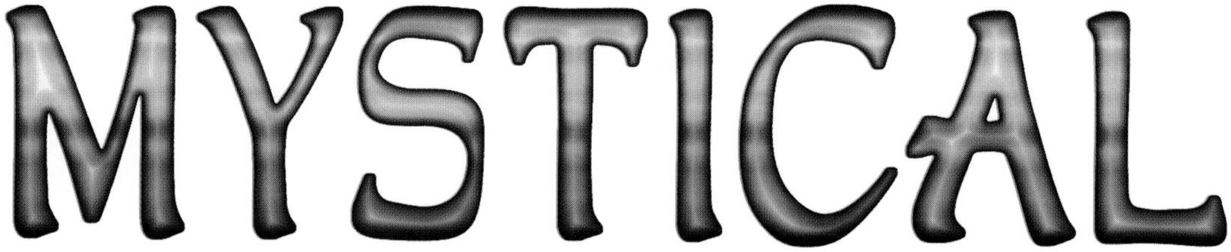

MYSTICAL

Figure 5–33   Color applied in KPT Gradient Designer using the Procedural Blend apply mode has transformed gray text to something of much greater value.

Digging for Gold Nuggets   Multiple applications of large transparent texture swatches strip away the tired familiarity of filter presets and produce sinuous drifts of golden color.

1. Open a copy of the 3D Master Text File that you created in the "Rounded-Corner and Embossing Effects" section of this chapter. Select the text.
2. Apply KPT Texture Explorer using the preset Metals: Golden Wood in Procedural Blend mode with a 512 × 512 pixel size.
3. Apply KPT Texture Explorer a second time using the preset Metals: Golden Wood in Procedural Blend mode with a 512 × 512 pixel size. While pressing and holding the mouse button, move the texture (located in the small preview box to the left of the large grid of textures) until the areas of highlight on the letters are to your liking (Figure 5–34).

Chiseled Heavy Metal   Sometimes worthwhile things take a bit more work to acquire. Sometimes it's worth it. This is one of those times.

If you add a thick black line around text, it becomes simple to select this area to form a chiseled edge. You can form highlights and achieve a realistic effect easily, using KPT Gradient Designer blends.

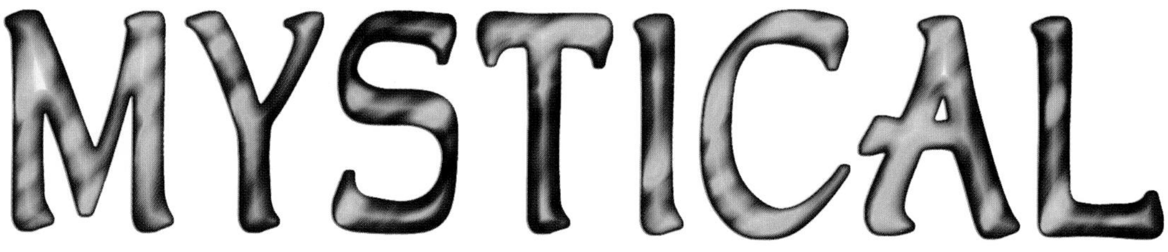

MYSTICAL

Figure 5–34   Transparent textures, applied several times using KPT Texture Explorer in Procedural Blend apply mode, add color and a unique sheen to a gray text sample.

NOTE: The Master Text File you made at the beginning of this chapter should have an alpha channel saved with it. To produce the chiseled edge, we will make an additional alpha channel.

1. Open the Master Text File.
2. Select All and fill the entire image with red. Load the preselected type selection.
3. Stroke the selection with a black line that is wide enough to cause the type to almost touch (Figure 5–35).
4. Deselect the type. Select the heavy black lines and save this as a separate selection.
5. Fill the selected black lines using KPT Gradient Designer with the preset Metallic: Golden Leonardo. The Repeat Twice option should be active (Figure 5–36).

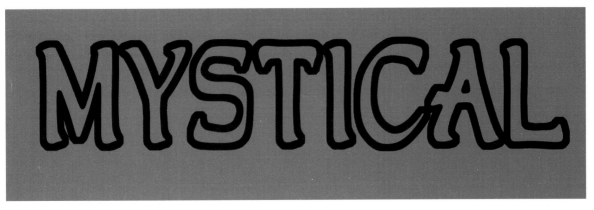

Figure 5–35   The black line was formed by stroking a selection of text.

Figure 5–36   The black area was selected and filled with a radial blend of golden colors.

Figure 5–37   A golden blend fills the original text area. Dodge-and-Burn tools in Photoshop help accentuate highlights, edges, and shadows on the chiseled text border

6. Load the original type selection and fill the type area using KPT Gradient Designer with the preset Metallic: Golden Leonardo 3.

7. Load the chiseled selection. Using the Dodge-and-Burn tools, darken and lighten areas of the chiseled area to achieve a more realistic play of light on metal (Figure 5–37).

CHAPTER **6**

Paper, Patterns, and Textures

An unlimited variety of textures, seamless patterns, and embossing tools are at your command when using filters. You can see the creative use of textures everywhere in today's design, multimedia, and illustration markets. Multimedia presentations—even the same, old boardroom point-by-point slide presentations—require numerous background sources.

The demand for textures and backgrounds is so hot that CD-ROM discs are filled with hundreds of them. Many businesses use this type of enhancement daily. Often, however, the cost of these CDs can be prohibitive.

Because a limited number of background and texture sets are on the market, presentations and multimedia videos can begin to look alike. Without new styles, designers risk boring the viewer, or—worse—producing projects that are predictable.

You can produce your own unique textures and backgrounds of unlimited variety for the price of a few inexpensive filters. In this chapter, we will review the techniques for executing any project with professional textures.

Homemade Textures

With just a few basic filters and some imagination, you can call these textures your own. You can follow along with the textures illustrated below *and* go beyond them. The important thing to remember when producing homemade textures is to *experiment, experiment, experiment*. Think of these examples as mere jumping-off points, beyond which you can colorize, emboss, swirl, resize, and embolden with reckless abandon.

Filters We Will Use

- *Adobe Photoshop*: Add Noise, Median, Gaussian Blur, Emboss
- *Kai's Power Tools 2.0*: Find Edges & Invert

1. Open a new 900 × 900 pixel grayscale file filled with 50 percent gray.
2. Apply the Photoshop Add Noise filter with a setting of 32 and with the Gaussian option active (Figure 6–1).

   TIP: **When used with the Add Noise filter, the Gaussian option yields a more random noise, which adds interest to textures.**

3. Apply the Photoshop Median filter at a setting of 6 pixels. The Median filter strips out enough of the grain data to make a distinctive set of textures possible.
4. Save this file as Master Texture File (Figure 6–2).

Options for Your Imaging Arsenal

We show several different "homemade" texture options in this section, in the hope that the basic concepts of producing your own textures will become evident. Filter combinations, along with variations in the size and density of pixels, are factors that can facilitate variety.

Figure 6–1
A great jumping-off point for creating a multitude of textures is to start with some basic noise.

Figure 6–2
Subtle differences in the surface of an image open the door to many filtering options for textures.

OPTION 1

1. Open a copy of the Master Texture File.

2. In Photoshop, choose the Image: Map: Posterize menu option and posterize the file to 6 levels.

3. Apply the Photoshop Emboss Filter using these settings: Angle 133, Height 10 pixels, and Percentage 100 (Figure 6–3).

OPTION 2

Here is a variation of a texture tip from Kai Krause, gleaned from *Kai's Power Tips and Tricks* (available through the HSC forum on America Online).

1. Open a copy of the Master Texture File.

2. Apply KPT Find Edges & Invert. The image looks almost white temporarily, but it won't stay that way for long.

3. In Photoshop, choose the Image: Map: Equalize menu option. Be sure to zoom into this image and notice the fine steel-wool-like threads running throughout (see Figure 6–4).

Homemade Textures with More Spice

Stuccoesque

The following exercise demonstrates an easy-to-produce stucco style texture for presentation backgrounds, print backgrounds, or as a bump map texture for 3D programs.

Filters We Will Use

- *Aldus Gallery Effects Classic Art Volume 1*: Ripple, Emboss
- *Aldus Gallery Effects, Classic Art Volume 2*: Grain
  ...or you can substitute
- *Adobe Photoshop*: Add Noise, Despeckle

1. Open a new grayscale file and fill it with 50 percent gray.

2. Apply the Gallery Effects Classic Art, Volume 2, Grain filter. Set the type of grain to Clumped, the Graininess to 50, and the Contrast to 50 (Figure 6–5).

NOTE: You can substitute the Add Noise filter with an additional application of the Despeckle Filter to achieve a similar grain effect.

3. Apply the Gallery Effects Classic Art, Volume 1, Ripple filter. Set the Ripple Size to 10 and the Ripple Magnitude to 12 (Figure 6–6).

4. Apply the Gallery Effects Classic Art, Volume 1, Emboss filter. Set the Relief to 10 and the Light Source to Top Right (Figure 6–7).

5. If you want a larger stucco pattern, enlarge the file after step 3 and then emboss the enlarged file (Figure 6–8).

Figure 6–3
You can achieve a pebbled texture by embossing.

Figure 6–4
In this image, produced using the KPT Find Edges & Invert filter and the Photoshop Equalize menu option, tiny threads are woven into a rich web of pixels.

Figure 6–5
The Gallery Effects Grain filter was used as a texturizer.

Figure 6–6
The Ripple filter mixes it up.

Figure 6–7
The Gallery Effects Emboss filter brings out the texture.

Figure 6–8
Enlarging the image file results in a larger stucco pattern for that southwestern look.

TIP: Changing the scale of an image as you work with portions of these texture experiments is a powerful way to obtain a much larger set of textures for later use.

TIP: Don't concern yourself with the softening of the texture file when you enlarge the size. Embossing is at its most jag-free when applied to a slightly blurred image.

Textures from Gradients

The examples up to this point have been about form rather than color. Yet, hue can be an important element in textures, and the easiest way to get lots of color jumping on the screen is to use KPT 2.0 Gradient Designer.

Textures from Images

Source material for textures is everywhere. CD-ROM image discs are a great source of data that can serve as a basis for textures. It may sound a bit silly to pay for high-resolution commercial images and then turn them into textures, but anyplace where colors and shapes reside is a great place to extract information for textures.

TIP: When using Photo CD images, open the low-resolution TIFF version. It is not necessary to work on high-resolution data at this point in the texture-creation process. Your focus right now should be the color and general shaping of image areas within the file. High-resolution data is required only for the strategic final steps of creating excellent print-quality textures.

Filters We Will Use
- *Adobe Photoshop*: Gaussian Blur
- *Aldus Gallery Effects, Classic Art, Volume 1*: Emboss
- *Aldus Gallery Effects, Classic Art, Volume 1*: Sprayed Strokes

1. Open any RGB image approximately 640 × 480 pixels in size. You don't need a CD-ROM image to do this exercise. You can use any scanned image or the Tiger image located in the Toolkit disc (Figure 6–9).
2. Apply Gallery Effects Sprayed Strokes using these settings: Stroke Length 20, Stroke Direction Left Diagonal, and Spray Radius 25 (Figure 6–10).
3. Apply the Photoshop Gaussian Blur filter set to 3 pixels.
4. Apply the Gallery Effects Emboss filter using a Relief setting of 15 and a Light Position of Top Left (Figure 6–11).

Figure 6–9
A low-resolution version of a Photo Disc CD-ROM image

Figure 6–10
The Gallery Effects Sprayed Strokes filter obliterates recognizable detail.

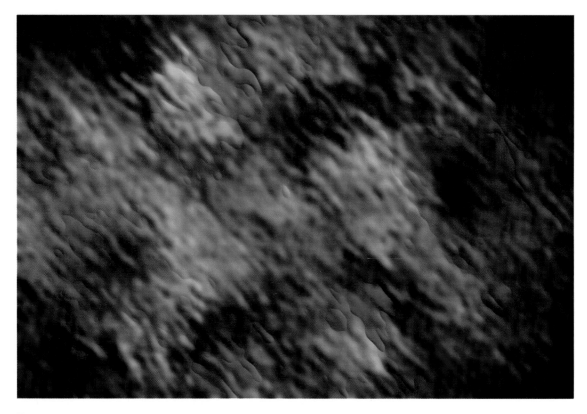

Figure 6–11   A new texture is formed after blurring and embossing.

Push-Button Textures

My math teacher taught me the importance of solving math problems in your head or on paper before picking up a calculator and having it do the work. The Homemade Texture section is an example of how to make textures the "old-fashioned way." KPT 2.0 Texture Explorer is a calculator of textures that you can use with a number of apply modes.

Texture Sets for Projects

Filters We Will Use
- *Kai's Power Tools 2.0*: Texture Explorer, Gradient Designer

Many commercial-art projects call for a suite of materials to be designed to work together. Let's assume a client requires the use of specific colors in a given project. With the help of KPT Gradient Designer and KPT Texture Explorer, you can use these specific colors in textural backgrounds.

1. The colors for the project need to be selected first. Open a new 400 × 400 pixel CMYK file and assign two "company" colors for the project. Apply each color to a distinctive area of the file.

2. Open KPT Gradient Designer and pull the Gradient Bar bracket to select the left half of the Gradient Bar. Fill one half of the Gradient Bar with a solid color. Slide the Gradient Bar bracket to select the other half of the gradient bar, and then fill this half with a contrasting solid color.

3. Name and save the gradient.

4. Open KPT Texture Explorer. Using the Gradient Bar in the upper left corner of the dialog box, select the corporate color gradient that you just saved.

   You now have the ability to create a number of color-coordinated textures that will match the color specifications of your project.

5. Make sure that the application mode in Texture Explorer is set to Normal. Click on the bottom ball of the Mutation Tree.

6. Click the ball until you see a color-coordinated texture (on the outside small squares) that will work for your project. Option-click on your favorite outer area texture blocks to protect them from change.

7. When you have a sufficient number of textures for the project, click on them to bring them to the center, and then save each one (Figure 6–12).

Figure 6–13 shows additional variations on the theme of this exercise.

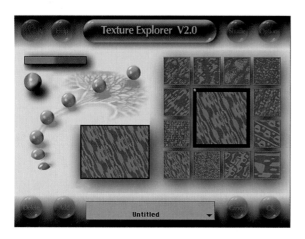

Figure 6–12
The red lines around the little textures indicate that they are locked and protected.

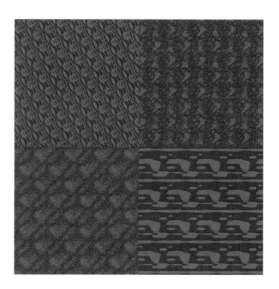

Figure 6–13
Examples of some of the possible variations for a corporate color scheme

Look Ma, No Seams

Photoshop and Painter allow you to fill an area with a pattern. If that pattern happens to be seamless, you will have access to an unlimited quantity of texture for backgrounds, presentations, or images. Let's look at the basic concepts behind the seamless texture technique and discover a few new twists.

Why are seamless textures important? By producing seamless textures, you can fool the viewer into seeing the area as a single sheet of texture. If the effect is not done masterfully, the effect is lumpy and awkward.

CLASSIC SEAMLESS TILES

Rather than use an existing image source, let's paint shapes and turn them into a seamless pattern. Remember that you can use this technique for anything you draw or scan.

To accomplish a seamless effect, we will use the Photoshop Offset filter. It allows you to see how the edges of the image on this file would abut each other if tiled endlessly together.

If we offset the image by half its size and select the Wrap Around option, all the outside edges of the file will meet in the center. With some creative cleanup or painting, we have a tile that will butt together with no visible seams.

Filters We Will Use
• *Adobe Photoshop*: Offset

1. Open a new 400 × 400 pixel grayscale file with a black background.

2. Set your foreground and background colors to white and black, respectively. Select a Gradient tool set to Radial/Lighten Only. Create spheres by pulling the Gradient tool at various distances across the file (Figure 6–14).

NOTE: This spherical gradient technique (Boobonics) is from Kai's Power Tips #12.

3. Select the entire file and apply the Offset filter at 200 × 200 pixels, which is exactly half of the file size (Figure 6–15). Set the filter to the Wrap Around option (Figure 6–16).

4. Use Clone and Smudge tools to make the center of the file look seamless (Figure 6–17).

NOTE: Don't paint on the edge of the file at this stage. Anywhere in the middle is okay.

5. With the entire file selected, choose the Photoshop Edit: Define Pattern menu option. Our tile is now in memory and ready to fill any selection.

6. Create an 800 × 800 pixel grayscale file and select All.

7. Use the Photoshop Edit: Fill menu option to fill the entire file with the pattern. All of the edges should match (Figure 6–18). Keep this file open for the next generation of manipulation.

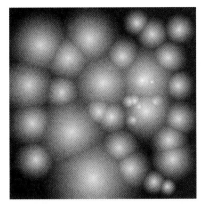

Figure 6–14
Little bubbles start the process of creating a seamless tile.

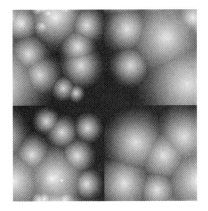

Figure 6–15
Offset bubbles need some fixing with the Offset filter.

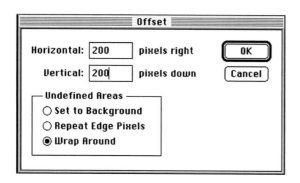

Figure 6–16
Be sure to select Wrap Around in the Photoshop
Offset dialog box.

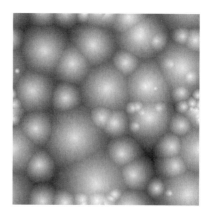

Figure 6–17
More bubbles added to cover
the seams

SEAMLESS CAN GET FLIPPY

Now that we have a file full of seamless tiles (strange-looking as it is), let's perform a simple technique to make the file more complex and more elegant.

8. Copy the entire file and paste it back on itself.

9. Flip the copy horizontally.

10. Use the Photoshop Composite Controls menu option set to Darken Only mode. Deselect All. You should have a more complex seamless image like the one in Figure 6–19.

SEAMLESS PHOTOREALISTIC TILES

Multimedia Library Inc. markets a CD named "The Art of Ancient Egypt." I find one image, called "Ram Head," especially fascinating. To create a professional-quality, seamless tile from it takes a bit more work. Sit back and enjoy the problem solving on this one!

1. Starting with the Ram image (Figure 6–20), carefully crop it in the area that has the best tile potential (Figure 6–21).

2. Offset the image with the Photoshop Offset filter to bring the outside edges into the inside (Figure 6–22).

3. You can see in Figure 6–23 that more than the seams have been retouched. I used the Clone tool to remove areas and blotches that would detract when multiple tiles were seamed together.

4. Save the tile as a pattern and generate a sheet of repeating rams (Figure 6–24).

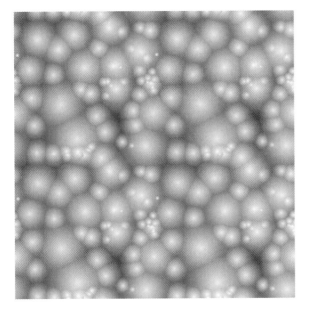

Figure 6–18
Filling the image with the newly defined pattern makes a bubbly brew.

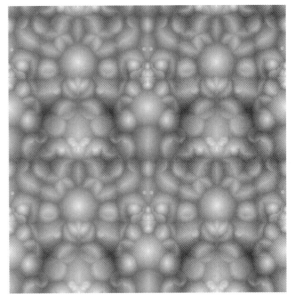

Figure 6–19
You might discover hideous or beautiful results, but they are seamless.

Figure 6–20
The original image from the Multimedia Library CD

Figure 6–21
The image is cropped to prepare it for tiling.

Figure 6–22
The image is offset to reveal the seams.

Figure 6–23
The seams have been retouched.

A DIFFERENT TWIST ON SEAMLESS

Tweaking an offset tile of texture is an art form and can require some rather advanced retouching skills. Here is a method that can produce some easy-to-accomplish merging of those harsh, divergent edges.

Filters We Will Use
- *Kai's Power Tools*: Gradient Designer
- *Adobe Photoshop*: Offset, Twirl

1. Open a new 400 × 400 pixel grayscale file.
2. Apply KPT Gradient Designer using the preset Metallic: Cool Metal Jacket A (Figure 6–25).

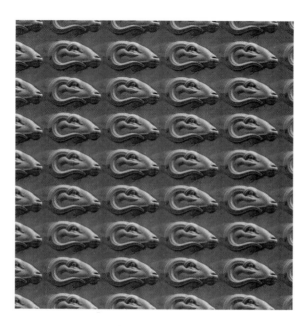

Figure 6–24
A wall of repeating rams

3. Apply the Photoshop Twirl filter at a setting of 240 degrees (Figure 6–26).

4. Apply the Photoshop Offset filter at an Offset setting of 200 × 200 pixels with the Wrap Around option active (Figure 6–27).

5. Apply the Photoshop Twirl filter at a setting of 240 degrees (Figure 6–28).

6. With the entire file selected, choose the Photoshop Edit: Define Pattern menu option. Our tile is now in memory and ready to fill any selection.

7. Create an 800 × 800 pixel grayscale box and select All.

8. Choose the Photoshop Edit: Fill menu option to fill the entire file with the pattern. All of the edges should match as in Figure 6–29.

NEWER, BRIGHTER, GNARLIER

Another approach to creating patterned textures is to use a distinctive pattern or element in the texture to your advantage. When tiled, these texture squares produce a gridded step-repeat. The important thing is to maintain control over these effects rather than be the victim of poor technique.

To make a very complex selection become seamless used to be quite a trick before the KPT 2.0 Seamless Welder filter entered the scene. The ease of use and imaging opportunities provided by Seamless Welder make this filter exciting and a rich source for experimentation.

Let's take a slightly more complex image and turn it into a serviceable repeating tile in Photoshop. In the classic seamless technique, we had to do some manipulation with the Smudge and Clone tools to reach the goal of seamlessness. None of that is necessary with the KPT Seamless Welder filter.

Figure 6–25
A radial blend starts the process of creating seamless tiles.

Figure 6–26
A twirl makes the source image pretty.

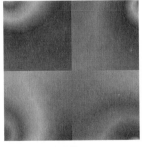

Figure 6–27
The Offset filter doubles our fun.

Figure 6–28
The Twirl filter seals the deal.

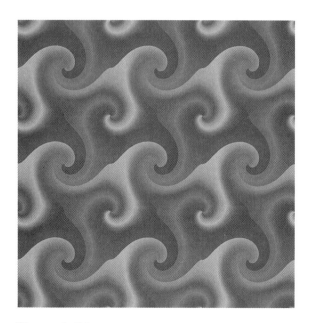

Figure 6–29
Oceans of seamless waves

Figure 6–30
This image from Photodisc Vol. IV displays
some interesting welding sparks.

Rather than matching just the edges, KPT Seamless Welder takes information from inside the selection to generate a smoothly blended transition.
Complex tiles that would be very difficult to produce can now be accomplished with ease.

Filters We Will Use

- *Kai's Power Tools 2.0*: Seamless Welder

1. Open an image containing an element that you want to make into a
   pattern (Figure 6–30).

2. Use the Rectangular Marquee tool to select an area of the element for
   tiling (Figure 6–31).

3. Apply the KPT Seamless Welder filter to the selection (Figure 6–32).

4. In Photoshop, use the Edit: Define Pattern menu option to generate
   a pattern from the selection.

Figure 6–31
This is the original area selected from the CD image.

Figure 6–32
The KPT Seamless Welder filter has altered the selection to prepare it for tiling.

Figure 6–33
The size of tiled images is unlimited.

5. Create a file that is larger than your tile selection. Select All and use the Fill with Pattern function in Photoshop to create a sheet of the new texture (Figure 6–33).

Textures on Your Textures

The use of filters like KPT Texture Explorer can produce jobs that have a recognizable "KPTness" to them. The algorithms producing these textures can also become too easily recognizable. Try some of these techniques to add uniqueness to your textural accomplishments.

There are several general approaches to making the most of this new harvest of variety. The first involves a change in scale. Try placing a small-to medium-sized texture over a larger texture of the same type. The result is a texture that is much richer than any that can be developed with a single-sized pattern.

Filters We Will Use

- *Adobe Photoshop*: Offset, Twirl, Wave
- *Kai's Power Tools 2.0*: Texture Explorer, Seamless Welder

A second approach to maximizing textural variety is to produce new textures by using the alpha channel modes of applying textures over one another. You can even enhance textures from CD-ROM sets using these techniques.

1. Start with a texture (any texture) and experiment with applying KPT Texture Explorer or Gallery Effects Texturizer. Use one of the seamless tiles we have produced earlier in this chapter.

2. Open a new image file. For example purposes, I used a 900 × 900 pixel RGB file.

3. Fill the image using the KPT Texture Explorer preset Eerie: Golden Alien Baby. I set the apply size to 512 × 512 pixels (Figure 6–34).

4. To enrich the texture, apply KPT Gradient Designer using the preset Minerals: Rustoleumesque in the Reverse Blend apply mode. The example illustration (Figure 6–35) uses an apply size of 128 × 128 pixels.

NOTE: You will need to apply differently scaled textures in a KPT Gradient Designer apply mode other than Normal. The Normal apply mode covers your first texture completely, which is not your goal.

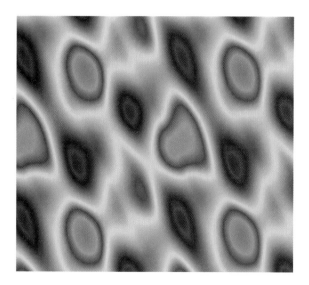

Figure 6–34
A large undulating texture was chosen as a base.

Figure 6–35
The texture was applied a second time to add more interest.

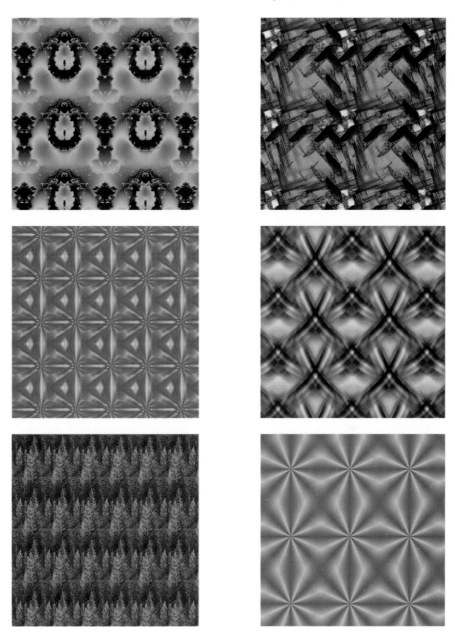

Figure 6–36
These images represent just a small sample of what you can accomplish with seamless textures.

The variety of potential seamless textures is almost endless, as evidenced by the examples in Figure 6–36. You can use samples of small sections of images or creative snippets from other filter effects. I encourage you to plant the seedlings for your own harvest.

7

Lighting, Halos, Fluorescent Effects

From track lighting to lightning to halos of angels, we are all aware of the emotional, powerful effects of light. The creation of glows and lighting has been one of the most difficult feats to achieve using digital media. The highest-quality 3D rendering effects require the most complicated of mathematical algorithms: *ray tracing*. This process takes into account all light sources and how they affect each surface.

With filter technology, you can easily create lighting effects of all kinds. New tools developed within the last year make these effects much easier for beginning to intermediate users of digital graphics programs to obtain. You can now generate illuminated cloud forms and electric eel effects without advanced drawing classes or programming skills.

In this chapter, we will examine ways to add a special glow to your images. Basic techniques for adding visual sparkle and more complex advanced imaging styles will be yours to command.

A Glow to Go

When you need to accentuate an image with a glowing effect, filters can perform the job flawlessly. Here are some ways to blast a friendly (or not so friendly) glow over anything.

Glowing Faces from This Planet

With so many filters to use, it is easy to produce powerful visual effects. It is difficult, however, to control these effects so that they work in your favor. When the goal is to put a glow on a face, be careful not to step over the line of propriety, or you'll have an alien on your screen.

Masking is the key to successful filtering on delicate areas such as faces. The sensitive areas are the eyes, nostrils, lips, and hairline. We will examine appropriate masking techniques as well as several filters that can generate acceptable glowing effects.

Filters We Will Use

- *Gallery Effects, Classic Art, Series 2*: Diffuse Glow, Glowing Edges

The original image used for this example (and also for the cover of the book) was a frame-grabbed image from a camcorder (Figure 7–1).

To produce the glowing face on the cover, we generated a mask (Figure 7–2) to protect the eyes and the lips from the effects of the Gallery Effects Diffuse Glow filter. The mask features a slight feathering to maintain an unobtrusive transition between the glowing areas and the masked areas.

After perfecting the mask, we applied the Gallery Effects Diffuse Glow filter using these settings: Graininess 4, Glow Amount 3, and Clear Amount 10. The filter tends to remove too much color from the flesh, so we used an airbrush to restore a slight blush to the cheeks (Figure 7–3).

The Gallery Effects Glowing Edges filter supplied the glow on the leopard hat. Since the effect of the filter was so intense, we used the Edit: Composite Controls menu option in Photoshop to blend the filtered hat with the original hat at a setting of 50 percent (Figure 7–4).

Figure 7–1
A rough image directly from a video source

Figure 7–2
A Quick-Mask was generated in Photoshop.

TIP: KPT 2.0 has Find Edges filters that are also useful for glowing effects, especially when you composite the filtered effects with the original image. You can also use the Photoshop Find Edges filter for this purpose.

TIP: To create the effect of an emanating glow, configure KPT Gradient Designer to generate a circular burst of color that is lightest in the center, fading outward to a darker tone.

To simulate a glow off the right shoulder of the woman, I used KPT Gradient Designer and set the lighter tone to rest just over the shoulder (Figure 7–5).

The use of KPT Texture Explorer set to the Difference apply mode allows the sheen of the gradient to remain visible. While the background was still selected, I used a large airbrush to paint along the hat with yellow to accentuate the figure and achieve an aura-like glowing edge (Figure 7–6).

Neon on a Budget

The rope trick described in the 3D chapter touched on the use of the Gradients on Paths filter from Kai's Power Tools 2.0. Neon glowing effects are built right into this filter, and you can change the component colors easily. Here is a quick technique to generate neon lettering without fuss.

Filters We Will Use

- *Kai's Power Tools 2.0*: Gradients on Paths

1. Open a new RGB file with the background of your choice and save the file.

Figure 7–3
The GE Diffuse Glow made the image seem more ethereal.

Figure 7–4
The Gallery Effects Glowing Edges filter makes the spots leap off the leopard hat.

Figure 7–5
KPT Gradient Designer was used for background coloring.

Figure 7–6
After applying a few
more effects, the image
is complete.

2. Make a new channel and set Color to Indicate Selected Areas. Select the channel only.

3. To hand-write something using a continuous stroke, use the Airbrush tool set to 15 percent opacity, with black as the foreground color (Figure 7–7).

Figure 7–7   Airbrushed freehand lettering in a new channel

Figure 7–8   KPT Gradients on Paths was used on the soft selection to produce a neon effect.

4. Load the newly-created channel as a selection and apply KPT Gradients on Paths (Figure 7–8).

TIP: **Gradients on Paths produces neon looks most effectively when the edges of the gradient are translucent and the center is almost opaque.**

Flexible Fractals

Fractals have left the realm of the pen-protector math nerd crowd forever with the advent of Kai's Power Tools 2.0 Fractal Explorer. In the not-so-distant past, an in-depth understanding of mathematics was required to get anything out of a fractal program other than a few canned effects. Other downsides included an 8-bit color (256 colors) limitation, extremely long rendering times, and lack of preview capability. Exploring the "wonderful world of Fractals" was a daunting task.

In Chapter 5, I mentioned the use of fractals to enhance backgrounds for presentations. Backgrounds are just one of a bevy of interesting applications, not the least of which is the creation of beautiful abstract art. The popularity of fractal-based images is sure to grow further as this technology becomes increasingly acceptable to artists. This section is certainly not intended as a comprehensive handbook on the use of fractals. The intent is to start you thinking about them creatively.

Here are some techniques for expanding the use of fractals without number-crunching knowledge.

Filters We Will Use

- *Kai's Power Tools 2.0*: Fractal Explorer

Using an Image for Colored Fractals

To generate amazingly complex fractal shaping using the colors you want, try the following technique. To illustrate it, I chose one of my experimental pieces produced with KPT Gradient Designer and Texture Explorer (Figure 7–9) and processed it using KPT Fractal Explorer. Fractal Explorer lets you wrap an image (not just a gradient) around a fractal, an option that gives you a vastly larger visual space to explore. You can follow along using any color images.

I opened a new file and used the "wrap image instead of gradient" function in the Options menu of the KPT Fractal Explorer dialog box. I chose a blue gradient to constitute the inside of the fractal, making it easy to select the center of the fractal for further processing. I then applied the fractal (Figure 7–10).

I then stripped a woman's face into the blue gradient area. I composited the colors and patterns of a section of the fractal with the face, using Photoshop's Edit: Composite Controls menu option with the Color apply mode selected. I then used the Smudge tool to blend the face with the fractal. A headdress became complete with nary a spiral fractal in sight (Figure 7–11).

Large Form Fractals

The ability to zoom into fractal space quadrillions of times opens up many possibilities. The potential exists to create large, soft shapes that can be flipped and composited with one another, resulting in images that belie their fractal origins.

The example illustration (Figure 7–12) demonstrates an experiment with this zooming capability. The soft forms were derived from one application of a zoomed fractal. The fractal was flipped vertically and composited with itself using the Lighten Only apply mode in Photoshop's Composite Controls dialog box. I then applied Photoshop's Diffusion filter and the Gallery Effects, Series 1 Emboss filter, using light settings (Figure 7–12).

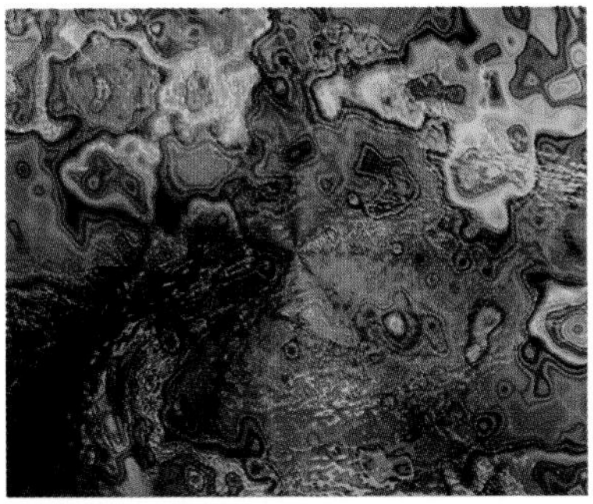

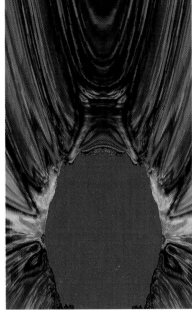

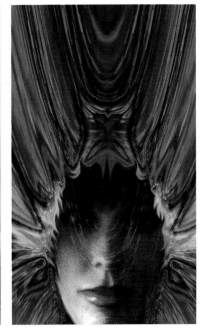

Figure 7–9
This experimental image, composed using numerous filters, served as a color source for a fractal.

Figure 7–10
KPT Fractal Explorer was used to make this stylized fractal.

Figure 7–11
A woman's face was stripped in to complete the image.

Electric Wizardry and Lightning

The occasional lightning rod or electric spark can come in handy in an illustration job. By spark, I mean real bolts of energy and strange sparks, not just the tame, standard starburst on the corner of a clean crystal glass.

We will examine two different approaches to producing "electric" effects. The first uses KPT Fractal Explorer, while the second uses a KPT Texture Explorer preset.

Find a Bolt

There are no exact spots in the Universe of Fractals where I can tell you to go to find a lightning bolt. I can point you in the right direction, however, and let you know that such discoveries are possible. Here is how to process a bolt of energy out of your discoveries.

Figure 7–12
Fractals can take on any
appearance you desire.

Figure 7–13
A diagonal fractal ready for pasting
into an alpha channel for
electrical effects

Figure 7–14
A fractal that can be stretched and
squeezed into a lightning bolt

Filters We Will Use

- *Kai's Power Tools 2.0*: Fractal Explorer

Here are the tips to assure your success. See Figures 7–13 and 7–14 for
visual examples.

TIP: In the KPT Fractal Explorer dialog box, go to the Color Outside
gradient control and select the Half Off gradient in the Transparency
category. This option yields a black-and-white fractal and assists you in
locating electric bolt-like areas. It also provides an automatic black
streak to use in a new channel when you utilize the bolt.

TIP: Once you find a fractal with a usable shape, you can squeeze it into
a narrower shape and use other filters, such as the Photoshop ZigZag or
Wave filters, to accentuate its spikiness.

Instant Lightning

Kai's Power Tools 2.0 Texture Explorer contains a preset in the Rips and
Tears and Shreds Category: Crackling Electricity. Although this preset can
produce instant electrical shapes, you usually need to perform some additional processing on them. The bright blue and red colors of the preset may
be inappropriate in many cases, but the shaping is good. You can extract
portions of the texture and place them into a new channel that you can use
as a mask for electrical effects (Figure 7–15).

Post-Lighting and Backlighting Effects

The ability to add professional lighting effects to your images *after* the photo shoot can be an important advantage economically. Some of the most costly aspects of doing ad work (or any photoimaging) involve the elaborate lighting scenarios and setups required to achieve the proper mood. Plug-in filters can provide endless ways to add light and color in the privacy of your own editing suite, and you don't have to recall the model or lose valuable setup time.

The technique involves channel operations, a scary proposition for some Photoshop users. Applying color in the Color Only apply mode (yes, that is a channel operation) is simple with KPT Gradient Designer. The previews make precise applications of color tints possible. You will hardly realize you are a channel master when the work is this easy.

Filters We Will Use
- *Kai's Power Tools 2.0*: Gradient Designer

Shaft of Light on a Landscape

1. I selected an image from the Vintage CD-ROM Sampler (Figure 7–16) because of its neutral-colored sky. You can follow along using any landscape image you have.

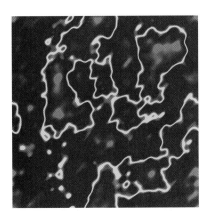

Figure 7–15
A KPT Texture Explorer preset with areas that can be extracted for electrical effects.

Figure 7–16
This base image originated from a Vintage CD (Seattle Support Group).

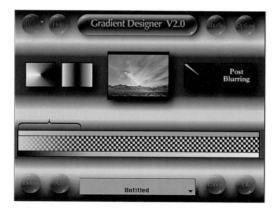

Figure 7–17
The preview window
shows how the gradient
will be applied using the
Procedural Blend
apply mode.

2. In KPT Gradient Designer, I set up a radial sweep blend that transitions from yellow to transparent. I used the Procedural Blend apply mode (Figure 7–17).

3. To move the center of origin of the gradient, I pressed and held the mouse button in the preview window and then dragged this center point to the cloud, which I had chosen as the origin of the shaft of light.

4. I applied KPT Gradient Designer to create the illusion of a shaft of light out of the clouds and a blush of light over the foreground (Figure 7–18).

**Sunset on
a Landscape**

1. I started with the same base image as in the previous section (Figure 7–16), but with a different time of day in mind.

Figure 7–18
The newly lit landscape
with an entirely new
weather pattern

Figure 7–19
KPT Gradient Designer
was set to apply the color
transparently over
the image.

2. In KPT Gradient Designer, I configured a radial blend that transitions from yellow to pink and then becomes darker. Once again, I chose and applied the Procedural Blend apply mode (Figures 7–19 and 7–20).

3. The Sunset effect required additional color modulation in the foreground. To this end, I prepared a second blend of purple color, using a transparent linear blend on the upper two-thirds of the image area. I applied this gradient in the Procedural Blend apply mode (Figure 7–21).

Figure 7–20
The first pass of the blend produced a perfect sunset sky effect.

Figure 7–21
A second pass of the filter added drama to the mountains and ground, completing the sunset color correction.

Liquid Aura

When you require an intense aura effect, you can use filters to create mysterious, almost palpable aura-like glows covering and surrounding objects. In this section, we will examine filters that can create these effects automatically and explore methods for producing them.

Beyond Liquid Shrink-Wrap

The Aldus Gallery Effects, Classic Art, Volume 3 Plastic Wrap filter makes it easy to place a liquid glow over an image. The thought of a plastic coating over an image may cause you to flash back to the movie *The Graduate* and recoil in horror, but be aware that this effect can be amazing over a properly prepared image. The Gallery Effects Plastic Wrap filter can produce a subtle glow effect that has little to do with plastic shrink-wrap.

Try this out with the Gallery Effects Plastic Wrap filter included on the Toolkit disc.

Filters We Will Use

- *Aldus Gallery Effects, Classic Art, Volume 3*: Plastic Wrap

1. Open a copy of Toolkit Tiger. Select All and choose Select: Float. You will perform all the following steps on this floating copy of the image.

2. Apply the Gallery Effects Plastic Wrap filter using these settings: Highlight Strength 10, Detail 15, and Smoothness 15 (Figure 7–22). The resulting image shows a glow effect already.

3. Let's take the effect a bit further. Choose Edit: Composite Controls and set Opacity to 55 percent, selecting the Luminosity apply mode. Apply these settings to the floating image and then select None to defloat it (Figure 7–23).

Homemade Liquid Light

Before Gallery Effects, Classic Art, Volume 3 came out in all its glory, I developed a way to obtain a similar look, using the Gallery Effects, Classic Art, Volume 1 Chrome filter and some manipulations. The effect is distinctive and offers some flexibility. The success and variations of this technique depend upon how you handle transparency compositing and the delicate colorization of the top glow layer. Don't worry—it's easy to do.

Filters We Will Use

- *Gallery Effects, Classic Art, Volume 3*: Chrome
- *Adobe Photoshop*: Gaussian Blur

1. Open a copy of Toolkit Tiger. Select All and then choose Select: Float. You will perform all the remaining steps on this floating copy of the image.

Figure 7–22
A high smoothness setting using the
Gallery Effects Plastic Wrap filter
helps to emulate a glowing effect.

Figure 7–23
By compositing the filtered image
with the original using the
Luminosity apply mode, a subtle
aura effect results.

2. Apply the Gallery Effects Chrome filter, using the settings Detail 1 and Smoothness 10 (Figure 7–24).

3. Fill the chromed floating selection with golden yellow using Photoshop's Edit: Fill menu option, selecting the Color Only apply mode.

4. Apply the Photoshop Gaussian Blur filter at a setting of 2 pixels to soften the edges of the golden chrome.

5. Choose the Edit: Composite Controls menu option in Photoshop, using settings of 66 percent opacity and a Screen apply mode. Apply these settings and then select None to defloat the image (Figure 7–25).

Rays of Light

You can apply precision light rays and complex colored light to produce more sophisticated images. The draftsmanship involved in producing dozens of precise, evenly spaced radiating lines used to be daunting. Now, however, Kai's Power Tools 2.0 lets you repeat the lines in a gradient up to 10 times.

Filters We Will Use

- *Kai's Power Tools 2.0*: Gradient Designer

1. Using KPT Gradient Designer, produce a pleasant background on which to place your glowing rays.

2. Open KPT Gradient Designer. Make the Gradient Bar totally transparent by selecting None as a color while pressing and holding the

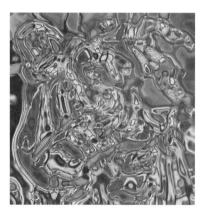

Figure 7–24
A full-intensity application of the
GE Chrome filter practically
obliterates the form of the
tiger image.

Figure 7–25
When composited with the original,
the colorized and blurred chrome
floating image produces a glow that
follows the form of the tiger.

mouse button on each end of the gradient bar consecutively. You
should see a Gradient Bar that is totally covered with a checkerboard
pattern, indicating total transparency as in Figure 7–26.

3. Pull the bracket located above the Gradient Bar so that the two ends
of the bracket are very close together on the left side of the Gradient
Bar. While pressing and holding the mouse button between the two
brackets, pick a golden color. As in Figure 7–27, you should see a
clear Gradient Bar with a small golden section on the far left side.

4. Press Command-C to copy the little bracket area, and then move the
Moveable Bracket over to paste the little gold bar next to the first
one. Be careful not to change the size of the Moveable Bracket when
you move it.

5. Paste the bar into the Moveable Bracket. You should now have two
gold sections (Figure 7–28).

5 Pull the left side of the Moveable Bracket all the way to the left so
that the Moveable Bracket covers both gold sections. Copy it by
pressing Command-C.

6. Move the Moveable Bracket to the right of the first two gold sections
and paste the copied gold sections into the Moveable Bracket. You
should now have four gold sections (Figure 7–29).

7. Repeat Step 5 so that you are copying all four sections.

8. Move the bracket and paste until you have filled the bracket bar
(Figure 7–30).

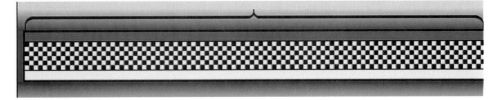

Figure 7–26   The Gradient Bar in KPT Gradient Designer with no color

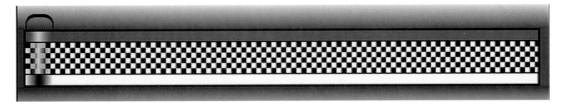

Figure 7–27   A narrow moveable bracket allows you to make a narrow band of color.

Figure 7–28   The gold band is copied and pasted next to itself.

Figure 7–29   The first gold bands are copied and pasted next to themselves.

Figure 7–30   The Gradient Bar is filled with bands of gold.

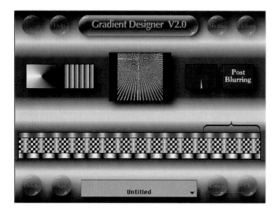

Figure 7–31
KPT Gradient Designer lets the user create blends
that would be a nightmare to paint by hand.

Figure 7–32
Five repeats of the Gradient Bar, radiating out from
the center, form a complex ray pattern.

9. Use Radial Sweep as the gradient shape, and make sure that Post
   Blurring is off. Now you must decide how many strings of light you
   wish to have. To add more, define the repeat number, which is located
   behind the second rectangle from the left in the top of the dialog box
   (I selected six times). Apply the gradient for a result like the one in
   Figures 7–31 and 7–32.

CHAPTER 8

Smoke, Mirrors, and More

The general public thinks of computer-generated graphics as sterile, pristine, unrealistic images. This is due in part to the lack of the atmospheric fogs, mists, and complex reflective surfaces that abound in everyday life. The good news is that you *can* develop these effects in still images without resorting to supercomputing or slavish airbrushing.

Smoke and mirror effects are as easy to produce with filters as the smoke and mirrors that the snake oil salesman of the Old West produced from the back of his wagon. In this chapter, you will learn to master techniques not only for conjuring smoke and mirrors, but also for generating the hottest chrome-object looks of today's high-tech movies.

Clouds and Smoke

The randomly shaped wisp of a cloud or the sinuous billowing of smoke are difficult to produce by airbrush alone. There are places for chaos rather than order in painting—star fields in a science fiction painting, for example, or clouds and smoke. While there are no true random-generator plug-in filters for clouds currently on the market, there *are* filters and techniques that can assist you greatly.

Many people think of fractals as spirals that have spirals that have spirals with more spirals wrapped around them. Kai's Power Tools 2.0 Texture Explorer has helped many persons discover the error of that stereotype. A college student named Chris Cox realized that this family of algorithms held a variety of mathematical formulas that could produce quite different effects. One of these effects he encased in a filter called Fractal Noise.

Fractal Noise fills a selection with a gray cloud-like pattern. The most powerful application for this filter is with feathered selections, compositing Fractal Noise images with portions of your pictures. The next two sections describe potential uses for this filter.

Filters We Will Use

- *Toolkit Disc*: Fractal Noise

In the Misty Moonlight

The object of this technique is to achieve a transparent misty fog using a filter. Feathered selections and transparent compositing are important, and having a filter to generate clouds or mist at any time is handy.

1. I selected a nighttime cityscape image of Seattle from a Vintage CD by the Seattle Support Group. Please use any landscape or image of your own to follow along.

2. Use the Lasso tool to select the areas you wish to fog, and feather the selections heavily.

3. Copy and float the selection on top of itself, and then apply the Fractal Noise filter to the selection (Figure 8–1).

4. Paste the selection onto the image at a 33-percent opacity. My result? A foggier Seattle (Figure 8–2).

Figure 8–1
The Fractal Noise filter applied to a heavily feathered floating selection

Figure 8–2
The filter-generated clouds were pasted onto the image at partial opacity.

Turbulent Times

Many artists find it difficult to reproduce the randomness inherent in quasi-chaotic forms such as clouds and fogs. The Fractal Noise filter can assist you with differences in paint density, while allowing you to determine the precise location of the mist.

To receive such assistance, you need to run the Fractal Noise filter in a new channel and paint with the filtered channel acting as a mask, as in the following example.

1. I selected a nighttime cityscape image from a Vintage CD by the Seattle Support Group. Please use your own image to follow along.

2. Create a new channel and apply the Fractal Noise filter to the channel.

3. Load the channel and pick a color for the mist. Use a large Airbrush with a 15-percent opacity to paint in mist selectively. The mask generated by the Fractal Noise filter will assist you in painting random mist (Figure 8–3).

TIP: Fractal Design Painter and Pixel Paint Professional respond similarly to Photoshop when you define an area of Fractal Noise as a paper texture.

Figure 8–3
Using the Fractal Noise filter to make an alpha-channel mask helps you paint drifts of mist in a naturalistic way.

Chrome Plating

Very few computer-generated images featuring shiny chrome with amazing reflections ever appear in print. Most of the chrome spheres you do see have been created in 3D applications that hold little appeal for many fine and commercial artists. Some artists have tried the Gallery Effects, Classic Art, Series 1 Chrome filter but stopped using it due to frustration, feeling that they could not control the filter's effects. The good news is that those days of helplessness are over.

I have made a concerted effort in this book to avoid complicated channel operations as a means of achieving powerful imaging effects. As the example of chrome effects demonstrates, filters have many more uses than their manuals and promotional materials suggest. Instead of learning a six-step channel trick here, you will learn how a few simple steps can produce chrome bumpers, cars, girls, teddy bears, and more.

You will learn how to add a *Terminator 2* chrome-like look to any object. Once you master this technique, you can then learn how to restore the original colors to the filtered object. As a finishing touch, you can learn how to project surrounding colors and objects onto the chrome object to create an unmistakably realistic chrome effect.

Controlling the Uncontrollable

The Gallery Effects Chrome filter can be frustrating to use, because the documentation does not fully explain how the filter works. The manual does say that you can adjust contrast or the balance of light and dark after applying the filter. Often, however, the filter generates too many reflections in the wrong places, and the result looks more like an indecipherable oil slick than chrome. Once you learn the inner workings of the filter, this problem is easy to fix.

Look at what a default application of the Gallery Effects Chrome filter does to the Toolkit Rooster (Figure 8–4). Notice how the image takes on the surrounding white of the background; edging has been lost and portions of the rooster comb obliterated. Even if I had selected only the rooster, the result would have been the same.

All is not lost, however. If you fill the area surrounding the rooster with black instead of white, select only the rooster, and then apply the filter, the result improves (Figure 8–5). All of the rooster is there and it could be quite useful as a chrome effect. It isn't quite right yet, but now we know that the brightness of the area outside the selection affects what we want to turn to chrome. The brightness and contrast values of the area *inside* the selection are also critical.

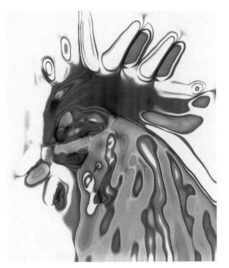

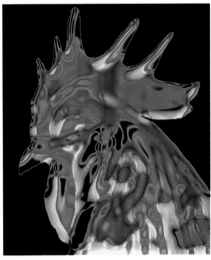

Figure 8–4
The Gallery Effects Chrome filter applied in default mode, resulting in a diffused image

Figure 8–5
The Gallery Effects Chrome filter applied in default mode on a black background, resulting in an improved, but still busy, image

TIP: Because it is critical to control the contrast between the selection area and the surrounding area, you will achieve better results if you copy to the Clipboard the area you want to process and then isolate it in a new file.

Filters We Will Use

- *Aldus Gallery Effects, Classic Art, Series 1*: Chrome

Here is a practical example of how to bring Chrome under control.

1. Open the Toolkit Rooster image included on the Toolkit disc. Select the rooster only and save the selection.

2. Select the entire image and fill with black at an opacity of 50 percent.

3. Load the selection so that only the rooster is selected. Apply the Gallery Effects Chrome filter at the default setting.

4. Use Photoshop Levels to adjust contrast and lightness to an attractive level (Figure 8–6).

5. Invert the selection area so that only the background is selected, and then fill it with black (Figure 8–7).

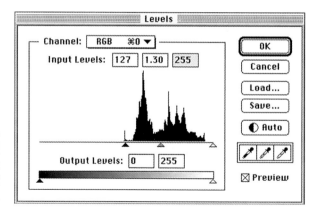

Figure 8–6
Photoshop Levels is used
to adjust the contrast
and lightness of
the rooster.

6. Save the file along with the selection, naming it Chrome Rooster. We will use it again in the "Colorizing Chrome" section of this chapter.

Colorizing Chrome

To inject the original color back into the object you chromed in the preceding section, follow the next group of steps.

1. Open the Chrome Rooster file you just made and load the saved selection. (Only the rooster should be selected.) Copy this selection to the clipboard.
2. Open the Toolkit Rooster image included on the Toolkit disc. Select the rooster only.
3. Paste the Chrome Rooster selection inside the selected rooster so that they line up exactly.
4. Using Photoshop's Edit: Composite Controls menu option, select the Luminosity apply mode. You should have a colorized chrome rooster like the one in Figure 8–8.

COLORIZING OPTIONS

The color of a chromed object does not have to be the same as the original object. Figures 8–9 through 8–12 demonstrate a few options for colorizing chromed areas.

Getting Those Reflections under Control

Although the colorizing techniques for enhancing chrome items are powerful, the 3D programs have the advantage of being able to reflect images over the surface of metal objects. There are ways to emulate this within paint and image-editing programs also. In the following example, you will learn one way to apply realistic reflections to metallic objects and get those reflections under your control. For this technical walk-through, I will use a

Figure 8–7
A much more realistic chrome effect results from changing the background color.

Figure 8–8
By compositing the Chrome Rooster image with the original, a glass Christmas tree-ornament effect is produced.

Figure 8–9
Kai's Power Tools 2.0 Gradient Designer applied to the Chrome Rooster using the preset Metallic: Gold Leonardo 3 in Procedural Blend apply mode

Figure 8–10
The colors in this cropped and resized tulips image (acquired from PhotoDisc Volume 2) will colorize the chromed rooster.

Figure 8–11
After copying and pasting the tulip image onto the rooster image, the Photoshop Composite Controls were set to the Luminosity apply mode to create the illusion of reflected flowers.

Figure 8–12
A glass Christmas ornament effect was created by using an Airbrush in Color Only apply mode to paint over the rooster.

photo from the PhotoDisc Volume 2 CD images. You can follow along with any image containing an area that you want to make reflective.

Filters We Will Use

- *Gallery Effects, Classic Art, Volume 1*: Chrome
- *Adobe Photoshop*: Zigzag

1. Carefully select the portion of the image that you want to chromatize. Copy the selection and place it in a new file (Figure 8–13).

2. After saving a selection, follow the procedure described in the "Controlling the Uncontrollable" section of this chapter.

3. Paste the chromed area inside the selection of the original file (Figure 8–14).

4. I selected the child and pasted a copy into a new file. You can select any area that you want to reflect into your chromed area.

5. I copied a photo of a tree and pasted it into the new file for the purpose of reflecting some trees onto the horse.

6. Apply the Photoshop Zigzag filter to distort the images you want mirrored into the chrome, making them appear more liquid (Figure 8–15).

Figure 8–13
An image from PhotoDisc Volume 2

Figure 8–14
The carousel horse's head stripped in after receiving
a chrome treatment

7. Paste the distorted reflections inside the chromed selection, using Color Only apply mode.

8. Finally, use a burn tool to deepen the color in selected areas of the final chromed image (Figure 8–16).

Vaporizing Any Object

When you want to destroy an image that has a pristine edge, you can do it in style with a bevy of filters designed to maim and shatter. You can slice, dice, diffuse, and scatter. You may even be able to make hundreds of julienne fries in seconds! (Just kidding.) You can atomize and explode pixels with a storm of destruction. You can also use the filters with some practical finesse.

In this section, we will examine a few of the many ways to disturb clusters of pixels with sophistication. Keep in mind that subtle selection techniques and channel selections are essential if you want to achieve something other than the straight "blast 'em all" filter defaults.

Incremental Destruction

Blur and diffusion filters used to be the primary tools for dissolving an image. Excessive blurring causes a greasy glass look, and the diffusion filters wind and wind pixels around an approximately four-pixel grid. When more diffusion is needed, more is available with third-party filters.

Figure 8–15
Selections prepared for use as reflections after an application of the Photoshop Zigzag filter

Figure 8–16
The completed chrome horse head with reflections

Because there are so many different diffusion options now, I have prepared a chart (Figure 8–17) to help sort out some of the styles and intensities of filtering destruction available to you. All are applied at the default setting.

These filter effects become much more interesting when you use them for actual imaging applications.

Into the Water, into the Sky

The following exercise describes how to control the transition of a solid into fluid and air using diffusion filters. The desired effect is one in which the pillar appears to dissolve into the water below; the pillar itself should disintegrate at the top and be encapsulated within a transparent bubble. Diffusion filters can assist greatly in achieving these effects.

Figure 8–17
Relative intensities of filtering destruction. Left to right:
(1) Photoshop Diffuse,
(2) KPT 2.0 PixelBreeze,
(3) KPT 2.0 Diffuse More,
(4) KPT 2.0 PixelStorm,
(5) KPT 2.0 PixelBreeze (applied on 50 percent gray)

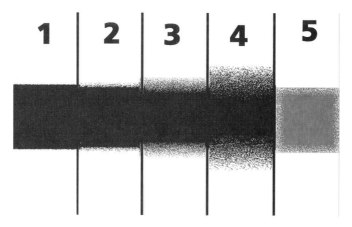

Filters We Will Use

* *Kai's Power Tools 2.0*: PixelStorm, Scatter Horizontal

1. I prepared an image (Figure 8–18) using techniques discussed elsewhere in this book. The ancient pillar is from Chapter 3, and the technique of laying on multiple transparencies of gradients and textures appears throughout this volume. I also used the mist-simulation techniques from this chapter, as well as tips from Chapter 10 on making frames. Try this with an image of your own making.

2. I selected a bottom portion of the pillar and some of the water on either side. Feather your own selection heavily, copy it to the Clipboard, and paste it onto itself.

3. Apply KPT PixelStorm once and then KPT Scatter Horizontal three times.

4. Scale the selection to a greater width and then paste it back into the image.

5. Using the Elliptical Marquee tool, I selected the top portion of the pillar and some of the sky on both sides, feathering the selection heavily.

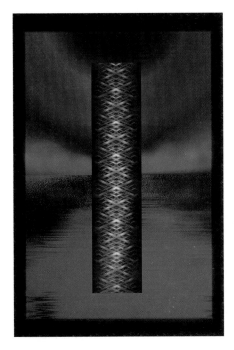

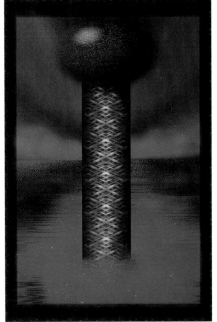

Figure 8–18
A pillar is pasted into an image, causing a need for integration.

Figure 8–19
Diffusion filters accomplish subtle integration effects.

6. Apply the KPT PixelBreeze filter, pressing the 9 key on the numeric keypad to achieve a strong application.

7. Apply KPT Glass Lens Bright to the feathered selection.

8. Finally, deselect all selected areas and use the Burn tool to produce a soft shadow (Figure 8–19).

Grained and Faceted Imaging

This chapter is built like an open-face sandwich. It has an enormous amount of meat piled on top of a fancy croissant. The fancy croissant refers to the eye-bending faceting techniques at the end of the chapter. The "meat"—the main portion of the chapter—is all about grain. Film grain, mezzotints, old printing techniques, and production-worthy information can come in handy on real-world jobs, day after day.

NOTE: This chapter contains exercises that use images not included on the Toolkit disc. I decided to give you more filters, presets, and goodies on disk instead of a complete set of work images. If you wish to follow along with some of the exercises, find a suitable image and experiment with various resolutions and adaptive settings. The concepts behind the techniques—not exact emulation of the exercises—is the important thing.

Grain with a Purpose

Photographers have a love-hate relationship with film grain. Film grain is the subtle-to-pronounced pebbly visual effect that various films and dark-room techniques produce. Film grain, while usually not evident to the consumer, nevertheless gives a velvety look to some contemporary photography. Depending on the size and intensity of the graininess in an image, you can simulate everything from a pointillist painting to a mezzotint effect. This section examines the wide variety of visual alternatives using grain-like looks.

It's Noisy in Here

There are a number of ways to make pixels zing around in an image like popcorn on a hot night. The issue is not whether you can do it, but rather, what kind of noise effect you want. What is the goal? I have prepared a chart (Figure 9–1) that demonstrates just a few types of noise.

This chart is not comprehensive; it merely shows how some of the filters operate. Once you understand that, you can harness noise and pixelating filters more effectively.

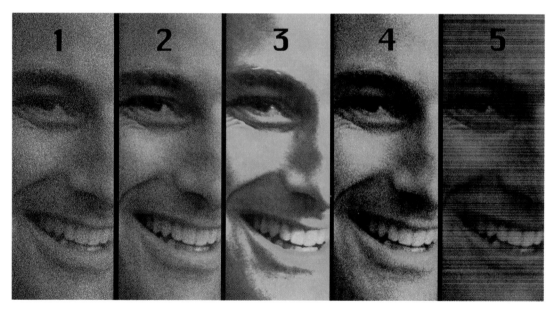

Figure 9–1   Figure grain chart
(1) The Photoshop Add Noise filter adds noise in the RGB channels, producing a uniform confetti-like graininess. The graininess is configurable in intensity, and you can place it into individual channels in the Luminosity Only mode, eliminating the color casts of the noise.
(2) The KPT Hue Protected Noise filter adds noise while staying within very close hue tolerances. Color casts are not added to the figure and the grain is uniform.
(3) The Gallery Effects, Volume 1 Film Grain filter lets you place grain in the darker areas, simplifying and almost posterizing the highlights.
(4) The Gallery Effects, Volume 2 Grain filter expands the options for adding grain, including greater hue protection. There is still color shift, however.
(5) Directional graininess is possible with the Gallery Effects, Volume 2 Grain filter. There is a noticeable graying of the image, which may be positive or negative, depending on the intended use.

Figure 9–2
A variety of colored
noise settings applied to
the tiger image

Colored noise is also possible. Filters such as the Fotomatic Color Noise filter feature color-configurable settings, which can be quite effective for some uses (Figure 9–2).

Mezzo Techniques

The term *mezzotint* describes an effect in which continuous-tone images are broken down into dots through the use of mechanical screens. You can generate mezzotint-like effects using filters and a few new twists of my own that will add interest to your projects.

Nineteenth-century stone lithography, a color printing process, uses fine-grained stones as plates. This printing method produced colored pictures before color photography became printable by today's methods. Stone lithography, with its sandstone-like colored dots, produced the beauty that makes California antique orange-crate-label art so collectible. Filters can emulate these techniques and expand upon them with lovely results.

Andromeda has been a force in writing custom filters for companies and special vertical-market needs. Sometimes the research from these projects evolves into a commercial product. The Andromeda Series 3 Mezzo filter is the result of some of this development. While the standard defaults can produce very good results, Figures 9–3 through 9–7 demonstrate some custom applications on our friend, the tiger.

Colorized Mezzo

I am one of many persons partial to the look of colored antique prints. The colors and graininess of 19th-century broadsides and posters are compelling. Computer graphics need not be left out of this aesthetic. We will examine several ways to achieve timely and lost-in-time colored looks.

Figure 9–3
The color tiger was changed to grayscale mode and then resampled up to 600 dpi in Photoshop. The background was replaced with a slight gradient blend around the head of the tiger. The tiger's contrast was enhanced using filter settings similar to Unsharp masking, and then a 120-worm-per-inch mezzotint screen was chosen to convert the grayscale to bitmap. The contrast adjustment (more or less mezzotint screen) and threshold adjustments (more or less black) fine-tuned the look and feel of the image.

Figure 9–4
The color tiger was changed to grayscale mode and then resampled up to 600 dpi in Photoshop. The photo was contrast-enhanced using functions similar to sharpening, after which an 85-worm-per-inch mezzotint screen was blended using a 40-line round dot. screen. The blend creates a knitted screen with a tweedy look. The blended screen was then used to convert the grayscale to bitmap.

Figure 9–5
The color tiger was changed to grayscale mode and then resampled up to 600 dpi in Photoshop. The photo was contrast-enhanced using built-in functions similar to Unsharp masking, after which a 110-worm-per-inch mezzotint screen was blended using a straight 30-line screen at 45 degrees. The blend creates a fiber-like screen. The blended screen was then used to convert the grayscale image to a bitmap.

CIRCUS TIGER

Although filters are the focus of this book, you sometimes have to do some "manual" work, too. By combining several mezzo techniques and a little hand-coloring, you can produce some effects that will have you smelling cotton candy(. . . and elephants?).

Filters We Will Use
- *Andromeda Series 3*: Mezzo
- *Ring of Fire*: Color Noise

1. Copy and paste several variations of Andromeda Mezzo filter tigers together, using Darken Only compositing to produce a richer and more complex mezzo effect.

Figure 9–6
The color tiger was changed to grayscale mode and then resampled up to 600 dpi in Photoshop. The image was created using a custom screen (a blending of a 35-line screen mezzotint and 45-line screen circular dot). The coarse line screen creates a grainier texture (in this case, white corn kernels) that is still a true black-and-white bitmap.

Figure 9–7
The color tiger was changed to grayscale mode and then resampled up to 600 dpi in Photoshop. The image was created using a custom screen (a blending of a 55-line screen mezzotint and a 15-line screen circular dot at 45 degrees). The coarse line screen creates a grainy texture consisting of clover-like clusters.

2. Paint in the color tints using the Airbrush tool at a low-opacity setting, set to Darken Only.
3. Apply the Ring of Fire Color Noise filter several times, using very low Coverage settings. Apply a red noise and a yellow noise to emulate color printing anomalies similar to some circus posters (Figure 9–8).

REVENGE OF THE CIRCUS TIGER

This section uses another set of filters and a different effect to reproduce the sandy look of old stone-lithograph circus posters. Yes, you have seen the old tiger a lot, but for circus poster emulation, how could I leave him out? This is starting to turn into a three-ring circus.

The key step in this technique is the resizing of the image at the end of the process. I will be using the Second Glance Chromapoint filter, which was designed to dither files for better output on color laser printers and wax thermal printers. In the grand tradition of this book, I will irreverently utilize the

Figure 9–8
With some hand-coloring and a little colored noise to emulate authentic dirty printing blanket nits, a mezzo becomes a circus poster.

Figure 9–9
While the Second Glance Chromapoint filter was made for printing to color printers, it can produce wonderful color-grained effects.

filter for a completely different purpose—to duplicate the dots of an antique stone lithograph almost exactly.

Filters We Will Use

- *Second Glance*: Chromapoint

1. Apply the Second Glance Chromapoint filter (located in the File: Export submenu) to the tiger. The source image file was 2 inches × 2 inches at 300 dpi. The filter automatically adds the word "point" to the filename.

3. Open the newly created filtered file and increase the size by 30 percent. For the book, I resized the file to 3 inches × 3 inches at 300 dpi. Figure 9–9).

TIP: The Chromapoint filter tends to produce lines and clusters of dots that would yield unattractive results when applied to flat color areas. Use full-color images, not posterized ones, to convert to Chromapoint for this technique.

Eagle-Eyed Noise

The grain game can be played a number of ways. A favorite strategy of mine is to generate noise on low-resolution files and then resample them way up in size for a distinctive effect. When coupled with the Photoshop Median filter—which tends to clump noise into larger areas when applied at low settings—this technique results in an attractive impressionistic effect.

The following steps describe how to achieve this particular effect. Do note that the number of applications of the filters and the settings should change according to the type of image and the size of the file.

1. I used an eagle photo from the Color Digital Photos CD by Digital Zone. I selected the low-resolution PICT file version of the image and actually reduced the resolution further to 500 × 400 pixels (Figure 9–10). Use an image of your own to try this exercise.

2. Apply the KPT Universal Hue Protected Noise filter five times at its full strength setting (Figure 9–11).

3. Apply the Photoshop Median filter at a setting of 1 pixel for the result in Figure 9–12. The noise turns completely to mush if you apply the Median filter at anything but a low setting.

4. At this point, double the size and resolution of the image to produce the desired effect.

Figure 9–10
A low-resolution eagle
ready for processing

Figure 9–11
KPT Universal Hue
Protected Noise was applied
heavily to the eagle.

Figure 9–12
The Photoshop Median
filter formed the noise
into clumps.

Figure 9–13
The enlarged image was given a finishing touch with a final application of KPT Universal Hue Protected Noise.

5. As the crowning glory for obtaining a quality image, apply the KPT Hue Protected Noise filter one more time. This filter sharpens the image and prevents visual softness (Figure 9–13).

Colored Scintillating Sands

I dedicate this section to Neil Sedaka and his famous tune, "Breaking up is Hard to Do." It's not really that hard if you want to break up an image into multicolored drifts of color.

Take advantage of the fact that there are now many filters available that break up an image into grainy variations. Success at this technique requires making copies of the original image. Don't panic about processing times and storage space; you can work in grayscale mode as I did and colorize each file just before you copy and paste it into the final image. Consider this as a "trash the work files as you go" technique.

The technique works with any image. Please don't go out racing around for a picture of an old building to try this one.

Filters We Will Use

- *Adobe Photoshop*: Crystallize, Find Edges
- *Chris Cox*: Skeleton
- *Kai's Power Tools*: PixelBreeze

1. I selected a Color Bytes CD-ROM image and made a copy (Figure 9–17). Make a copy of the image you wish to use.

2. Convert the copy to grayscale mode.

3. Apply the Photoshop Find Edges filter to the grayscale image and make two more copies of it.

   NOTE: Remember that the original color image is still unaltered; only 3 grayscale copies are being processed. The original is needed again at the end of this process.

4. Apply the Chris Cox Skeleton filter to one of the grayscale images. Set the Skeleton filter to a Threshold value of 188 to drop out some of the gray and obtain a cleaner line (Figure 9–14).

5. Apply the Photoshop Crystallize filter to another of the grayscale images, creating a watercolored area for later use (Figure 9–15).

6. Apply the KPT PixelBreeze filter to the third and last grayscale image. This filter creates the shimmer needed in step 7 (Figure 9–15).

7. Convert each of the three grayscale files to RGB and colorize them. I colored the pixels of the Skeleton filtered image with purple, the Crystallize filtered image with pink, and the PixelBreeze filtered image with yellow (Figure 9–16).

8. Paste these files one at a time onto the original color image. Use the Composite Controls dialog box in Photoshop to eliminate the white background, pulling the right side of the floating item slider bar toward the left (Figure 9–17).

Figure 9–14
The original photograph from Color Bytes

Figure 9–15
The building was processed with (left to right) the Chris Cox Skeleton filter, the Photoshop Crystallize filter, and the KPT PixelBreeze filter.

Figure 9–16
Colorizing the three filtered grayscale images (left to right): purple for the Skeleton-filtered image, pink for the Crystallize-filtered image, and yellow for the PixelBreeze-filtered image.

Figure 9–17
The final result of layering the three colorized treatments on top of the building photograph

Kaleidoscopic Madness: Faceted Imaging

Hand-painting the same object over and over is one of the most time-consuming things an artist can do. Tedium and a low tolerance for mistakes are his or her lot.

The computer, however, is not constrained by such limitations. It has the power not only to replicate, but also to mutate those replications into some really twisted, beautifully strange formations. Using the filters described in this section, you can produce art that any bee would love.

HSC has developed two filters that multiply a selection by itself. Since making the most of distortion filters requires that you understand what they do to an image, I have prepared a special grid (Figure 9–18) to illustrate the effects of these new filters.

The first filter is called Vortex Tiling. It duplicates an image thousands of times, wrapping all the duplicates into a vortex that converges toward a central point as shown in Figure 9–19.

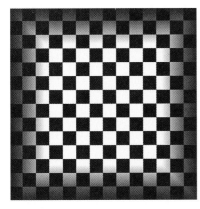

Figure 9–18
A special pillow grid helps illustrate what type of distortion a filter is producing.

Figure 9–19
KPT Vortex Tiling applied using default settings

Figure 9–20
KPT Video Feedback applied using default settings

The second filter, called Video Feedback, produces a series of repetitions that twist and repeat as if you were gazing into a deep well of repeating twisted tiles (Figure 9–20).

You can see that the Vortex Tiling filter is hellbent to produce symmetrical wrapping. That can be a definite plus or a horrible constraint. There's a bit of the rebel left in me, so I immediately look for a way to bust through that symmetry. Following are a couple of experiments in those directions. As you know by now, I encourage you to take the experiments further.

1. Using KPT Gradient Designer, prepare a blended tile that radiates from yellow on the bottom to pinkish on the top. Apply a second radiating blend off-center over the first (Figure 9–21).

2. Since the primary focus of the image was off-center, applying the Vortex Tiling filter started to form zigzags into the lines, making things more interesting (Figure 9–22).

Cloud Eagle

You will want to experiment with the many possibilities offered by this technique. I offer one of my studies.

1. I prepared an eagle image using a background filled with Xaos Terrazzo Filter seamless tile. Yes, the gridded appearance of the green (Figure 9–23) is deliberate.

2. The KPT Vortex Tiling filter normally causes the grid of the background to form a rosette pattern. I adjusted the image size so that the eagle would wrap around the outside of the image to form a cloud-wing effect (Figure 9–24).

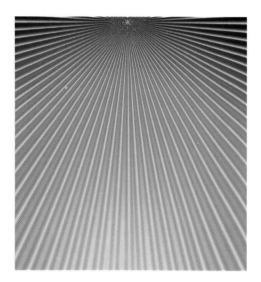

Figure 9–21
An asymmetrical blend with off-center rays

Figure 9–22
The KPT Vortex Tiling filter affects the offset blend differently.

Figure 9–23
The Digital Zone "Eagle on a Post" image was surrounded by the Xaos Terrazzo filter tiles.

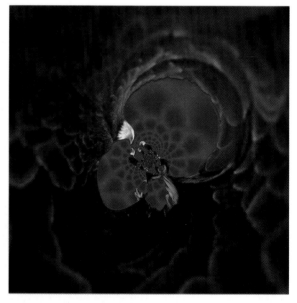

Figure 9–24
The KPT Vortex Tiling filter was applied to generate the "surround the image" effect.

Tapestry Tango with cMulti

Illustrator and designer Ruth Kedar, owner of Ruth Kedar Designs in Palo Alto, California, is well known for her mastery of the Andromeda filters. Many of us have played with the Andromeda cMulti filter on occasion. It comes with Photoshop as a sample filter and can be put to some very powerful use, as evidenced in the image that Ms. Kedar prepared for us.

Ruth Kedar produced the image in Figure 9–25 as an experimental piece for a poster project. What struck me about the technique was its utter simplicity—an elegant idea sheathed inside several simple, yet significant, steps.

Filters She Used

- *Andromeda Series 1*: cMulti

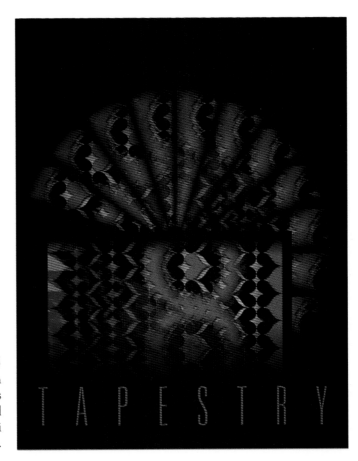

Figure 9–25
The final image by Ruth Kedar, "Tapestry," shows the fabric rectangle and Andromeda cMulti radiating pillows of color.

1. The main reclining rectangular section was drawn in Adobe Illustrator. The repeating pattern was broken up using the Andromeda cMulti filter to produce the two rings in the fabric pattern. Because the cMulti filter was applied so densely and tightly, the filtered areas appear to be solid decorative rings.

2. The fabric pattern rectangle was placed on a large black background and cMulti was applied.

3. The Spoke Transition checkbox was activated and the transition set to its highest setting. It was especially important to place the fabric rectangle on a black background. The result of this attention to detail is a very convincing radial lozenge effect.

4. The original tapestry pillow with a black border was pasted back onto the filtered fan of colors (Figure 9–25).

CHAPTER 10

Oils, Pastels, and Other Digital Deceptions

Many people viewing computer-generated images are surprised when they recognize styles that mimic oils and watercolor. These traditional media have a classic and timeless appearance and have always been extremely popular among artists and art lovers. Now, thanks to filters, they can be generated with push-button ease. However, don't be content just to push buttons. For this chapter, we will explore *advanced* uses for these filters and discover new ways to obtain unusual (and sometimes surprising) effects.

The first filter sets by Aldus (Gallery Effects, Classic Art 1) could turn a photograph into an oil painting, watercolor, or pencil sketch with the click of a button. When these painterly filters were marketed to the graphics community, the advertiser's battle cry was "You don't have to be an artist!" These push-button painting filters put new fear into illustrators' and photographers' minds. The gleam of new money glistened in the eyes of copyright lawyers as mountains of scanners were plugged into desktop computers and virtually every image in print was rescanned and processed through these filters.

After a few years of this push-button painting, most of us have become more sophisticated and can spot canned art filter effects as easily as some sports fans recognize baseball team uniforms. However, painterly filters are not outmoded. Used in combination with one another and applied at various opacities, they can produce subtle results. No filter will make a person an artist, but with some intelligent finesse, they can be as effective as any traditional artist's palette and brush.

On the Way to a Painting

Simply pushing a button to produce a painting effect from a photo can be unnerving for some artists. For them, and for others who would like to develop their own painting styles, let's look at some basic techniques that you can apply on the way to a painting.

Filters We Will Use

- *Adobe Photoshop*: Median, Ripple, Unsharp Mask

1. Make a copy of the Toolkit Tiger image on the Toolkit disc.
2. To strip out unnecessary detail, apply the Photoshop Median filter at a setting of 7 pixels.
3. Apply the Photoshop Ripple filter with the Amount set to 90 and the Ripple size set to Medium.
4. Apply the Photoshop Unsharp Mask filter at 400 percent, using a Radius of 3 Pixels and a Threshold of 3 Levels (Figure 10–1).

NOTE: This is a 72 dpi image. You would have to adjust the settings differently for print-quality 300 dpi images.

The basics of painting at within your grasp. There are many variations to this type of filtering. While you can accomplish much with the native Photoshop filters, I like adding a few third-party filters to the mix.

Variations

Save the file that you just finished as Painted Tiger and try some of the following variations generated with other filters.

Filters We Will Use

- *Adobe Photoshop*: Crystallize, Diffuse, Minimum, Maximum
- *Aldus Gallery Effects, Classic Art, Series 1*: Emboss

VARIATION 1

Using the Painted Tiger image, apply Gallery Effects Emboss at a Relief setting of 8 with a Light Position of Top Left. As shown in Figure 10–2, this filter accentuates the soft-colored shapes in the image and creates the illusion of thick impasto brush strokes.

Figure 10–1
The completed Painted Tiger

Figure 10–2
A thick oil-paint effect

VARIATION 2

For a soft, fluffy paint effect, apply the Photoshop Maximum filter to the Painted Tiger file at a setting of 3 (Figure 10–3).

VARIATION 3

For a daubed paint effect, apply the Photoshop Crystallize filter to the Painted Tiger image at a setting of 10. Follow up with the Photoshop Diffuse filter at the Normal setting (Figure 10–4).

NOTE: These techniques, while easy to control, are time- and CPU-intensive because multiple applications of filters are necessary.

Figure 10–3
A nice fluffy tiger

Figure 10–4
A cottonball tiger

TIP: You can use some of the foregoing variation techniques to prep a photo for further manipulation in Fractal Design Painter, which features natural media painting tools.

Roulette Wheel of Styles, or, Beyond Canned Filter Effects

Own a compendium of painterly effects that can solve quick design problems in a pinch. Let's play with some of the filters that are made to produce painting effects, and some that weren't thought of that way, and load up on an arsenal of painterly techniques that belie a simple click and wait.

Oily and Crusty

To simulate oil paint with filters, it is important to strip back initial detail. The thicker the paint, the more you want to simplify. Embossing techniques produce the simulated depth of the paint.

To illustrate the varieties of paint looks, this section uses a fine rooster (Figures 10–5 through 10–8) that I extracted and prepared from the Multimedia Library Image, Volume 3. If you are interested in trying some of

Figure 10–5
The rooster head is a 266 dpi image designed to illustrate paint styles.

Figure 10–6
The Gallery Effects, Classic Art, Vol. 1 Fresco filter was applied using a Brush Size of 6 and Brush Detail of 8. Gallery Effects, Classic Art, Vol 1 Craquelure was applied using a Crack Spacing of 15, a Crack Depth of 6, and a Crack Brightness of 9.

Figure 10–7
The Photoshop Crystallize filter was applied using a cell size of 10. Gallery Effects, Classic Art, Vol. 1 Craquelure was applied using a Crack Spacing of 15, Crack Depth of 5, and a Crack Brightness of 9.

Figure 10–8
The Gallery Effects, Classic Art, Vol. 1 Poster Edges filter was applied using an Edge Thickness of 2, Edge Intensity of 0, and Posterization of 3. Gallery Effects, Classic Art, Vol. 1 Emboss was applied using an Upper Left Light Position and a Relief of 7 pixels.

these, open the Toolkit Rooster from the Toolkit disc and resample the image up to 266 dpi.

TIP: These techniques are extremely resolution-dependent. Check a sample of the effect on a small selection before exposing a file to these settings.

TIP: The Gallery Effects, 1 Craquelure filter produces wonderful embosses on irregular tones. The filter forms grid-like patterns if there are white or single-colored areas. For a crusty painting effect, deselect these flat areas or paint in some tones to give the Craquelure filter something to facet.

TIP: The Gallery Effects, 1 Fresco filter can make images extremely dark. Try using the Levels or Curves controls in Photoshop to restore a better balance of tones.

TIP: The Gallery Effects, Classic Art 1, Craquelure filter can change character dramatically, with even a slight change in crack depth. Be sure to use the preview window in the dialogue box to view detail-sensitive areas and very light areas.

TIP: If the black grain of the Gallery Effects, Classic Art, Vol. 1 Poster Edges filter produces too much contrast for the image, use the Magic Wand tool to select all of the black pits in the image and then fill these with a lighter color.

Chalky and Grainy

Filters can also help you simulate rough surfaces with chalk. Aldus makes several filters that do this in one pass (see Figures 10–9 through 10–11). You can extend the range of capabilities of these preconfigured filters by experimenting with scaling and filter combinations. The next section explores techniques for generating alternative paper patterns.

Figure 10–9
The Gallery Effects, Classic Art, Vol. 2 Rough Pastels filter was applied using a Stroke Length of 17 and a Stroke Detail of 11. The Texture Control settings are Type, Sandstone, Scaling 81 percent, Relief 34, and a Top Left Light Position. Gallery Effects, Classic Art, Vol. 1 Craquelure was applied using a Crack Spacing of 56, Crack Depth of 1, and a Crack Brightness of 10.

Figure 10–10
The Gallery Effects, Classic Art, Vol. 2 Colored Pencil filter was applied using a Pencil Width of 2, a Stroke Pressure of 15, and a Paper Brightness of 37. Gallery Effects, Classic Art, Vol. 2 Texturizer was applied using settings of Type, Sandstone, Scaling 100 percent, Relief of 4, and a Top Left Light Position.

Figure 10–11
The final image has been adjusted using the Levels controls in Photoshop and retouched slightly with the Clone tool.

TIP: You can use the Gallery Effects, Classic Art, Vol. 1 Craquelure filter to modify the stringent regularity of the Gallery Effects, Classic Art, Vol. 2 Rough Pastels Filter.

TIP: When you use the Gallery Effects, Classic Art, Vol. 2 Colored Pencil filter in Photoshop, the current background color becomes the paper color. Pick a paper color that enhances the image and is attractive at the bright setting in the filter dialog box. If the current background color is a bright one and you use a low brightness setting, the Colored Pencil filter grays and dirties the paper color.

TIP: The Gallery Effects, Classic Art, Vol. 2 Colored Pencil filter tends to wash out the color in the original image. Use the Levels controls in Photoshop to restore saturated color and improve the visual punch.

TIP: Regardless of settings, the Gallery Effects, Classic Art, Vol. 2 Colored Pencil filter can strip out the color of the original image in inappropriate places. To cover those bare spots in Photoshop, use the Clone tool set to Clone Aligned. Dodge and Burn tools can also help increase highlights and shadows for an attractive final result.

Painting over Paper Textures

The next step in your acquisition of digital painting magic is to understand and use paper textures within programs that do not provide them automatically. The trick is to create your own paper textures that serve as masks for manual painting or for other filters.

If you use Fractal Design Painter or Pixel Paint Professional, you are already familiar with the way paper textures affect the application of paint. Paper textures in these programs reside in a new layer or channel and behave like masks.

Once you understand the principles behind using paper textures, your results with filter effects will be richer and many new avenues of imaging will open up to you.

In Chapter 5, I demonstrated the seamless tiling technique and its many variations. Classic uses for paper textures include using seamless tiles for masking.

The Toolkit disc contains a seamless tile with the filename Toolkit Tile to get you started with the following exercise.

1. Open the Toolkit Tile file and select All.

2. With the entire file selected, use the Edit: Define Pattern menu option in Photoshop. The tile is now in the memory, ready to fill any selection.

3. Open the Toolkit Rooster file located on the Toolkit disc and make a new channel (in Photoshop, click on the triangle in the upper right corner of the Channels dialog box and select New Channel).

CAUTION: Be careful not to copy the pattern into any other part of the image but the new channel.

4. Select All in the new channel and choose the Edit: Fill menu option to fill the entire file with the pattern. All of the edges should match.

5. Switch to regular viewing mode and load the channel that you filled with pattern in step 4, and hide the edges of the selection.

6. Save a copy of this file that includes the new channel so that you can experiment.

Try some of the combinations illustrated in Figures 10–12 through 10–16 and start working on your own combinations.

Figure 10–12
The Photoshop Burn tool was used with the channel loaded. Gallery Effects, Classic Art, Vol. 1 Emboss filter was applied to accentuate the edges. The contrast and lightness were then adjusted using the Photoshop Levels controls.

Figure 10–13
The Kai's Power Tools 2.0 PixelStorm filter was applied with the channel loaded.

Figure 10–14
The Kai's Power Tools 2.0 Sharpen Intensity filter was applied twice with the 9 key on the numeric keypad pressed both times. This key applies the filter at maximum strength. The Photoshop Levels controls were used to adjust the contrast and lighten the image.

Figure 10–15
The Xaos Paint Alchemy filter was applied using the preset Molecules Full. The Gallery Effects, Classic Art, Vol. 1 Emboss filter was applied to accentuate the edges.

NOTE: All the techniques shown in Figures 10–12 through 10–14 are resolution-dependent. To do print-quality work, you should adjust the settings upward in the dialog boxes of the respective filters to compensate for the higher pixel density.

NOTE: The KPT PixelStorm filter produces a significantly different effect when you apply it through a textured selection.

NOTE: The Xaos Paint Alchemy filter with the Molecules Full preset contrasts well with the chiseled edges of the texture loaded in the channel.

Directional and Organic Paint

Certain filters respond to specific characteristics of an image. The Gallery Effects, Classic Art, Vol. 1 Craquelure filter, for example, changes the spacing between cracks based on changes in the intensity of lightness and

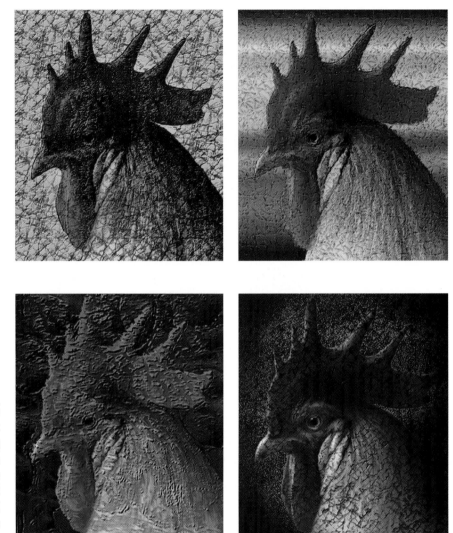

Figure 10–16
These images represent several variations using techniques explored in this chapter. All of these images were produced using a channel containing one or more seamless textures.

darkness in an image. Xaos Paint Alchemy filter takes this style of image feedback even further.

The number of options in Xaos Paint Alchemy are daunting to some, but within this extensive painting engine are controls that allow brushes to respond directly to an image to produce a wide variety of effects. Once you grasp the concepts, you can control painting tools that follow your slightest whim with amazing results.

In this section, you will examine painting techniques that eliminate the mechanical slickness of computer graphics from your images. You will first experiment with the preset styles found in Paint Alchemy and then examine the underlying principles behind getting customizing brush strokes to go in a desired direction. You will also examine ways to modify the style presets included with Xaos Paint Alchemy. Finally, you will see examples of filter combinations that disguise the identities of any particular filter being used.

Painting in the Right Direction

The ability to control the direction of paint strokes sets Paint Alchemy apart from its plug-in competitors. Paint Alchemy comes with a preset called "Threads." This preset paints using a needle-like stroke that follows the brightness of the image. Strokes run horizontally over perfect midtones, curve upward when passing over darker color values, and curve downward when passing over lighter ones (Figure 10–17).

The woman's face featured in Figures 10–18 through 10–22 has been extracted from an image on the Volume 2 CD by PhotoDisc. This face contains a variety of tones, making it an excellent subject for experimentation.

TIP: When configuring Xaos Paint Alchemy to follow an angle by hue, saturation, or brightness, use a brush that fades to black on one end. Such a brush allows the strokes to blend over one another, yielding a more refined result. Any sharp changes in brush angle are softened with a faded brush.

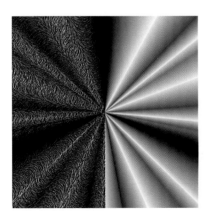

Figure 10–17
Any shape, regardless of complexity, can be followed by the brushstrokes.

Figure 10–18
This face is the sample image used to illustrate Xaos Paint Alchemy directional paint techniques.

Figure 10–19
The Xaos Paint Alchemy filter applied using the Threads preset. For a cleaner outcome, the Standard Line brush was replaced with the Standard Line-Fade brush.

CAUTION: Regardless of Paint Alchemy settings, there is always the potential of unappealing results around eyes and teeth when you apply this filter to faces. Consider either partially masking the eyes and teeth or using a cloning tool to brush them back to a pleasant appearance.

TIP: If a highlight or color shift in an image gives you an undesirable result when using directional brushes, correct the image before applying the filter.

TIP: Xaos Paint Alchemy does not work with grayscale images. To simulate scratchboard, convert a color image to grayscale after you apply the filter, or set the brush color to white instead of defining brush colors from the image. When you use the Color from Image setting, the brush strokes will have shading when you convert the image to grayscale mode.

Once you become familiar with directional brushes, using different styles of brushes will expand your filtering-trick bag exponentially.

Figure 10–20
In this example, the brush angle was set to change according to hue instead of brightness.

Figure 10–21
In this example, the brush angle was set to change according to saturation levels in the image. This setting causes the stroke angle to follow the contours of the woman's face more closely than any others.

Figure 10–22
The Xaos Paint Alchemy filter was applied using the Threads preset. The brush angle was set to follow the saturation values in the image, with a sepia tone defined as the background color. A custom brush named Toolkit Smooth Fade (included on the Toolkit disc) was used. The Clone tool with the From Saved option restored sensitive areas obliterated by the filter.

Modified Paint Alchemy

As with all filters—especially the paint filters with preset styles—output from preset-processed images can start looking alike. When you begin using additional filters to modify an already powerful filter, however, more options open up. I like to think of Paint Alchemy as an extension to the textures that you can form out of a little noise. With a base painting or photo, there is a quantum leap in possibilities. Paint Alchemy's powerful brush engine gets the pixels going in the right directions, and you can take them the rest of the way.

Basic Xaos Modifiers

I have prepared a number of variations to illustrate just a few Paint Alchemy options. You can follow right along with the first six examples (Figures 10–23 through 10–28); I used the default settings and presets for as many of the filters as possible to simplify your experimentation. The second set of six images (Figure 10–29) is designed to show the tip of the iceberg of possible effects using these filter combinations.

NOTE: The 12 filtered images that appear in Figures 10–23 through 10–29 began with the Toolkit Rooster included in the Toolkit disc. I

Figure 10–23
The Xaos Paint Alchemy filter was applied using the Ripple Detail preset. To accentuate the edges, the Gallery Effects, Classic Art, Vol. 1 Emboss filter was applied using default settings.

Figure 10–24
The Xaos Paint Alchemy filter was applied using the Molecules Medium preset. To accentuate the edges, The Gallery Effects, Classic Art, Vol. 1 Craquelure filter was applied with default settings.

Figure 10–25
The Xaos Paint Alchemy filter was applied using the Vortex Layered preset. The Photoshop Median filter was applied with a 1 pixel setting. To accentuate the edges, the Gallery Effects, Classic Art, Vol. 1 Emboss filter was applied using default settings.

resampled the images upward from 404 Kb to 1.57 Mb and did some sharpening to prepare them for print-quality files.

TIP: The Molecules presets in Paint Alchemy produce a strong pattern of bubbles, which assures that the Craquelure filter will not produce a grid pattern. This filter combination can also produce a great paper texture.

TIP: The Photoshop Median filter, when applied at a low setting, can soften and simplify Xaos brush stroke edges. This softening effect protects the image from jagged, torn edges when embossed.

Variations Galore

The next set of six images (Figures 10–46 through 10–51) don't have filter walk-through settings provided with them. They are examples of custom settings and combinations intended to show some of the variety of effects possible— combinations of filters, seamless patterns placed in channels, and special blends added as backgrounds—when you use the Xaos Paint Alchemy filter as a base. The basic techniques to achieve these and more variations are described throughout this book.

 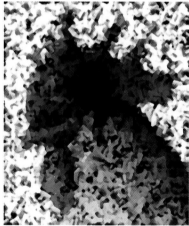 

Figure 10–26
The Xaos Paint Alchemy filter was applied using the Diagonal Brick preset. The Kai's Power Tools 2.0 Gradient Designer filter was applied using the Surprises Galore: Arabian Tiles Pass B preset. To reduce possible banding during printing, the Kai's Power Tools 2.0 Hue Protected Noise filter was applied.

Figure 10–27
The Xaos Paint Alchemy filter was applied using the Cubist preset. The Photoshop Gaussian Blur filter was applied with a 1 pixel setting. The Kai's Power Tools 2.0 Sharpen Intensity filter was applied without modifier keys. To accentuate edges, the Gallery Effects, 1 Dry Brush filter was applied with default settings.

Figure 10–28
The Xaos Paint Alchemy filter was applied using the Colored Pencil preset. The Kai's Power Tools 2.0 Texture Explorer filter was applied using the Nature: Bach Lava Rach preset in the Procedural Blend apply mode.

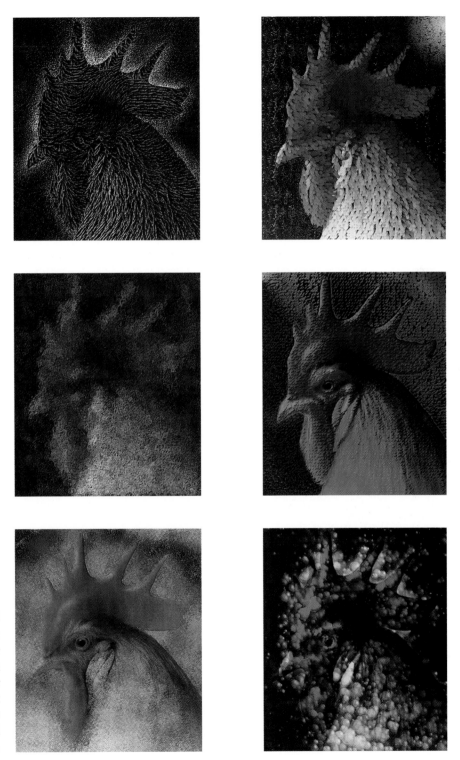

Figure 10–29
The Xaos Paint Alchemy filter works well when combined with other filter techniques. Paint Alchemy was the base filter used on these images.

11

Picture Frames

Using just a few steps, you can surround images with a variety of shaped and textured frames. If you elaborate on these techniques, you can emulate any frame design—from simple frames with drop shadows to bombastic Baroque creations.

The basic technique involves the use of the KPT Gradient Designer filter. The ability to pick None as a color allows you to produce a clear pocket for your image. I have produced frames which are quite delicate and light for projects. I also do some very garish baroque frames that require a number of steps to produce. We will examine the techniques step by step, building up from light and bright frames to massive frames with patterned liners and swelling forms.

NOTE: It can be helpful to study the art of frame-making throughout history, using reference books or visiting nearby art museums.

Filters We Will Use

- *Kai's Power Tools 2.0*: Gradient Designer, Gradients on Paths, Texture Explorer
- *Adobe Photoshop*: Pinch, Twirl, Spherize

Basic Frame from Presets

Kai's Power Tools has a series of presets that can get you started on your trip down frame-lane. KPT Gradient Designer presets constitute a wonderful starting point on the journey toward understanding the underlying principles of frames.

All the frames in this chapter will be made from one file, so let's create a Master Frame File to make things easier.

1. Make a new 450 × 600 pixel grayscale file.
2. Apply KPT Gradient Designer using the preset Framing Effects: Grayt Gray Frayme with the rectangular burst setting (Figures 11–1 and 11–2). Save the file with the name Master Frame File.
3. Keep this image on the screen. You will add a texture to this image in the next section.

NOTE: Select None as a color to view the inside of the frame. Transparent areas appear as a checkerboard in the dialog box.

Wrapping a Texture Around a Frame

You can composite complementary patterns onto the surface of your frames, and multiple applications of textures make for an even richer crop of frames. This section describes some basic techniques for adding textures to frames.

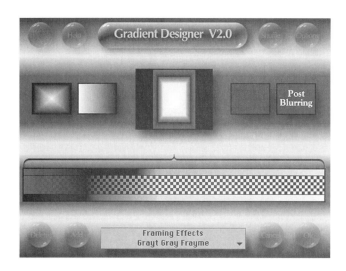

Figure 11–1
The KPT Gradient Designer dialog box shows the transparent right half of the Gradient Bar.

Figure 11–2
KPT Gradient Designer makes the frame, including a translucent blend that affects the image.

1. Using the frame you created in the preceding section, select just the dark gray-to-black area on the outside of the frame.
2. Apply KPT Texture Explorer with the preset Marble: Alpine Blue Marble, using a pixel size of 128 × 128 and the Procedural Blend apply mode. Do not deselect the outside of the frame.

NOTE: A second application of texture yields a much richer result.

3. With the outside of the frame selected, apply the KPT Texture Explorer preset Minerals: Rustoleumesque in the Procedural Blend apply mode with a pixel size of 96 × 96 (Figure 11–3).

NOTE: I have placed enlarged insets of the top corners of the frames to help you see the results.

Ogee Frame Making

Traditional frame patterns were used for centuries in art and as architectural molding. The term *ogee pattern* refers to an undulating frame profile that resembles the letter "O" and the letter "G" placed side by side.

Figure 11–3
The KPT Texture Explorer was applied twice.

To produce molding on a ceiling, a flat board with a metal cutout profile of the design was used. This stiff, metal-lined profile was pulled along a long, straight edge on top of a heavy coat of plaster. The result was a long, straight strip of decorative molding that followed the ceiling shape.

You can reproduce this visual form with some modifications to KPT Gradient Designer. Instead of cutting a profile in metal, you will be creating highlights and valleys, forming frames that appear to have been made the old-fashioned way.

Filters We Will Use

• *Kai's Power Tools 2.0*: Gradient Designer

NOTE: Due to the nonnumerical nature of the **Gradient Designer,** you need to follow the steps visually. If you find yourself confused regarding the use of the customizing tools available with **KPT Gradient Designer,** refer to the documentation within the dialog box for clarification

1. Open a new grayscale file 500 pixels high and 400 pixels wide.
2. Open KPT Gradient Designer and select the preset Translucent: Fabric Folds Transparent. Select the Rectangular Burst Gradient from the top left square in the dialog box (Figure 11–4).
3. To clear the center of color and make a frame, pull the right side of the Gradient Bar Bracket to the center of the Gradient Bar.

   The left half of the gradient bar should now be covered by the Bracket. Select None as a color at each side of the bracketed area. The preview window in the dialog box should show a rather wide frame with a clear center (Figure 11–5).

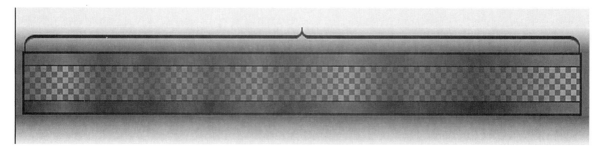

Figure 11–4   The Gradient Bar in the KPT Gradient Designer dialog box for the Transparent: Fabric Folds Transparent preset

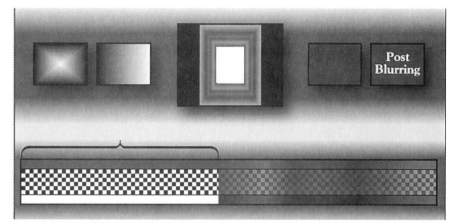

Figure 11–5
The left side of the Gradient Bar is made transparent by selecting the color None. The result is an open area surrounded by a translucent frame.

4. Double-click on the top center of the Gradient Bar Bracket to make it automatically expand to select the entire Gradient Bar. Press and hold the Option key while you drag the gradient within the Gradient Bar to the right. You should see the frame narrow and the clear area inside become larger.

5. When you reach an attractive width for the frame, release the mouse (Figure 11–6) and apply the blend (Figure 11–7).

I have prepared a few custom applications of this technique. To become proficient at custom frame-making with KPT Gradient Designer takes practice and a keen understanding of how the Gradient Bar Bracket works, as well as some finesse with the Eyedropper (Figure 11–8).

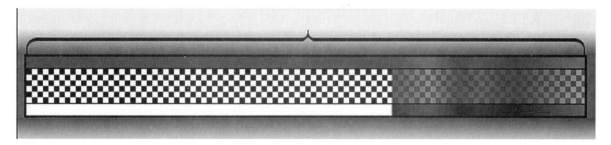

Figure 11–6 Pressing and holding the Option key as the gradient is dragged to the right in the Gradient Bar results in narrowing the frame width.

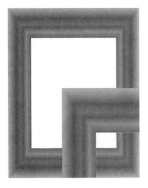

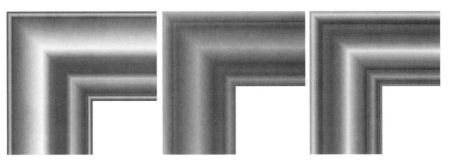

Figure 11–7
The completed Ogee
style frame with a
detail insert

Figure 11–8
A variety of traditional frame shapes like these examples can be produced using
KPT Gradient Designer.

Frame Liners

Another frame style popular in the Victorian era was the lined frame. An extra pattern of embossed leather or woven material was placed on a board, which formed a visual break between strips of gesso and plaster. No taste was spared in combining more designs than you could shake a whalebone corset at.

Victorian excess at its finest can be yours. I am sure that inquiring minds want to know how this is done, so. . .onward to visual complexity.

Filters We Will Use

- *Kai's Power Tools 2.0*: Gradient Designer, Texture Explorer

1. I created a complex blend with KPT Gradient Designer, using the techniques explained in the "Ogee Frame Making" section. I made sure there was a flat section in the blend to serve as a frame liner (Figure 11–9).

   TIP: When performing this technique on a color image, use a contrasting color for the liner area to make selection of the liner area easier.

2. I selected the liner area and applied KPT Texture Explorer, using a custom texture set to a medium size pattern.

3. I then used the Burn tool on the selected liner edges to accentuate the liner form (Figure 11–10).

Figure 11–9
A complex blend produced in KPT Gradient Designer and applied using the Rectangular Burst setting. The wide flat area will be used as a frame liner area.

Figure 11–10
The flat area becomes a frame liner when a KPT Texture Explorer custom texture is applied.

Baroque Bulges and Twists

Now that you can lay in patterns on your frame, a bit of Rococo flourish could top off a frame properly or be used in a tongue-in-cheek send-up.

The Baroque Concept

The trusty native Photoshop distortion filters can help you achieve some bulges and twists in your frame imaging. Let me hammer home the idea of experimentation yet again. The framing techniques described in the following steps are rich territory to explore, with many more implications than a few simple bulges on frames.

Filters We Will Use

- Kai's Power Tools 2.0: Gradient Designer, Texture Explorer
- Adobe Photoshop: Polar Coordinates, Twirl, Shear

1. I made a frame with a simple frame blend and applied some texture using KPT Texture Explorer. The texture is a result of multiple applications of textures flipped over and pasted onto themselves, then composited together in the Darken Only apply mode.

2. I selected All and applied the Photoshop Pinch filter at a setting of 40 (Figure 11–11). Save the file as Master Pinched Frame.

Flipping Frames for Accuracy

Though the concept is simple, any further distortion of the frame can cause symmetry problems. Frame-flipping techniques are extremely difficult to apply in exactly the same fashion on all four corners or sides of a frame. Let's examine mirroring, flipping quarters of frames for flawless symmetry.

1. I selected the top right quarter of the Master Pinched Frame, copied it to the Clipboard, and pasted it into a new file (Figure 11–12).

   TIP: In Photoshop, you can set the Rectangular Marquee to a certain size by calling up its dialog box. Check the size of your frame and set the marquee for half of the pixels in height and width. You will automatically select one-quarter of the frame when you move the selection into a corner of the frame image.

2. I applied the Photoshop Twirl filter with a setting of 81 degrees (Figures 11–13 and 11–14).

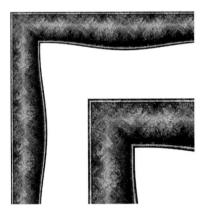

Figure 11–11
A rounded frame produced with KPT Gradient Designer and KPT Texture Explorer has curves produced by a single application of the Photoshop Pinch filter. The insert shows the smooth transition made possible with the Photoshop Pinch filter.

Figure 11–12
To assure that all corners of the manipulated frame are symmetrical, one-quarter of the frame is selected to receive further processing.

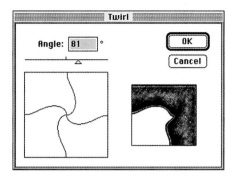

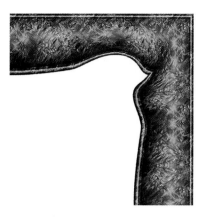

Figure 11–13
The Photoshop Twirl filter is applied at a setting of 81 degrees.

Figure 11–14
The corner of the frame takes on an organic shape after an application of the Twirl filter.

3. By applying the Photoshop Twirl filter with a setting of –100 degrees, the frame corner becomes much more organic (Figures 11–15 and 11–16).

4. A new file four times the size of the quarter frame was created. The quarter frame was pasted into the file and flipped, copied, and pasted until all four corners had a new frame corner and all edges were aligned (Figure 11–17).

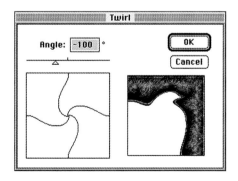

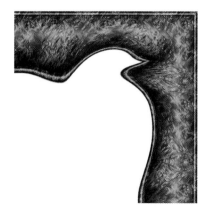

Figure 11–15
The Photoshop Twirl filter applies a twist in the opposite direction if you input a negative number.

Figure 11–16
The application of the Photoshop Twirl filter at a setting of –100 enriches the frame corner.

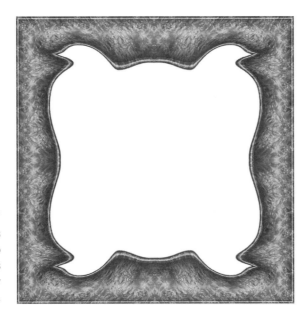

Figure 11–17
The frame corner is flipped and copied to make up all four corners of the new Baroque frame.

Shearly You Jest

There are many ways to alter the outside of the frame also. I used the Photoshop Shear filter on the Master Pinched Frame to reproduce the shape of an old TV screen.

1. I added white canvas area surrounding the Master Pinched Frame.
2. In the Photoshop Shear filter dialog box, I selected points that would bend the top corner of the quarter frame to the left (Figures 11–18 and 11–19).
3. The top right corner of the frame was copied and flipped to create a full frame, using the technique described in the "Flipping Frames for Accuracy" section (Figure 11–20).

NOTE: It is important to extend the canvas beyond the image you are shearing to assure that you have clear space for the distortion.

Ovals and Circular Frames

Your grandparents knew that frames didn't have to be square or rectangular. Circular and oval frames are easy to make using a variety of techniques. Selection and masking options are the key to generating a variety of surfaces, and some easy distortion techniques will round out your frame-making.

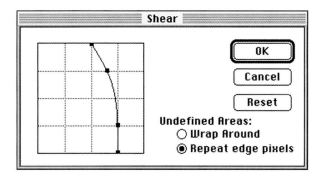

Figure 11–18
The Photoshop Shear filter is used to bend the top of the frame to the left.

Figure 11–19
The result of the Photoshop Shear filter

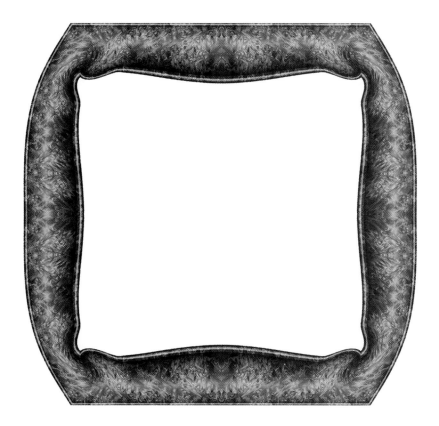

Figure 11–20
The new 50s TV frame

The Photoshop Polar Coordinates filter is the workhorse for generating oval and circular frames. To make these shapes more interesting, I am including some techniques for simulating classic wooden effects and edge fillets.

Filters We Will Use
- *Kai's Power Tools 2.0*: Gradient Designer, Texture Explorer
- *Adobe Photoshop*: Polar Coordinates

Basic Round Frame

1. To begin creating a round frame, open a new square file. Select a narrow area in the center that spans the entire width of the file.
2. Apply a texture using any of the texture filters, a gradient blend, or an image pasted into the rectangular selection (Figure 11–21).
3. Select the entire file and apply the Photoshop Polar Coordinates filter, using the Rectangular to Polar setting (Figure 11–22).

Basic Oval Frame

To create an oval frame, open a new rectangular (not square) file and follow the steps outlined in the "Basic Round Frame" section (Figure 11–23).

Figure 11–21
A rectangle spans the full width of a square file as a preliminary to creating a circular frame.

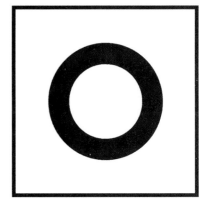

Figure 11–22
The Photoshop Polar Coordinates filter pulls the rectangle into a circle.

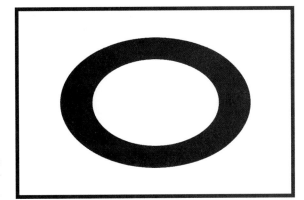

Figure 11–23
When the same steps are
applied to a rectangular
file, the result is an oval.

Woody Frames

There are several distinctive ways to generate wood-like frames. The choice depends on how you want to construct them.

For example, the wood can appear to wrap over the entire area, so that the frame appears to be constructed of a single piece of wood. Or the wood can appear to be bent, *à la* the Vienna School of bentwood furniture.

Bentwood Frame

You can give any texture on the frame the appearance of a single strip of wood bent around the round frame shape. This technique is based on two concepts:

- To achieve a realistic wood slab effect, you must apply an appropriate texture to a square and stretch it into a long slab.
- To bend wood, you must apply the texture before using the Photoshop Polar Coordinates filter for the bending effect.

Here is how to bend some wood without resorting to steam and wood-clamps.

1. Make a small rectangular selection and fill it by applying KPT Texture Explorer using the Wood: Ark Bark preset in Normal apply mode.
2. Use the Scale menu option in Photoshop to stretch the small rectangle into a long slab of wood (Figure 11–24).
3. Create a new square grayscale file as wide as the stretched selection of wood.
4. Paste the stretched selection of wood into the middle of the new file.
5. Select the entire file and apply the Photoshop Polar Coordinates filter using the Rectangular to Polar setting (Figure 11–25).

Figure 11–24
A rectangle was filled with a KPT Texture Explorer wood preset and then stretched to produce a slab of wood.

Figure 11–25
The Photoshop Polar Coordinates filter bent the wood texture into a frame without the use of steam.

NOTE: Because KPT Texture Explorer makes seamless tiles, the edges of the stretched strip in the above example matched when the Photoshop Polar Coordinates filter joined them together. This is not always the case when other textures and effects are added to the stretched or prestretched slab.

Beyond Bentwood

The techniques described in the Bentwood Frame section have far-reaching implications. You can stretch any complex textures into long areas and further process them using additional textures and gradients. Fun can certainly be yours when you let the infinite options start percolating in your imagination.

Figures 11–26 and 11–27 show a few samples of how far you can "stretch" these techniques.

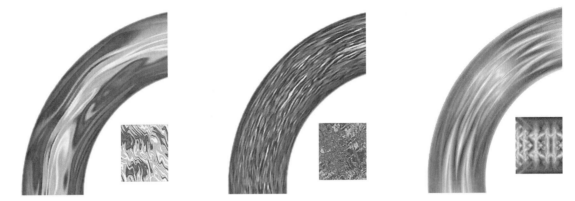

Figure 11–26   Three examples of KPT Texture Explorer and additional textures being stretched into a round frame shape

Figure 11–27   Three examples of merging the Ogee Frame techniques and Bentwood techniques to achieve more dynamic visual options

CHAPTER **12**

Gigantic Files and Seamless Composites

The print and advertising industries are responsible for both the liabilities and opportunities brought about by huge image files. A magazine cover image can consume as much as 25 to 60 Mb of disk space. Poster-sized 8×10 transparencies can occupy 300 megabytes.

Pixel-based programs grind to a digital crawl when they have to grapple with files of this size. Filters do exist, however, that can boost productivity incredibly when you work with huge files destined for the production pipelines of Mac, PC, Scitex, or Quantel systems. With current plug-in technology, there is no reason to access the entire image when you need to change just a portion of a file. This chapter examines filters that lessen the temporal pain of opening and working with such huge files.

After scanning, cropping, and sharpening, the most time-consuming function in the digital imaging business is merging a part of one image with another. This practice, called *compositing*, is the bread-and-butter business of the finest "Top Guns" in the imaging industry. Operators can command large sums to do this type of work due to the difficulty of masking out undesirable portions of each image. This must be accomplished without allowing any visual trace of seams between the combined images.

New filter technology exists to assist average users in the production of sublime and subtle composites. Investment in a filter of this type can pay for itself in one job.

Extracting the Offending Portion

When I talk to a digital artist doing print-quality work, I am always surprised if he or she hasn't heard of Total Integration's FASTedit TIFF or Alaris's Apertura filters. These allow you to retouch huge images without having to manipulate the entire file. This is especially helpful for the photographer who is doing digital retouching. Huge files take a long time to open, and they consume vast quantities of RAM and scratch disk space.

The time factor for opening files may not seem significant to some of you. If you are in multimedia and routinely work with screen-resolution images, or if most of your work involves small files, you may find this information less than useful. What is a small file versus a large file? To a person doing imaging for print media, a small file is anything under 5 to 15 Mb. A medium-sized file is 15 to 50 Mb, and large files run 50 Mb and up.

If you have art directors or editors who request incessant changes to an image, or if you can't seem to make up your own mind as to when an image is done, read on. If you are a production facility and need to do spot corrections on files—lots of files—you *really* need to read on.

CAUTION: The information in this chapter will save you enormous amounts of time and money.

Both FASTedit TIFF and Apertura are accessible from within Photoshop's Acquire: Export submenu. Since I am best acquainted with FASTedit TIFF from Total Integration, I will use that product as an example in this chapter.

No-Stick Gumballs

It is an advantage to extract a single section of an image, retouch it, and then pop it back into place seamlessly. It is a "wild and naked in the sun" advantage to be able to slice out multiple sections of an image and then compare the corrections side by side. The next time you find yourself immersed in a "Gitty-up" deadline, try the following technique.

1. An absolutely huge file of gumballs (Figure 12–1) needed to have some of the balls enhanced (Figure 12–2). For the purpose of illustrating this

Figure 12–1
An image needing some enhancement
to the gum balls

Figure 12–2
The Total Integration FASTedit TIFF
filter allows multiple extractions from a
file for enhancement purposes.

technique, I color-desaturated the source image (from the D'pix Folio 1
CD Pro) in advance.

2. I used the Total Integration FASTedit TIFF filter to segregate four
separate snippets of the big file for enhancement of the gumballs.

3. I then used the KPT Texture Explorer and KPT Glass Lens Bright filters to enhance the gumballs, snippet by snippet (Figure 12–3).

4. I then used the Write or Update TIFF portion of the FASTedit filter
to put the four sections back into place (Figure 12–2).

Figure 12–3   The FASTedit filter pops extracted elements back into the image perfectly.

Amazing Image Merging

One of the most often touted features of Photoshop is the ability to composite two images together. Actually, both Fractal Design Painter and Photoshop include a number of masking and frisket-making options to make this possible. For example, you can use a Magic Wand to select a range of colors. You can paint a red-tinted mask or paint into a single color channel. You can also use the Pen Paths tool in Photoshop to generate hard-edged masks.

What do *Terminator 2, The Demolition Man, Memoirs of the Invisible Man,* and Photoshop have in common? All of the movies—and Adobe Photoshop—have been touched by the intelligent masking tools of Ultimatte. Film fans may fondly recall the special effects in early movies—when Godzilla, for example, found himself in a situation in which the rubber suit and balsa-wood set weren't convincing enough, you could see the fuzzy glow of a bad composite surrounding the ol' green guy. That fuzzy area (sometimes fuzzy *blue* area) was the result of traditional *blue-screen compositing.*

Blue-screen compositing is a method of photographing subject(s) in front of a blue screen for simple isolation and stripping into a separately photographed background scene. When successful, the subject can be placed seamlessly and realistically into the new location.

Blue-screen compositing is the most effective method for isolating fine and translucent elements for naturalistic composites. It allows very fine hairs, and even glass surfaces, fog, and smoke, to be isolated and composited into another photographic or graphic scene without any blur, color casting, or harsh edging. Even shadows cast by the subject on a blue-screen background can be extracted and placed into the new background image.

Ultimatte is already the foremost provider of digital blue-screen imaging technology to the motion picture industry. Now, it has developed PhotoFusion, a plug-in that generates sophisticated blue-screen composites on high-resolution digital files within Photoshop plug-in compatible applications.

The Ultimatte PhotoFusion process completes its work in three steps. It first generates a mask by producing an alpha channel. It then uses this mask to process the foreground. This second step, which is user-configurable, removes any color cast from the blue-screen contamination. The third step uses the mask to composite the foreground image into the background.

You will have a hard time producing masks as clean as the ones that Ultimatte PhotoFusion generates. I tried to do it, using every technique imaginable—and I failed. Ultimatte explains that the PhotoFusion algorithms are proprietary and therefore unique.

Here is an example of just how unique PhotoFusion is. When you use a magic wand tool in Photoshop, the pixel is either selected or not selected. A selected pixel made into a mask is a high-contrast mask—black-and-white, in other words. An Ultimate PhotoFusion mask, on the other hand, is grayscale and can behave much more subtly.

The Ultimatte filter can perform blue-screen-type compositing on images shot on red and green backgrounds as well. The predominant colors of the foreground image should be the factors that determine which color background should be used in the photo shoot.

The filter comes with two interfaces. One interface serves as a cute and friendly training tool, yet it is also a complete and functional filter. The second interface is more Mac-like and menu-driven. For the book, I will be using the training version. I like showing my coffee buddy. . . well, you will see.

I Can See through Your Drinking

This title has nothing to do with a substance abuse problem. It refers to the ability to composite tinted glass into another picture in such a way that the original background does not contaminate the new one. Jeff Foster, of Foster Digital Imaging in Brea, California, prepared a series of images (Figures 12–4 through 12–11) for a real-world tinted-glass test of the Ultimatte PhotoFusion filter.

To prepare for the test, a model (Figure 12–4) was photographed against a specially-painted blue-screen backdrop. Please note that the blue color bleeds through the glass and contaminates other portions of the image through reflections. A background photograph was also taken for compositing with the model in the final ad comp (Figure 12–5).

Figure 12–4
A specially prepared blue background was used in this photo.

Figure 12–5
The coastal scene will form the background for the model in the final composite image.

The challenge of removing the blue cast from the glass, and the complications of extracting an accurate mask, would be daunting under any circumstances. Certainly, no pen-path traced around the bottle could generate a sufficiently professional result. We haven't even mentioned the problems of extracting fine hairs and removing the color contamination from them—that would pose an even greater challenge. PhotoFusion lets you surmount such obstacles as easily as in the following example.

1. The PhotoFusion filter first asks you to select a portion of the image containing the color you want to mask out (Figure 12–6).

2. PhotoFusion shows you the mask and asks you to select an area that is completely white, yet has noise in it. This gives the filter the information it needs to clean up the mask (Figure 12–7).

3. You are asked to select an area of the mask that is completely black. This selection gives the filter the information it needs to adjust the density of the mask (Figure 12–8).

TIP: The Ultimatte PhotoFusion filter is most effective when you complete the processes of building the mask and compositing the foreground and background images totally within the filter.

4. Once you have selected the background, PhotoFusion shows you one last tweaking dialog box. The Flare Controls sliders (Figure 12–9) allow you to determine how much of the color contamination you want to remove and/or keep. An excellent composite (Figures 12–10 and 12–11) is the result.

Figure 12–6
Selecting the blue screen color to generate the mask

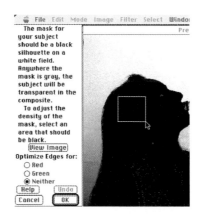

Figure 12–7
Removing noise from the mask

Figure 12–8
Setting the density of the mask

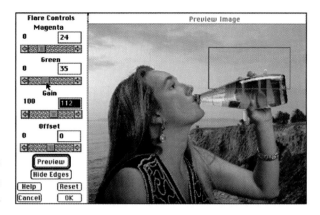

Figure 12–9
Calculating the
flare suppression

Figure 12–10
A close-up of the mask
and composite

Figure 12–11
The final composite is
extremely clean.

Production Tips

Production time is a valuable commodity. Here are some tips designed to give you back some of that time and allow you to smell the roses.

Reducing Banding and Enhancing Noise

KPT Universal Hue Protected Noise is perfect for adding noise to color blends. Why would you want to do this? Long, continuous blends of color can band when printed, because of the limitations of 256 colors per channel in 24-bit color mode. A gradient that is visually appealing on the screen may still band when printed. Adding some noise to the gradient can help soften banding effects and produce a smoother transition. The noise does not have to be very apparent to be effective. Some artists (myself included) feel that a little noise even adds richness to a gradient. Subtle distinctions like these help the eye appreciate the lushness of the pixel medium of digital art.

Ways and Means of Noise Effects

Photoshop's native Add Noise filter generates random colored noise that is influenced by the RGB phosphors of the monitor. The result is rather confetti-like and can be distracting on flesh tones.

You can eliminate the confetti-color effect either by using native Photoshop filters alone or by enlisting the aid of third-party filters. The Photoshop-only technique involves floating a selection, applying the Add Noise filter, and using the Edit: Composite menu option to apply the filtered selection by Luminosity only. This is a rather RAM-intensive means to an end, but it works. The KPT Hue Protected Noise filter, on the other hand, saves you the step of floating the selection, because it changes the pixels within the same hue range, eliminating the confetti discoloration. Gallery Effects includes several applicable options in its Classic Art, Series 2 filters, and the Andromeda Series 1 Design filter lets you generate mezzotint effects for this purpose.

Quick Edits for Filmstrips

If you edit Adobe Premiere filmstrips within Photoshop, you can use FASTedit Filmstrip to open and edit just the frames needing changes. This product revives the old-fashioned technique of strip-editing.

Extracting Images from Gang-Scans

When a single file contains a gang-scan of multiple images, you can extract the image you want into its own separate file using FASTedit TIFF. Think of this process as choosing an image from a contact sheet.

Timesavers for Prepress Scanner Operators

Because of the large previews, scanner operators use FASTedit TIFF to preview their scans for correct subject and data integrity. This can result in impressive timesaving.

Keep Those Names Short

FASTedit TIFF can add between one and five numbers to the end of each original filename. Make sure that the images you want to edit have short enough filenames to permit this addition.

Collage Special Effects

FASTedit filters can help you produce collages and special effects. Give your new art component the same filename as the FASTedit clip extracted from the image. Then, strip in the new collage element, using the File: Export: Write or Update TIFF option. Since the numbers added to the filename indicate the xy coordinate location of the extraction, FASTedit will automatically resize the new collage element into the pixel space of the original extraction.

13

Animation and Video Magic

Photoshop filters not only make excellent tools for enhancing and transforming still images, but they also can serve as powerful special-effects engines for animation and video. This chapter shows you how to use filters on time-based still images or video sequences for incredibly dynamic results.

All the examples that follow are based on the standard computer screen/NTSC video size of 640 × 480 pixels. Keep in mind that if you apply filters to smaller multimedia-sized images, you can quickly overwhelm the image (and if you zoom the image on playback, your finely detailed effects will look like coarse scratchings). After waiting (im)patiently for filters to be applied to larger high-resolution images destined for print media, working with 640 × 480 images might seem like a breeze—until you remember that it takes 30 such images to make up a single second of playback. This could add up to a pretty long night.

Ashes to Ashes, Pixels to Rust

In video and animation, images are often destined not for the printed page or the computer screen, but to be encoded into an analog video signal that is recorded onto metal oxide-coated magnetic tape and played back on an ordinary TV.

TIP: Subtle brushes and fine paper textures don't hold up as well on TV as they do in the high-resolution world of print, particularly if compressed. Crank up the effect and record a test to tape before committing.

The video medium has a much narrower color range than that of either RGB monitors or CMYK print media. If you record an "illegal" color to tape, it will vibrate, bleed, and possibly even create a signal that is technically not legal to broadcast(!). When in doubt, apply your program's "NTSC-safe" filter as your last effect and check the images on an NTSC monitor.

Okay, enough with the propeller-head stuff. Let's get moving.

Random Thoughts

Here's a test to try. Place a still image in your QuickTime program, extend it over one second, apply Gallery Effects, Classic Art, Series 1 Charcoal, and make a movie. Pretty unexciting, eh? Every frame looks the same. Now change the filter to Gallery Effects, Series 1 Chalk & Charcoal and render again. What a difference! This is because some filters, such as Chalk & Charcoal, actually randomize their effect each time they are applied. Every new frame of the movie triggers the filter to apply its effect again, resulting in an animated appearance.

Although few filters actually randomize, don't feel discouraged. Digitized video has inherent noise and motion, so most filters yield exciting effects. However, if all you have to work with is a *still* image, choose your filter carefully.

Filters that do randomize include those in the KPT Scatter and Noise family, as well as the following Gallery Effects, Classic Art selections: Chalk & Charcoal, Craquelure, Film Grain, Mosaic, Ripple, Smudge Stick, and Spatter (Series 1); Grain, Notepaper, and Sprayed Strokes (Series 2); and Reticulation, Sponge, and Torn Edges (Series 3). Since most noise filters randomize, you can also apply one to a still image *before* any other filter to fake the random effect.

TIP: Xaos Paint Alchemy 1.02 now uses the "magic number" 13 as the Randomization value to force a reseed on every frame. If you need to update your version 1.0 filter, you'll find an updater and instructions on the Toolkit disc.

Frenzied Filters

If you find that brush strokes animating at 30 frames per second (fps) is a little hard on the retina (it can often look like noise), then make a movie at a lower frame rate so that new brush strokes are created only every second or third frame.

TIP: If you apply a randomizing filter to a still for a long duration, save time by rendering for just a second or so and then loop the resultant movie. You'll never notice the pattern repeating!

Another useful technique for video captured at 30 fps is to apply the filter, render a movie at 30 fps so that every frame is filtered, and then time-stretch the filtered movie. In the slow-motion result, you will see every discrete frame in the video, and the brushes will appear to randomize less frequently.

Animating Filters the Hard Way

It *is* possible to apply filters to video without a QuickTime program, but you had better have plenty of patience. This "manual" method involves opening each frame in Photoshop and filtering it individually. If you want the filter to animate, you have to change the parameters for each frame before reapplying. If this doesn't sound like a great way to spend your life, CE Software's QuicKeys and/or Equilibrium's Debabelizer can help automate the process. Currently, these are the only products that can animate some of Photoshop's distortion filters.

TIP: You can use the Calculator DA to automate the process of animating filter parameter values. While recording a Sequence in QuicKeys, have the Calculator repeatedly alter the previous value and paste the new sum back into the filter's dialog box. If you experience trouble playing back the Sequence, insert a short Pause after each value change to allow time for the Calculator to come forward.

Striptease

The FilmStrip format was developed by Adobe as a way to transfer MooVs between Premiere and Photoshop. The process is a bit cumbersome, and when a full-frame movie is exported from Premiere as a FilmStrip, it can average around a megabyte per *frame*. Still, if you have enough RAM, you can get some stunning effects (you can also paint directly on video clips and their alpha channels with all the tools offered by Photoshop). The Premiere 3.0 manual has a great required-reading section on the "care and feeding" of FilmStrips.

Here are brief instructions on how to generate instant MTV:

1. Export a clip from Premiere as a FilmStrip and open the file in Photoshop.

2. Run KPT Texture Explorer. Test a small area before applying the filter to the entire file, and be sure to experiment with Procedural, Lighten Only, and other options. Then run the filter, take a coffee break, and save the file.

3. Import the FilmStrip file back into Premiere and generate the movie. Your home movies of Aunt Edna will never be the same.

Animating Filters the Quick(Time) Way

Here, we offer a sampler of easy-but-powerful filter effects that you can execute in your favorite QuickTime editor.

Look Ma, No Selections

In Photoshop, applying a filter to a selected area is a breeze. In QuickTime-based programs, which don't offer "selections" per se, you can achieve the appearance of applying a filter to selected areas by the use of masks and layering or by the use of mattes. The following exercise uses CoSA After Effects to demonstrate how to apply the Gallery Effects, Classic Art, Vol. 1 Chalk & Charcoal filter to just the center of an image (courtesy D'Pix Peeping ROM CD):

1. After you have your clip (Figure 13–1) ready to go as a layer in a composition, duplicate the layer so that you have two copies stacked on top of one another.

2. Apply Gallery Effects, Classic Art, Vol. 1 Chalk & Charcoal to the top layer.

3. Now open the clip's Layer window and make an oval mask to taste (Figure 13–2). You can feather the edge of a mask in After Effects,

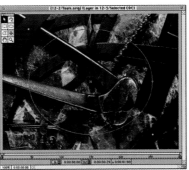

Figure 13–1
The original image

Figure 13–2
An oval mask applied to the top
layer in the Layer window (note
that you don't see the effects of the
filter or the mask in this window,
only in the Comp window)

Figure 13–3
The final composed frame, with
the filtered image on top and a soft
feather added to its mask

just as you can feather a selection in Photoshop. Figure 13–3 shows
the final composited image.

**TIP: In After Effects, the mask and mask feather are calculated before
you apply the filter. If the filter messes up the feather, reverse the
process by applying the filter in one comp, and masking and feathering
in a comp one level higher.**

**NOTE: To achieve the same result in Premiere, place the clip in Track
A and in the S1 track. Create a still image with a white-to-black radial fill
(or go wild with any grayscale texture created with KPT Texture
Explorer) and apply this to the S1 track as an Image Matte in the
Transparency Settings dialog box. The gradation in the radial fill will composite the images with a soft edge.**

Bandit Squirrel

So you got a job processing scandalous video for a tabloid news program—
but you need to hide the identity of the perpetrator by applying a "mosaic
mask" to the face (or other parts of the anatomy) and then tracking these
parts as they move. Here is how to do it (refer to Figure 13–4):

1. Make a copy of the movie and process it with the Photoshop Mosaic
   filter. (Premiere offers a similar filter.)

Figure 13–4   Left to right: The unfiltered clip, the Mosaic'd clip, the result of masking just over the face, and tracking the culprit's moves

2. Layer the filtered clip on top of the unfiltered clip in CoSA After Effects, and use a soft-feathered mask to apply the filtered clip to the area in question.

3. Set a Keyframe for the Mask position, step through the video in the Layer window, and move the mask to keep track of the *major* changes in position (let the program interpolate the in-between frames).

Scatter Brains

When you apply a filter to a clip that has an alpha channel (or has been cropped with the Mask tools in After Effects), you may be surprised to find that most filters don't treat the alpha. Special acknowledgment goes to some of the KPT Scatter filters for offering "4-channel" support. Notice the different effect achieved when KPT PixelBreeze is applied first to just the RGB image (Figure 13–5) and then to the RGB plus Alpha (Figure 13–6).

NOTE: Write to your graphics district congressperson and insist that all Photoshop filters work on the alpha channel as well.

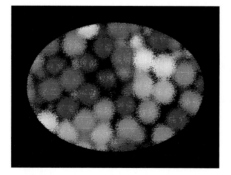

Figure 13–5
KPT PixelBreeze applied in After Effects as a "3-channel" filter. Notice that the edge of the mask remains pretty solid (Photo from D'Pix Folio 1).

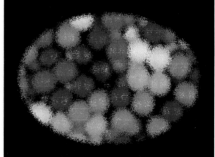

Figure 13–6
Applied as a "4-channel" filter, KPT PixelBreeze scatters the edge of the mask also.

Figure 13–7   Left to right: three stages of an image zooming up, with the fourth image unblurred because it has arrived (Photo © Aris Multimedia Entertainment, Inc. 1991. All Rights Reserved)

Life's a Blur

...at least when it's captured on video or film. If any on-screen object is moving, it will be blurred as the camera keeps its shutter open while recording each frame. When animating otherwise-still objects, you can artificially add this motion blur to them. Try adding a Radial Blur to an object zooming up in Adobe Premiere—it makes the effect much more convincing (Figure 13–7).

1. When zooming up a movie or still, cut it into two sections—one that lasts the duration of the zoom, and the other that continues on before or after the zoom.

2. Apply the Photoshop Radial Blur filter to the section that is zooming. Make sure you set the radio button to Zoom (amounts of 20–30 work nicely).

Party Animal

Let's have some fun creating a "dancing" title (Figure 13–8). The object of this exercise is to create variations on the initial design, sequence these stills back to back, and make a movie. Each PICT should play for just 2 or 3 frames, or to taste.

1. Create an RGB image and fill it with a gradient from KPT Gradient Designer. Add a fourth channel and create your type in the alpha channel as white text on a black background (or hand-paint your text for a rotoscoped look). Save this file as a 32-bit PICT.

2. Now, create some variations on the theme. For example, apply the Gradient again in the RGB channel using a different angle or colors, and in the alpha channel, mess with the title using any of the Photoshop Distort filters.

3. When you have created 6 to 10 variations (enough so that a pattern isn't obvious as they loop), sequence them over a background in your QuickTime program (Figure 13–9).

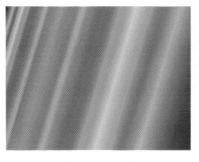

Figure 13–8   Left to right: The color for the type fills the RGB channel; the type is placed in the alpha; and the alpha is used by the QuickTime program to cleanly drop out the background.

Figure 13–9   Four titles sequenced against a KPT Texture Explorer background. (A drop shadow has been added to enhance the contrast.)

> **NOTE:** Preparing text art correctly for compositing is not an intuitive process. The secret is to not only place text in the alpha channel in Photoshop, but also to fill the RGB channel completely with the color for the type. If the RGB channel contains text against a white background, you will see a fringing effect or halo around the type after compositing. Adobe Premiere offers a White Alpha Matte to help alleviate this problem.

Cross-Dressing Color Channels

VideoFusion is a favorite program among those who like really wild special effects. One notable feature is its ability to split an image or movie into component channels—alpha plus RGB or Hue, Saturation, and Brightness—and treat them individually, later swapping the processed channel(s) back into the composite image.

Even more fun ensues when you swap a processed channel for a different one than it came from. The Brightness channel is an especially good target, since this is the one that contains most of the detail in an image—mess with it and you repaint the picture (Figures 13–10 and 13–11). Try this one for yourself:

1. Choose an image that has a strong red, green, or blue component to it (white counts too, since it contains all three). A blue sky with white clouds makes a good example. Extract the blue channel.

2. Apply to this channel a filter that leaves the white area alone but mangles the gray or black areas. Gallery Effects, Classic Art, Vol. 2 Graphic Pen was used here; it is one of the strongest such filters, in addition to which it randomizes every frame.

3. Swap this filtered image back in for the Brightness channel. Note that the sky remains untouched, while the rest of the image is transformed.

TIP: **You can filter any channel that looks interesting. Try extracting the Hue channel, processing it with the Gallery Effects, 3 Cutout filter, and swapping it back in for the Brightness channel. The result is a variation on the posterized look.**

Pan-Demonium

Need to create an energetic, fast-cut background but don't want to make 10 variations in Photoshop? The following exercise uses After Effects to pan around a large still image using the Hold interpolation option. Because the image jumps (instead of moving gradually) into a new position every 3 frames, it appears that multiple frames were prepared (Figure 13–12).

Figure 13–10   The original image; the extracted blue channel (now a grayscale image); and the blue channel after Graphic Pen has been applied

Figure 13–11
The final image when
the filtered Blue channel
is swapped in for the
Brightness channel.
(Photo © 1991 Chris
Kitze, Photographer ©
Aris Multimedia
Entertainment, Inc.
1991. All rights reserved)

1. Use or create an oversized image (a photo with pixel dimensions of 675 × 1017 was used here). Apply the Gallery Effects, Classic Art, Vol. 3 Torn Edges filter, and mix it back in a little with the original if desired.

2. Set the first keyframe using Hold interpolation, and move the image into a new position every third frame.

3. Set keyframes (using Hold interpolation) for the Background color also, so that the color changes with every move.

TIP: CoSA BONUS: Some Gallery Effects filters will turn a process-color image into a two-color image, the colors of which are determined by the foreground and background colors of the host application. CoSA After Effects has the ability to not only set the foreground

  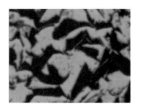 

Figure 13–12   Left to right: the original image; with Gallery Effects, Classic Art, Vol. 3 Torn Edges and Background color applied; image panned to a different position and color-modified; the final composited with the foreground image (Photos from D'Pix Peeping ROM CD)

Figure 13–13
The Effects Floater in After Effects lets you blend a filtered image with the original and animate foreground and background colors of filters from Gallery Effects

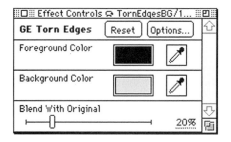

and background colors, but also to animate (cycle) these colors over time using various interpolation methods. Try using it with the Gallery Effects, Classic Art, Vol. 3 Glow filter—animating the foreground and background colors will turn your glow into a light show (Figure 13–13).

TIP: CoSA DOOR PRIZE: All images filtered with third-party Photoshop-compatible filters can be composited with the original image using an intuitive Blend With Original slider in the Effects Floater. You can also animate the mix to control any number of fade-ups and -downs. Well worth the price of admission.

Fire, Matte with Me

When you use a matte to composite one image with another, the matte serves as a window to knock out parts of the foreground image to reveal the background—and gradient images make great mattes. Now, what if the matte itself is moving over time? In the following example, a large grayscale image is rotated using CoSA After Effects, and the output from this animation is used as a "traveling matte" (see Figures 13–14 and 13–15).

1. Create an interesting Radial Sweep grayscale gradient in Photoshop with KPT Gradient Designer, about three times larger in size than the video frame.

2. In After Effects, create a new comp ("KPT Comp"), place the center of the gradation below the Comp window, and set it to rotate clockwise about one revolution every 15 seconds.

3. Make a new comp and drag in KPT Comp, Image B (background), and Image A (foreground), in that order. Turn off the video for KPT Comp.

4. Use the After Effects Set Matte filter to have Image A "Take Matte from Layer: KPT Comp" and to use the luminance (grayscale) values of the layer for the matte.

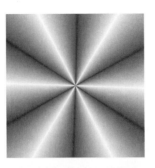

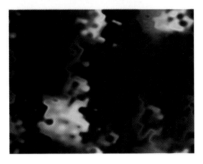
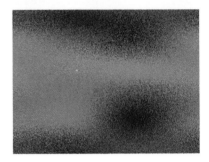

Figure 13–14
Top row, left to right: the radial sweep gradation (1800 × 1800 pixels) created in Photoshop; the gradation when placed in a 640 × 480 comp in After Effects. Bottom row, left to right: Image A (KPT Texture Explorer using the preset Fire: Billowing Smoke); and Image B (KPT Texture Explorer using the preset Fire: Diffracted Inferno).

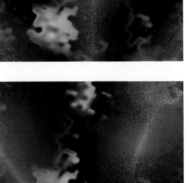
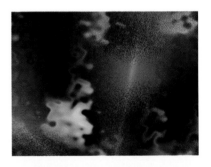
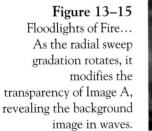

Figure 13–15
Floodlights of Fire... As the radial sweep gradation rotates, it modifies the transparency of Image A, revealing the background image in waves.

QuickTime Techniques

The following techniques are all worthy of step-by-step treatment and humorous example images. Because of space limitations, we ask you to try them out on your own to see how fun they can be.

Check Your Pulse

Cross-dissolve between two versions of a video clip: one processed with a wild filter like KPT PixelBreeze, and one unfiltered. Time these dissolves to match the beats of a music video for a pulsating effect.

Rainy Reflection

Apply the Gallery Effects, Classic Art, Vol. 1 Spatter filter to obtain the effect of rain falling on an image reflected in a pond. This filter randomizes every frame, just like real raindrops.

Organic Edges

When using an edge detection-type filter on two or more overlapped images, apply it to the group rather than individually. Soft, organic edges will appear where the layers overlap.

TIP: QuickTime applications create links to filters. If you move the project to another computer for rendering, make sure the filters are available on the other system. (If necessary, assist the program in finding the path to the filters on the new system.)

TIP: Some filters designed with Photoshop in mind may reopen their dialog boxes every time you move to a different frame (Andromeda Series 1 are so inclined). Convert your movies to PICT sequences and then apply these filters to your frames in Photoshop.

14

Power User Combinations

In previous chapters, we have examined scores of techniques for producing special effects with Photoshop-compatible filters, and now, no doubt, you are beginning to see the power of integrating several different types of these tools. So let's pull out all the stops and take a dip into the world of power user filter combinations. This is the territory of some of today's most exciting digital art.

Think of graphics programs as power tools and filters as a toolbox full of hand tools and specialty gizmos. A unified vision is still necessary to achieve a great image, but with an understanding of all of the tools, any effect is obtainable. The most powerful aspect of filtering is knowing how filter combinations work together.

You have seen how important it is to understand the power of the selection and masking tools in the programs you are using. To make sense out of filter combinations, you need to know how to control the areas and intensities of their application.

This chapter examines several real-world projects produced in professional environments. I have chosen projects that exemplify varied styles and applications to illustrate the versatility of filtering techniques in the fine and commercial arts. This is truly "the good stuff."

All the World's a Stage

Several different cover concepts were under consideration during the development of this book, and one of them is the "Plug-in Stage" image shown in Figure 14–1. Although the comps described in this section did not make the final cut, they nevertheless serve as excellent examples of how to make real-world use of many of the techniques described throughout this book.

The "Ancient Pillars" techniques discussed in Chapter 3 were used to frame the stage. The "Colorizing Chrome" tips from Chapter 7 helped to create the glowing metallic appearance of the plug. To provide dramatic stage lighting, I used the alternative lighting techniques (using KPT Gradient Designer for color casts) from the "Post Lighting and Backlighting Effects" section of Chapter 6. The Sucking Fish filters helped with the plug pattern at the back of the stage. Many other techniques explored in the book make minor appearances on the stage of these comps.

Pillars and Lintels

Using KPT Gradient Designer, I created custom blends to simulate the lintel and pillars. Thanks to careful color picking, even the purple color casts of the shadows could be built into the one-pass application of the blend (Figure 14–2).

To achieve the ancient textural effect on the top lintel, I applied custom textures using KPT Texture Explorer. For the first application of the filter, I used the Difference apply mode, compositing the filter with the original blend (Figure 14–3).

Although the pattern of the first application of texture had the shaping I wanted, the lintel was too busy to allow the title header of the book to stand out. To quiet the lintel visually, I used KPT Gradient Designer to apply another blend in the Difference apply mode (Figure 14–4).

The side pillars received a KPT Texture Explorer custom texture applied in the Procedural Blend apply mode. The Gallery Effects, Classic Art, Volume 1 Emboss filter brought out the detail. I also applied some manual dodging and burning (Figure 14–5).

Stage Rear and Floor

To continue the plug-in theme, I pasted in a series of wall plugs as a pattern on the back of the stage. I produced the holes of the plug and the lines around them by filling or stroking rectangular selections. The Sucking Fish filters helped to bevel the edges. To generate the stylized wood grain, I applied a KPT Texture Explorer custom texture in Procedural Blend apply mode (Figure 14–6).

I produced the floor tiles by capturing the icon of a plug-in filter from the screen and then enhancing it. Using the Edit: Fill menu option in Photoshop, I used the Fill with Pattern option to generate a sheet of floor

Figure 14–1
The final cover comp with a plug-in on center stage—appropriate for a book on plug-in filters.

Figure 14–2
The KPT Gradient Designer filter put to use as a 3D object builder

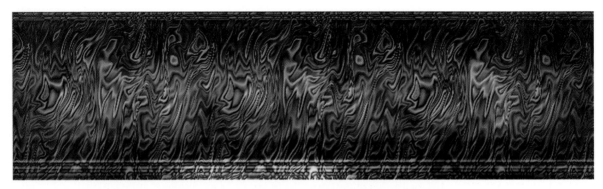

Figure 14–3   KPT Texture Explorer was applied in Difference Apply mode.

Figure 14–4   KPT Gradient Designer was applied in Difference Apply mode.

Figure 14–5
The pillars were texturized and embossed.

Figure 14–6
Small samplings of plugs were created and then texturized.

Figure 14–7
The wall plugs and icon-patterned floor were generated using Photoshop's Edit: Fill menu option with Fill with Pattern selected.

tiles. I then distorted the sheet of floor tiles using the Perspective tool and pasted it into the image. The same method produced the wall of plugs (Figure 14–7).

Stage Lighting

To achieve the effect of light streaming onto the stage from the side, I used KPT Gradient Designer as a translucent colorizing tool (see Chapter 6, "Post-Lighting and Backlighting Effects," for a description of the techniques). After masking out the pillar on the left and the lintel on top, I applied a translucent radial gradient that faded to transparent (Figure 14–8).

A Rosy Glow

In another of the comps, I produced a glowing rose as a replacement for the painted plug (*à la* Magritte). I produced the glow over the rose, using the Gallery Effects, Vol. 1 Chrome filter as described in the "Homemade Liquid Light" section of Chapter 6. I processed the rose in a separate file and then pasted it into the master image (Figures 14–9 and 14–10).

Ovoid Light Rays

Another of the cover comp concepts featured a mysterious, glowing light emanating out from the center. Here, in brief, are the steps that produced it:

1. I selected an oval area and feathered it heavily.
2. Deleting the feathered selection left a soft white rectangle.
3. I used KPT Gradient Designer to create a fine-lined, light-ray gradient, using the technique described in the "Rays of Light" section of Chapter 6.

Figure 14–8
KPT Gradient Designer was used to make a translucent glow loom across the stage.

Figure 14–9
A rose was placed at stage center.

Figure 14–10
A detail of the rose with its liquid aura-like glow

4. I applied the new gradient to a larger feathered selection. The enlargement of the selection allowed the rays to emanate beyond the white glow (Figure 14–11).

Plug-In Plug

In the first round of book-cover dreaming, I came up with the idea of a plug to drive home the concept of plug-ins. Subtle, eh? While the concept may have been overkill, the result exemplifies several important filtering techniques outlined in the book. Here is how I arrived at it:

1. I created the winding electrical cord by drawing the cord shape in black.

2. I selected the cord and filled it with a KPT Gradient Designer blend in Normal apply mode. The custom blend (a Circular ShapeBurst blend) yielded a tubular effect, which I used as a base from which to customize the shadows and highlight areas with the Dodge-and-Burn tools.

3. I created the plug head by cutting out a section of a circular blend produced with KPT Gradient Designer (Figure 14–12).

4. I further enhanced the plug cord using a harlequin pattern manually painted in Fractal Design Painter.

5. Using the techniques described in the "Colorizing Chrome" section of Chapter 7, I produced the color and glow of the plug head with the help of the Gallery Effects, Volume 1 Chrome filter.

6. I manually painted the glow surrounding the plug in Fractal Design Painter (Figure 14–13).

Figure 14–11
An egg-shaped glow produced with the glow effects covered in Chapter 6.

Figure 14–12
The plug and cord with filter-produced and hand-painted blends

Figure 14–13
The techniques shown in Chapter 7 paved the way to produce this type of colored chrome.

7. In the final version of this comp, I used the KPT Page Curl filter to produce a dramatic location for the description of the Toolkit disc (Figure 14–1).

Angel

The Angel image (Figure 14–14) was created for a Japanese magazine, using a complex series of manipulations, transformations of video sources, scans, and natural media painting techniques. Photoshop, Painter X2, and a freeware filter by Chris Cox were the predominant tools for this project.

Torso and Head

Here is a brief description of how I produced the torso and head of the angel:

1. The torso for the Angel began as a frame-grab of a model from a video shoot that I did in my studio using a Hi-8 video camera (Figure 14–15). The image was very rough and the color was not very good.
2. I used the Photoshop De-Interlace filter to help solidify the base image and then applied the Photoshop Median filter (set to 3 pixels) to homogenize the roughness of the frame-grab.
3. I resampled the torso from 72 dpi to 300 dpi (Figure 14–16) and used the Photoshop Unsharp Mask filter to remove some of the softness in the image resulting from the resolution change (Figure 14–17).
4. Since the frame-grabbed image had no face, I used another black-and-white video image of a face that was in the right position. I colorized it by generating a KPT Gradient Designer blend composed of colors from the torso (Figure 14–18).
5. I elongated the face, repainted it manually, and composited it with the base image. KPT Hue Protected Noise helped to blend in the facial changes and eliminate banding in the soft shifts of color (Figure 14–19).
6. I needed a hair reference, so I bought an inexpensive costume wig and digitized it using a flatbed scanner. After pasting the hair into the general target location, I used cloning tools in Fractal Design Painter X2 to make the hair flow more perfectly. I painted portions of the hair one strand at a time using various paintbrushes.

Wings

What angel could fly without wings? My angel sprouted hers this way:

1. I scanned in an actual black-and-white wing that a friend found on an Indian reservation in the American Southwest (Figure 14–20).

Figure 14–14   The completed angel

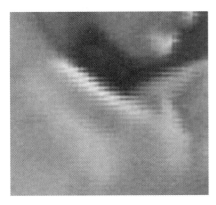

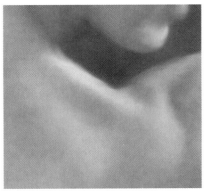

Figure 14–15
The model's back was frame-grabbed from a Hi-8 camcorder source.

Figure 14–16
The video source image was enhanced with filters.

Figure 14–17
The model's back after cleanup and colorization

2. Using the KPT Cyclone filter, I generated an arbitrary color map to change the colors of the wing to those of a peacock.

3. The wings were quite short and wide, so I reshaped them using the Distort submenu filters in Photoshop (Figure 14–21).

4. I then pasted the wings into the base image and blended them into the shoulders using the Clone tool. Dodge-and-Burn tools helped to highlight and darken portions of the wings to make them more dimensional.

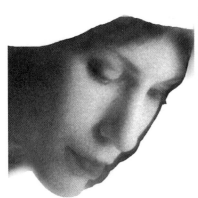

Figure 14–18
A face from another source was used.

Figure 14–19
The back and head were carefully composited together.

Figure 14–20
A bird wing was scanned directly on a flatbed scanner at 300 dpi.

Figure 14–21
The stretched wing was colorized with the KPT Cyclone filter.

Clouds

One basic element—a cloud formation—was still lacking. I created it like this:

1. After compositing the wings, head, and hair, I created and saved an alpha channel mask. The Fractal Noise filter, located on the Toolkit disc in the Chris Cox filter set, generated the background. This filter produces a gossamer cloud-like effect (Figure 14–22).

2. I used Dodge tools to darken the background in some areas and tinted other areas with Color Only applications of the Airbrush tools.

3. I then applied the KPT Grime Layer filter to feathered selections to simulate drifts of stellar material (Figure 14–23).

Finishing Touches

With the selection mask protecting the angel, I used the Airbrush tool and the Dodge tool in Fractal Design Painter to paint the aura of light around her body and wings. Afterward, I applied various colors to give variety to the color of the light around her. Using the Airbrush in Fractal Design Painter X2, I added color tints to the angel's skin tones. Areas of the torso received slight applications of the KPT Hue Protected Noise Minimum filter.

To finalize the stardust effect and the sparkles of energy around the angel's head, I used the Photoshop Airbrush tool with the Dissolve apply option active (Figure 14–24).

Figure 14–22
The Fractal Noise filter was applied to generate the basic background.

Figure 14–23
Dodge-and-Burn tools were applied to simulate clouds. Areas were colorized to add visual interest.

Figure 14–24
The aura was added as a finishing touch.

Alien King

The unusual Alien King image was an experiment in merging filter-generated seamless textures using 3D bump-mapping techniques. It is my personal "Token Science Fiction" image for the book.

The production of the alien is a study in program hopping. I generated the initial blend for the 3D texture with KPT Gradient Designer from within Fractal Design Painter X2. I processed the blend within Painter with further filtering and brought it into StrataStudioPro. I created the filter-produced frame and handled the final output processing in Adobe Photoshop (Figure 14–25).

1. I produced a metallic blend in KPT Gradient Designer within Painter and the Blobs function was applied to this blend (Figure 14–26).

2. I transferred the texture to Photoshop, where I made it seamless with the help of the Photoshop Offset filter.

3. I imported the seamless texture into StrataStudioPro and configured it as a 3D texture with a bump-map (Figure 14–27).

4. Next, I applied the texture to a complex wire-frame model in StrataStudioPro and rendered it.

5. In Photoshop, I opened the rendered version and produced the jewelry using techniques described in the "Golden Jewelry" section of Chapter 3. I produced the gems, using the KPT Texture Explorer and Glass Lens Bright filters.

6. The background behind the figure is a Fractal produced with KPT Fractal Explorer. I produced the frame through multiple applications of KPT Gradient Designer, Texture Explorer, and Gradients on Paths and then embossed it using the Aldus Gallery Effects, Volume 1 Emboss filter.

NewMedia Yogi

The annual *NewMedia Magazine 1994 Multimedia Tool Guide* cover was the assignment, and I was blessed with free reign to have fun and come up with a "cool cover." I chose to illustrate a Tibetan Bodhisattva sitting on a lotus throne holding multimedia products in his hands.

I researched original, traditional antique paintings in my studio to complete the project. Subtle blends were one of the striking features in the original paintings, and I chose KPT Gradient Designer to emulate the effect. The yogi came about like this:

Figure 14–25   Alien King—an image produced using a wide mix of applications and filters

1. I hand-drew and scanned the line work into Photoshop.
2. Using KPT Gradient Designer, I produced basic blends to begin shaping the yogi's lotus platform. Dodge-and-Burn tools helped develop the areas further (Figure 14–28).

Figure 14–26
A seamless texture produced in
Painter, using KPT Gradient
Designer and the Blobs function
in Painter

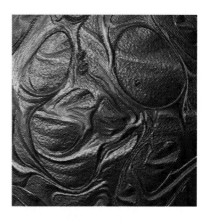

Figure 14–27
The same texture rendered with its
accompanying bump-map in
StrataStudioPro

3. I wanted to use CD discs to emulate the rings of curls on the heads of
traditional Tibetan *thangka* paintings. All of the CD sources I had
were lame, and I couldn't get a good scan of one. I made a custom CD
image, using a custom gradient set to Radial Blend in KPT Gradient
Designer (Figure 14–29).

4. I sized the CDs and pasted them onto the head. The headset itself I
also made with KPT Gradient Designer (Figure 14–30).

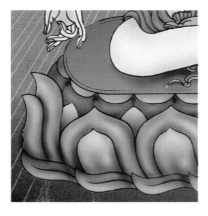

Figure 14–28
Smooth blends served as a basis for
the soft shaping of the platform.

Figure 14–29
A custom KPT Gradient applied in
Radial mode made up the CD disc.

5. To create a rainbow glow in the background, I used KPT Gradient Designer to produce the custom blends and KPT Hue Protected Noise to reduce the chances of later banding problems during output.

6. KPT Gradient Designer generated the radiating glow; the resulting rays were so thin that they appeared jaggy when applied. I used the Photoshop Diffuse filter to blend them into the background blend without loss of fidelity (Figure 14–31).

7. The client supplied slides of the multimedia products, and I simplified the resulting files using the Gallery Effects, Volume 1 Dry Brush filter applied at a very fine setting (Figure 14–32).

8. The client added the magazine header and copy (Figure 14–33).

Figure 14–30
The CDs were pasted on the yogi head.

Figure 14–31
Complex KPT Gradient Designer blends were diffused to homogenize the background.

Figure 14–32
The products were
simplified with the
Gallery Effects, Vol. 1
Dry Brush filter and
composited into
the picture.

Figure 14–33
The final masthead and
type were added
to complete the
magazine cover.

Professional Applications

I began this book by discussing the "Filter Controversy"—the buzz surrounding the "push-button" nature of filters. You may be able to click on a confirmation button to apply filters, but there is no "create" button. In this final chapter, let's look at some "real" creating by some of the world's top digital artists.

I have assembled images from a distinguished group of professionals who use this technology every day. Notice the diversity of styles and functions exemplified by their filtering techniques. These individuals represent only the tip of the creative iceberg.

Jeff Foster

Jeff Foster, of Foster Digital Imaging in Brea, California, produces multimedia and Hollywood film projects as well as digital imaging of all sorts. Using a variety of applications and filters, he produced the "Sing by the Sea" poster for a concert (Figure 15–1). This is a particularly good example of how a series of programs and filters can work together to get a job done.

Sing by the Sea

Foster produced the image background from a photo of a beach, which he had flipped and then distorted using Valis Flo, a morphing program (Figure 15–1). The penguins and logos were scanned and composited into the image, and the headline was rendered with Pixar Tapestry.

Figure 15–1   Sing by the Sea (Jeff Foster © 1993)

To produce the glow effect in the upper right area of the image, Jeff applied the Photoshop Lens Flare filter. The happy little star was the happy result of the Photoshop Spherize filter.

The frisbee began as a photograph, which the artist squashed after applying the Photoshop ZigZag filter set to Pond Ripples. The Andromeda Velocity and cMulti filters make the frisbee appear to be flying.

Laurence Gartel

Laurence Gartel, a photographer producing fine and commercial digital art, has a long list of exhibitions to his credit. Based in Floral Park, New York, his work is filled with densely packed, collage-like imagery. "The Playroom" (Figure 15–2) is from a recently produced series of fantasy-filled, surrealistic landscapes.

Figure 15–2   The Playroom (Laurence Gartel © 1994)

The Playroom

As building blocks for this image, Laurence used still video captures and scanned photo elements, which he then filtered individually. He also included a number of 3D objects rendered in StrataStudioPro 3D.

Custom KPT Texture Explorer textures helped produce the floor and wall backgrounds. To generate the perspective for the floor, Gartel applied Studio 32 to one of the textures.

The water in the pool, including the reflected fish and dog, received applications of the Photoshop Wave and ZigZag filters. To the cone—produced in StrataStudioPro—Gartel applied KPT Texture Explorer in Procedural Blend mode.

The cyber disk, located behind the bust on the pillar, originated as a scan of noodles, to which Gartel applied the Photoshop Wave filter followed by the Photoshop Polar Coordinates filter.

The sky in the upper right corner of the piece was treated with the Gallery Effects, Classic Art, Vol. 2 Angled Strokes filter. The butterflies were enhanced with the Gallery Effects Fresco filter.

John Goodman

John Goodman, proprietor of the Chicago-based Goodman Studio, is a digital illustrator and 3D animator. His work exemplifies a deep understanding of Renderman imaging and textural effects. He utilizes Photoshop-compatible filters optimized for use with Silicon Graphics (SGI) workstations. Goodman's work is a good example of cross-platform use of filters in digital imaging today.

Watermap

This variation of the Corbett logo (Figures 15–3 and 15–4) is suggestive of liquid textures. Goodman describes his techniques this way: "KPT Texture Explorer was applied in a tall, narrow selection, which was stretched to mimic the effect of waves. The Photoshop Wave filter heightened this effect, along with a subtle KPT Gradient Designer blue-green blend. The sky and horizon were created with KPT Gradient Designer, and clouds from a PhotoCD completed the effect of an expanse of cloudy ocean."

Firemap

The textures and color schemes of the second variation of the Corbett logo (Figures 15–5 and 15–6) evoke flames. Goodman describes his creative process: "I used KPT Gradient Designer to simulate a vertical shaft of fire, which was then warped using the Photoshop Wave filter. Strokes of black were feathered in and further waved, twirled, and scaled to create a fluid fire effect."

Figure 15–3
The filtered water environment map

Figure 15–4
The Corbett Water Logo (John Goodman © 1994)

Renderman Environments

Here is how Goodman describes the process of creating a series of logo renderings (Figure 15–9) using textures with a 3D rendering application: "After creating an initial texture, specially prepared Pixar Renderman environment maps were made from the textures. Each texture was made into the front, back, left, and right panels of a seamless virtual "cube." Once created, they were assembled by Renderman into a cubic environment map, which may be used in a scene. The scene, modeled in VIDI's Presenter Pro, was then rendered on a Silicon Graphics INDY workstation."

Figure 15–5
The filtered fire environment map

Figure 15– 6
The Corbett Fire Logo (John Goodman © 1994)

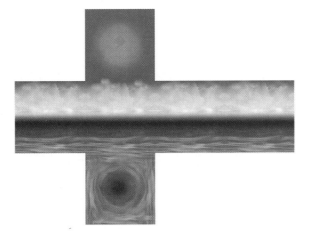

Figure 15–7
A cubic environment map prepared for Renderman

Ruth Kedar

Ruth Kedar, best known for her playing-card designs, is an illustrator and designer based in Palo Alto, California. She uses Adobe Illustrator, Adobe Dimensions, and Photoshop together with third-party filters. The "Mirage" image (Figure 15–8) is one of a series of fine-art digital paintings she has produced based on mirages and desert winds.

Figure 15–8
Mirage
(Ruth Kedar © 1994)

Mirage

Ruth stripped in bottles generated using Adobe Dimensions. The wavy element in the background is parchment, which she scanned and then distorted with a variety of Photoshop distortion filters to achieve the tortured effect. To make the scintillating background screen, she applied the Photoshop Tile filter using a slight offset.

To lend a sense of visual motion to the upper bottle, Kedar applied the Andromeda Velocity filter. She produced the mirage of the bottle at the bottom of the image by first applying the Andromeda Reflection filter, and then inverting the bottle and placing it into the alpha channel. After selecting this processed reflection and saving it, she pasted the original bottle on top and offset it to obtain the embossed effect evident in the final image.

Kai Krause

Kai Krause (the K in KPT) is a digital artist, experimentalist, and interface designer based in Malibu, California. Krause has prepared three example images for this chapter. The set of two images produced with KPT Bryce (Figures 15–9 and 15–10) were altered using Kai's Power Tools. The Chaoscene image (Figure 15–11) is one of a series of experiments in "chaotic motion."

The first two images—"Surreal Whirlwind" and "Horizon Doppler Beacon" (Figures 15–9 and 15–10)—are variations on an imaginary scene produced with KPT Bryce. KPT filters were used to alter the basic scene. This pair of images is an excellent example of using filters creatively in ways that diverge from their original intent and design.

Surreal Whirlwind

An original landscape was produced using KPT Bryce, to be used as a base image for variant experiments. To produce this variant (Figure 15–9), Krause applied KPT Fractal Explorer in Procedural Blend apply mode, using a translucent blend for the seed gradient. The placement gives the effect of a cosmic wind washing through the Jovian desert valley.

Horizon Doppler Beacon

The "Horizon Doppler Beacon" variant (Figure 15–10) features liquid bronze waves, which Krause produced by applying KPT Texture Explorer to the alpha channel in the lower area of the image. Krause generated the beam in the horizon of the Jovian desert by applying a translucent radial blend in KPT Gradient Designer.

Chaoscene

Kai describes the process of producing the "Chaoscene" image (Figure 15–11) thus: "First, a series of KPT textures was overlaid at angles using Difference apply mode, yielding subtle color fields and the rainbow sheen

Figure 15–9
Surreal Whirlwind (Kai Krause © 1993)

Figure 15–10
Horizon Doppler Beacon (Kai Krause © 1993)

Figure 15–11　Chaoscene (Kai Krause © 1994)

in the upper left. A terrain was derived from scanned portions of hair (!), which were composited using KPT gradients as variable-opacity masks to create a feeling of depth and perspective. The tree was born as a separate element: Multiple levels of very deep Julia sets (KPT 2.0 fractals) were overlaid and branch-like features copied and combined. Using Photoshop Levels, the fractals were rendered as a monochromatic black-on-white and multiplied into the scene as a stark tree shape. An early version of an upcoming new filter—the Convolution Kernel Explorer or KPT Convolver—was used to add horizontal blur and vertical relief embossing."

NOTE: For more information on developing your own variations on these techniques, refer to the "Post-Lighting and Backlighting Effects" section of Chapter 6. The technique described there uses KPT filters.

Mark Landman

Illustrator Mark Landman of Cotati, California, known for his hilarious postcards, produced the intriguing "Enolith" image (Figure 15–12) using a photograph taken by Jay Blakesberg. The subject is the famous musician, Brian Eno, whose normally smooth face was merged with an image of a mountainous rock.

Enolith

Mark says: "I applied the Photoshop Emboss filter to a scan of a black-and-white photo. I pasted a section of a mountain face, using varying Color Only, Darken Only, and Lighten Only settings in Photoshop's Composite Controls dialog box to build up the complex rock look. I then used the Hue/Saturation controls to arrive at a color scheme befitting a desert landscape.

"All the other component images—skies, desert, mountains—had to be de-moiréd because they had been scanned from printed material. I obtained good results by applying the Photoshop Despeckle filter several times, until the flat areas were almost smooth enough. I then followed with the Photoshop Median filter to smooth any remaining rough edges.

"I used the Photoshop Add Noise filter to add detail to the heavily cloned and painted foreground area. A light application of the Photoshop Unsharp Mask filter helped compensate for any softening during printing."

Pieter Lessing

Pieter Lessing, a photographer and digital artist based in Los Angeles, specializes in photographing entertainment industry personalities. His

Figure 15–12
Enolith (Mark Landman
© 1993)

photographs are syndicated by Visages. The images shown here (Figures 15–13 through 15–16) are from a set of portraits utilizing subtle filter effects.

Michelle Pfeiffer

Lessing says of his Michelle Pfeiffer portrait (Figures 15–13 and 15–14): "I wanted to use a subtle approach that would complement Michelle's classic, refined beauty. I increased the contrast and brightness of the image to burn out most minor details and create a more graphic image. I then applied the Photoshop Find Edges filter. To tame its overpowering effect, I created a mask channel to protect the important facial features. The edge of the feathered mask allowed the Find Edges effect to taper off from full application in the corners to no effect in the center."

Billy Idol

Lessing describes the process of creating the Billy Idol portrait (Figures 15–15 and 15–16): "Billy Idol had just put out his Cyberpunk album, and I wanted to create an image that would echo this new direction. I applied the Aldus Gallery Effects, Classic Art, Vol. 1 Poster Edges filter. I then used the Photoshop Image: Adjust: Curves menu option to obtain "false color"

Figure 15–13
Michelle Pfeiffer (Lessing/Visage © 1993)

Figure 15–14
Dreamy Michelle Pfeiffer (Lessing © 1993)

values by drawing short, horizontal lines with the arbitrary mapping function. The surface of Billy's glasses was created by applying a repeating linear blend with KPT Gradient Designer."

John Lund

John Lund, a studio digital photographer based in San Francisco, is known for his incredibly clean photographic composites. He has produced an experimental piece, "New Tori" (Figures 15–17 and 15–18), using a combination of filter-manipulated photography, straight photography, and a filter-generated background.

New Tori

Using the Andromeda, Series 2 3D filter, Lund wrapped the photograph of a circuit board around a virtual cylinder (Figure 15–17). He rotated the angle of the circuitry from within the filter for direct inclusion in the final composite.

Figure 15–15
Billy Idol (Lessing/Visage © 1993)

Figure 15–16
Cyberpunk Billy Idol (Lessing © 1993)

The Andromeda filter actually curved and distorted the image of the circuitry board, yielding a realistic effect when the circuitry was merged into the final image (Figure 15–18). Lund placed the additional wires onto the circuit-board arm from within Photoshop. A background simulating radiating energy was produced using a radial blend created in KPT Gradient Designer.

Glenn Mitsui

Glenn Mitsui, based in Seattle, Washington, is a fine-art and commercial-art illustrator and designer. His finely crafted, complex graphic constructions are often seen in the pages of *MacWorld* Magazine. "Game" (Figure 15–19) was featured in *MacWorld* and serves as an excellent example of seamlessly integrating filters into illustration projects.

Figure 15–17
Andromeda Cylinder
(John Lund © 1993)

Figure 15–18
New Tori (John Lund © 1993)

Games

The "Games" image (Figure 15–20) was prepared for *MacWorld* magazine's "Game Hall of Fame," an article rating computer games. The figure was inspired by an Indian petraglyph (an ancient style of painting), with the line-art components produced in Aldus Freehand and then imported into Photoshop.

Mitsui produced all the blends in the image using KPT Gradient Designer. The KPT Glass Lens Bright filter helped stylize the eyeballs, shoulders, crown balls, and theater stanchions. To generate the textures on the sides of the TV screens, the artist used "Simple Patterns" paper textures in Painter. He also applied the Photoshop Lens Flare filter to the TV images to simulate screen glare. The gyroscopes originated as imported Aldus Freehand line drawings, which Matsui blended into the wallpaper with the help of the Photoshop Gaussian Blur filter.

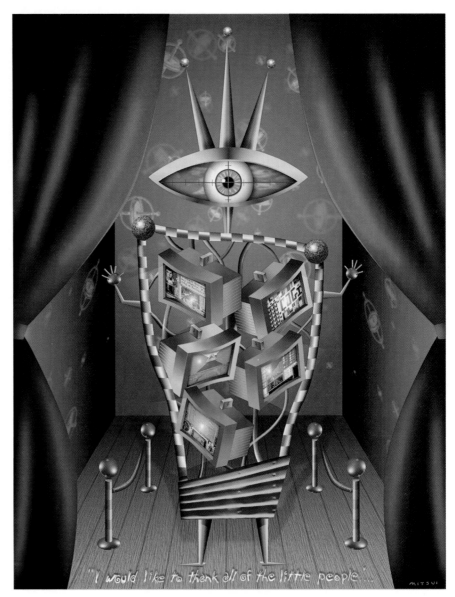

Figure 15–19
Game
(Glenn Mitsui © 1993)

Jeffery Schewe

Jeffery Schewe is an advertising photographer and digital imagist based in Chicago. He produced the novel set of custom computers shown in Figures 15–20 and 15–21 using the Andromeda, Series 2 3D filter. These are good examples of jobs in which typical 3D imaging would not yield a sufficiently convincing photographic look.

Mad Dog

Jeffery says: "The job was for Valentine-Radford, a Kansas City ad agency, and their client, Ambassador Systems (a division of Hallmark). The client wished to convey the custom aspect of their computer systems and therefore provided Hallmark wrapping paper for scanning as the texture wraps of the computers.

"I separated the photograph of the computer into its basic geometric shapes by digitally removing any logos and blemishes. I used the Andromeda Series 2 3D filter to distort the wrapping paper scans likewise into primitive shapes. I used the Viewpoint controls to alter perspectives and the Photo controls to rotate, size, and precisely position the scans. I purposely did not use 3D's Shader controls, because I wanted to use the component's own shading.

"I used the 3D shapes as a source to fill the computer elements with wrapping paper. Through a combination of Color mode, Luminosity mode, and Multiply mode fills, I was able to colorize the computer elements while preserving the details of the computer itself.

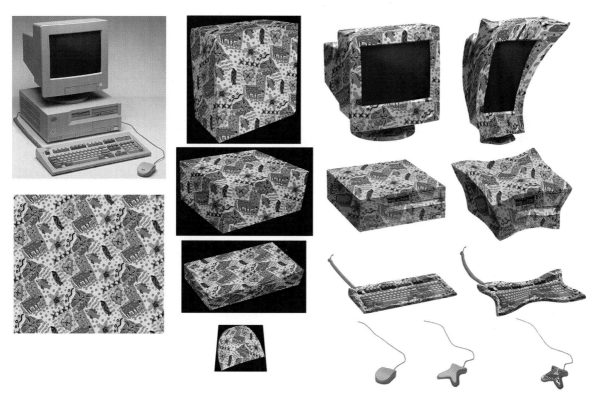

Figure 15–20   Mad Dog assembly (Jeffery Schewe © 1993)

Figure 15–21
Mad Dog
(Jeffery Schewe © 1993)

"I used MetaFlo from The Valis Group to stretch and warp the computer elements. Using selection techniques, I pasted the computer elements back together and created the drop shadows in Photoshop."

Lee Varis

Lee Varis is a studio photographer and digital imagist based in Los Angeles. He produces large-scale posters for the movie industry, using his digitally manipulated photography. "Swamp Thing" (Figures 15–22 through 15–24) is an experimental piece that resulted from fortuitous play with high-resolution fractals—a great tribute to the benefits and fun of uninhibited play with filters and imaging in general.

Swamp Thing

The basis of "Swamp Thing" was a high-resolution fractal generated by KPT Fractal Explorer (Figure 15–22). Varis then applied the Photoshop Polar Coordinate filter using a Polar-to-Rectangular setting; he also set the

Figure 15–22
Swamp Thing Fractal
(Lee Varis © 1993)

Figure 15–23
Swamp Thing Polarized
(Lee Varis © 1993)

hue to green for a more chlorophylled effect (Figure 15–23). Details and enhancements were hand-applied with Photoshop brush tools. The artist used the KPT Glass Lens Bright filter to generate the creature's eyes in the final image (Figure 15–24).

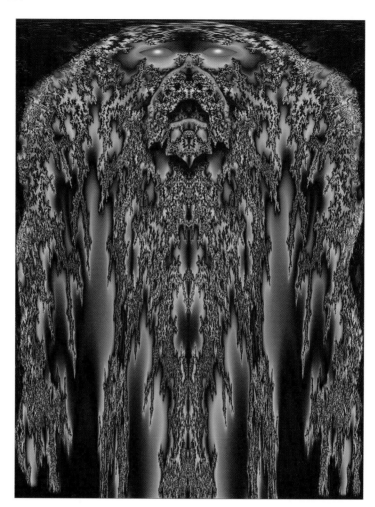

Figure 15–24
Swamp Thing
(Lee Varis © 1993)

Index

Optronics Exposes Color Digital Proofing Technology

I t's inevitable. Children do it. Engineers and artists do it. Maybe you're doing it right now as you hold this book. A function of creative curiosity is to wonder how something, in this case a book, is made. Our level of curiosity is probably correlated to the level of complexity of the the the process that leads to the end result, the product. The discovery process begins as we study *Photoshop Filter Finesse*, particularly its production. As we delve into the layers of detail and technology behind the book, we expose the complete picture, much in the same way light exposes film or photographic paper to reveal a colorfully vibrant image.

The copy of *Photoshop Filter Finesse* you are holding is the result of the collaborative efforts of several groups of individuals and product vendors, specialists in different phases of the production cycle. Each brought to the proverbial drawing board their own contribution to the overall process of producing the book from concept through to print.

The New Direct Digital Proofing: Imagesetter and Proofer in One

The author exercised his expertise and creativity generating all of the images in the book using Photoshop 2.5. The images were calibrated on a Macintosh in RGB mode, and saved as RGB TIFF files.

They were subsequently integrated into QuarkXPress 3.3 pages and converted to CMYK TIFF through a batch scripting program, PhotoMatic, recently released by DayStar Digital of Flowery Branch, Georgia.

The files were then sent to Optronics, An Intergraph Division, based in Chelmsford, Massachusetts, a manufacturer of high quality desktop scanners and imagesetters. The application files were imposed at Optronics on a Macintosh Quadra 950 workstation using INposition 1.5, a Quark XTension imposition software package by DK&A of San Diego, California.

The next step was invoking the Optronics imagesetter interface, CSLink, from within the application Print Menu, allowing the user to write PostScript files directly to the imagesetter spool, or queue for output from the Macintosh. Specifying the desired screen resolution, angles, and even dot gain profiles to achieve direct digital proofs and, ultimately, film output from CSLink is a simple matter.

This process differs from the typical production approach in that the imagesetter, Optronics' ColorSetter 4400 with IntelliProof, generates both color digital proofs and film. IntelliProof is a new direct digital color proofing (DDCP) system, developed by Optronics, which combines the advantages of digital proofing with the halftone screening of conventional proofing systems.

Traditionally, the process of generating color proofs has been iterative, costly, and time-consuming because films must be generated in order to make proofs. If changes are required, films must be regenerated.

Photoshop Filter Finesse represents the perfect opportunity to put this newly developed technology to the test. One of the biggest challenges in producing a color book of the caliber of *Photoshop Filter Finesse* is ensuring color fidelity of the original images.

Therefore, it was important to check the color quality of the electronic files created in Photoshop prior to imaging the job on film and running it on press. To ensure utmost color fidelity, the IntelliProof was calibrated with customized dot gain tables to match printed press sheet samples from the targeted press. With IntelliProof, the digital proofs used to check the electronic files also served as guides for the printer at press time.

IntelliProof is the first digital color proofing system that doubles as a laser imagesetter, enabling it to produce both four-color proofs and color separated films. It is based on the Optronics' ColorSetter 4400 imagesetter, a high-performance, external drum imagesetter that generates color-separated films from PostScript files.

IntelliProof takes advantage of the same software-based RIPs, eight-beam laser technology, 2000 or 4000 dpi resolution, and 33- to 300-lpi halftone screening which the Optronics ColorSetter 4400 imagesetter uses to output film separations. The resulting proofs, which are generated on photosensitive paper instead of film, closely predict how a job will look on press.

An IntelliProof system adds red and green lasers to the standard blue argon-ion laser built into the ColorSetter 4400 to record full-color images, text, and computer-generated graphics, complete with halftone dot structures, in a single

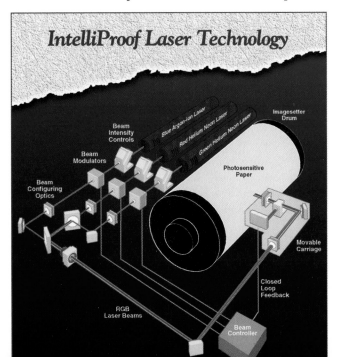

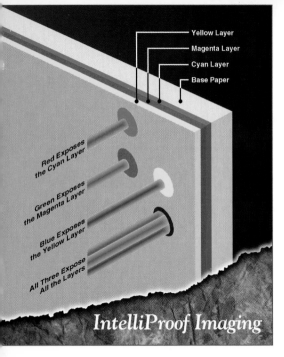

Yellow Layer
Magenta Layer
Cyan Layer
Base Paper

Red Exposes
the Cyan Layer

Green Exposes
the Magenta Layer

Blue Exposes
the Yellow Layer

All Three Expose
All the Layers

IntelliProof Imaging

pass. The cyan, magenta, and yellow dyes in the Konica Konsensus photographic paper, which Optronics chose for its ability to match press inks closely, make the RGB laser beams yield CMY when processed. The convergence of all three laser beams on the same spot produces the fourth process color, a deep black (K).

IntelliProof includes tools to calibrate laser intensity and balance, dot gain targets, and linearization tools. A variety of color controls, including SWOP/GAA standards, are supported to ensure color consistency from proof to finished product. Standardized look-up tables (LUTs) provide close matches to widely used press systems and can be modified to suit custom requirements.

IntelliProof digital proofs were evaluated by *Photoshop Filter Finesse* author, editors, production specialists, and printer prior to making color separated film. After final approval, the job was ready to image on film and go on press. The menu option, films, was selected on the imagesetter monitor, and 20" x 26" color-separated films were generated with the same halftone dots that appeared on the proofs and that were printed on press.

In addition, IntelliProof makes it possible to achieve remote proofing and film imaging. Through various communication network interfaces, a company with IntelliProof-equipped ColorSetter 4400s at multiple sites can, for example, transfer a file from one site for proofing at another to see how that file will print on the presses at the remote site.

By combining the latest laser imaging technology with easy-to-use software controls and user interfaces, IntelliProof makes it possible to output repeatable, high-quality color proofs imaged with halftone dots as routinely as sending a document to a printer.

The production process of *Photoshop Filter Finesse* has allowed us to explore the layers of color expertise that has brought Optronics IntelliProof technology from a drawing board concept to a multi-functional imagesetter and color proofing device.

Scans for this article were produced on the Optronics ColorGetter II Pro using ColorRight 4.0 software. Illustrations were created using Adobe Illustrator 4.0, Fractal Design Painter 1.0, and Adobe Photoshop 2.5. Pages were composed using QuarkXPress 3.3, and output on Optronics IntelliProof at 2000 dpi, and 150 lpi. Text and graphic design by Rosa DeBerry King. Illustration and graphic design by Mark A. Wing.

Optronics
An Intergraph Division

Performance in Precision Imaging

7 Stuart Road • Chelmsford • Massachusetts • 01824 • (508) 256-4511 • Fax (508) 256-1872

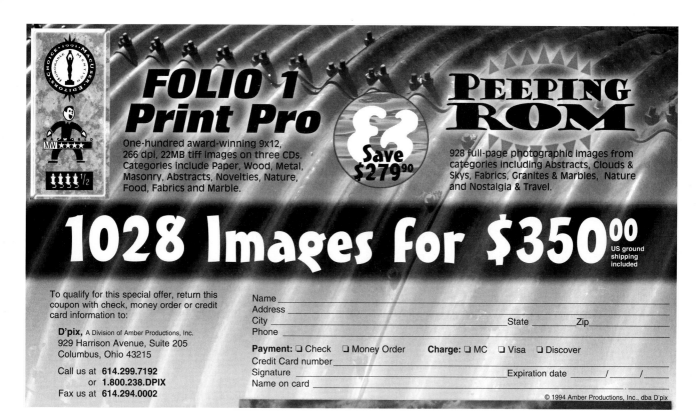

SPECTACULAR FULL PAGE IMAGES

Order the *ColorBytes Mini Sampler* **before** December 31, 1994 at the special *Photo-shop Filter Finesse* price of only $19*—saving over 75% off the retail price of $79.

The *ColorBytes Mini Sampler* is a great way to get 20 first class images—backgrounds, textures, nature, wildlife, environment, business, industry, and more. With ColorBytes you get more than just a disc full of pictures. You get images selected by a team of graph-ics professionals, high-end drum scanning at up to 4,000 dpi, careful color-correction and balance; and images optimized for a full-page bleed, CMYK separation, and 200 line screen printing. And best of all, the images are *royalty free!*

Ideal for Macintosh® or PC, these images are sure to capture the attention of your audi-ence. Each image is saved in several formats and resolutions, and the disc comes with a full-color printed reference guide and a *30-day money-back guarantee!*

To order, call 1-800-825-COLOR. Be sure to mention this ad when you call you will also save over $150 on *ColorBytes Sampler One* or *ColorBytes Sampler Two!*

ColorBytes, Inc.
2525 South Wadsworth, Suite 308
Lakewood, CO 80227
1-800-825-COLOR •303/989-9205
303/988-6463 (FAX)

    * Add $6 per disc for shipping and handling

"The images from ColorBytes are crystal clear. Just the way I like them!"
—*Bill Niffenegger, Digital Artist & Author, Photoshop Filter Finesse*

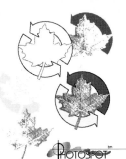